FULFILL
YOUR
SOUL'S
PURPOSE

FULFILL YOUR SOUL'S PURPOSE

*Ten Creative Paths to
Your Life Mission*

NAOMI STEPHAN, Ph.D.

STILLPOINT PUBLISHING

STILLPOINT PUBLISHING
Building a society that honors the Earth,
Humanity, and The Sacred in All Life.

For a free catalog or ordering information, write
Stillpoint Publishing, Box 640, Walpole, NH 03608, USA
or call
1-800-847-4014 TOLL-FREE (Continental US, except NH)
1-603-756-9281 (Foreign and NH)

This book is manufactured in the United States of America.
Cover and text designed by Karen Savary.

Published by Stillpoint Publishing, Box 640
Meetinghouse Road, Walpole, NH 03608

Fulfill Your Soul's Purpose:
Ten Creative Paths to Your Life Mission
Formerly *Finding Your Life Mission:*
How to Unleash That Creative Power and Live With Intention

ISBN: 1-883478-00-6

Library of Congress Cataloging in Publication Data
94-67881

3 5 7 9 8 6 4 2

This book is printed on chlorine-free recycled paper
to save trees and preserve Earth's ecology.

To Sue for her love and support
Du bist geschlossen in meinem Herzen.

Sigh for the Divine.

—HILDEGARD VON BINGEN

LEARN TO THINK LIZARD

Learn to think Lizard
Learn to think watercress,
Subtle and crisp.
Learn to see clean, unblinking
Into cool shadows that hide from the dust
Of afternoon light.

Learn to think lizard
Slink past the obvious
To the underneath leaf
And there in canny damp twilight
Of cucumber truth
Breathe with your skin
The peace of the rain, the pond, the fern.

—SUE MOORE

CONTENTS

ACKNOWLEDGMENTS

This book is like a musical composition. It has a creator, but she can be heard only with the help of others. In my case, in addition to Sue, I am grateful to my sister Judith, who spent many hours after a long working day reading (and rereading) the various stages of this manuscript, making valuable editorial and textual suggestions and never failing to include words of encouragement. Thanks go also to Robin Ladd, who gave a certain rigor to the process, challenging me on many concepts and ideas. Posthumous thanks go to Richard Byrne, who understood the urgency of my message and encouraged me to continue my mission of transformation.

I am grateful to all those people who asked about the progress of the book, listened to me, and then gave me fresh perspective on my material. Special thanks go to all my clients, whose paths and pilgrimages I was privileged to share.

I am thankful to a number of people who have affected my life. Especially do I wish to gratefully remember my mother Irene, who in 1993 made her transition. Bless her, she recognized my musical gift early on. It provided a great bond between us.

Other posthumous thanks must also be meted out. Thanks to my father, Curtis, who although he did not get to see this book gave me an appreciation of language, linguistics, history, theology, and the importance of dedication to one's calling.

Thanks to Hildegard of Bingen (1098-1179), truly a Renaissance woman of immense inspirational genius, whom I have been privileged to meet via her music, paintings, and words. And thanks to another musical mentor, J.S. Bach, whose divinely inspired music, in the words of a family friend, Dr. Paul Nettl, was indeed "Naomi's daily bread."

I am further grateful to Madame Dorothee Manski, my first voice teacher at Indiana University. A woman of another era, Madame Manski was blessed with infectious humor, a generous heart, a magnificent voice, and belief in my talent.

Three other people deserve honored mention. Each one, although beset by personal health crises, nevertheless gave me sustaining and abiding love. Fond thanks to Mary Williams, trusted friend, writer, and ingenious spiritual advisor, to Janet Hargrave, a brave World War II pilot who for so long went without recognition, and who understood my journey and cheered me on with just the right wise phrase for the moment, and to my dear friend Pat Taylor, who encouraged me to continue developing my musical talent, which she alone had recognized many years ago.

Thanks also to Terry Musch, colleague and dedicated Life Missionary, whose praise and admiration of the Life Mission model sustained me through this process. Bravo to Edward Cansino, whose talented choir I Cantori performed my first composition so beautifully.

To everyone at Stillpoint Publishing I am grateful for their continued belief in the timeliness of my message, especially to Meredith Young-Sowers and Errol Sowers who gave me incisive and sound advice for the reshaping of this book. Thanks to Dorothy Seymour for her wise and insightful editing. Grateful thanks go to editor Ann Weil Richards for her keen eye for detail, for her commitment to absolute clarity of thought, and to the success of this book.

See you at Carnegie Hall.

PREFACE

LIFE IS A PERSONAL MISSION

This book is about conscious discovery of that mission—the reason for which you are living—and to establish a most powerful connection between your mission and your soul.

You have a purpose that exists only for you and that only you can fulfill. This purpose is a call from your soul, and it takes courage and self-love to answer that call. Being faithful to that calling is the only way to lead a committed, rewarding life. It's also the most natural way to be. As the Zen master said to the student: "Zen is eating when you are eating." Life is living your personal mission.

Your only obligation is to carry out the mission you are meant for, not what your father, mother, mate, or friends say you should do. No one can go through your life, tell you what it is or how to live it, except you.

We're talking about self-care here: releasing the need to please others so that you take care of yourself! Every one of you has an individual mission to manifest. Each of you has an individual part to play in that process. There are no substitutes for you, no actors standing in the wings to play your role. And there is no need or time on this planet to meddle in each other's roles! Your mission will begin to take shape in you when you consciously follow your own inner wisdom.

Your mission is the most important gift you will ever receive in your life. It has only one requirement: that you follow the inner voice of your soul. You have no excuses for missing the mark because it's *your* mark. The ultimate source for your answers is an inside job.

The beauty of experiencing your Life Mission is that through it, you get in touch with that special spiritual assignment from your soul that only you are qualified to fulfill. Then, filled with a sense of direction and purpose, you will be equipped to give that gift to others and support them on their own mission path.

INTRODUCTION

If you want to lead a life that expresses your innermost being, if you want to be in consonance with yourself, this book is for you. It doesn't matter where you are coming from. Maybe you haven't the foggiest notion of what your mission is, perhaps you doubt that you even have one, or maybe you simply need a boost of courage to pursue your own destiny.

All you need is the desire to find your mission. This book gives you the tools to achieve it.

The goal of *Fulfill Your Soul's Purpose* is for you to develop authenticity, self-trust, centeredness, insight, faithfulness, self-love, creativity, spiritual growth, and—most important—to realize your unique destiny. Live your mission and success, prosperity, and happiness will follow.

REASONS FOR THIS BOOK

Life is difficult if you do not accept—or manifest—your personal mission. My father, for example, was someone who did not completely manifest his desires. He looked upon his ministerial office with enormous reverence and referred to it as a call coming from a divine source. But he chose his head over his heart by listening to the voice of "logic." He followed family tradition and rather than responding to his own passion for ancient history and academic research, became a clergyman like his father. Because his passion was not totally fulfilled, he experienced periods of stress, melancholy, sadness, and depression.

My mother, too, never completely embraced her one true desire: to sing in the service of her God. To be sure, she found one way of manifesting this musical mission, choosing to direct the church choir and play the organ. Yet the vocal performer in her languished in the background for many years. For both my parents, life at times seemed tedious instead of tantalizing, because both had only partly addressed their missions.

Following their example for more than twenty years, I put my energy into pursuing a path that didn't entirely satisfy me, even though I was very good at what I did. Like my parents, I experienced bouts of despair, unhappiness, and frustration—proof that something was lacking. By neglecting my musical gifts I could feel the pain caused by that neglect. Because I had slighted the very core of my soul, for years I had less of my true self to draw upon.

WHY MISSION?

I figured if intelligent people like my parents experienced difficulty in expressing their mission, there might be a lot of others experiencing it too. Then one day I had an important realization: that the concept of a calling applied not just to the strictly religious interpretation my father had, but to life in its totality. Everyone had a mission!

That insight became the seed for this book. From my personal experience, I became convinced that most people fail to answer their personal callings fully because they lack the tools to see a mission on a deeper (if you will, soul) level. The indicators of "starvation of the soul" are everywhere: ignoring a passion for drawing as a youngster, doing what friends want, taking the "practical" route through college (to get that "good" job), marrying too early or the wrong person or even at all because "that's what one is supposed to do." You can see it when people abandon careers that languish in the corner of their hearts or cancel a longed-for trip to Europe in favor of a bigger house in the suburbs. Even if they are sick to death of the life they are leading, they still deny love and commitment to the ones who need it most: themselves.

Lives are at odds with desires. It hasn't always been that way. When you were a baby and cried, you had specific needs: a hug, milk, or a warm blanket. Asking for what we want gets lost over time. Instead, we adults, rather than affirming our need for love, fulfillment, and creative self-expression, often displace our unfulfilled desires onto a career, expensive hobbies, or mortgages.

Are you staying with that stultifying job (or even an okay one) to buy freedom for retirement, turning a deaf ear to your inner calling because "it won't pay the rent," living in the city when the country beckons, remaining in a relationship for anyone's sake but your own, or even contracting a serious illness rather than ceasing self-abusive behavior? Now is the time to examine the one question that matters: what is my soul's path in this life: my Life Mission?

The inevitable emotional consequences of a missed or partly fulfilled mission are discomfort, disappointment, distress, and discouragement. Job failure, addictions, loss of productivity, relationship problems, or dis-ease are some visible symptoms.

BENEFITS OF THE LIFE MISSION PROCESS

After reading this book, you'll be able to access an inner landscape of intentional guidance, what I call the voice of your soul. Through this process, you'll discover a clarity of purpose, an ability to live your calling daily because you'll be able to connect with the path you were designed to follow. You'll no longer need to respond to any negative messages from your inner critic or others. You'll know how to manage your life as your mission unfolds.

Living your mission will afford you a sense of clarity, direction, and purpose. Rather than being on the receiving line of "chance," you'll create your own fortune. When opportunity knocks you'll hear it, because you'll recognize it as opportunity. You'll feel a connectedness to your Source, and thus feel nurtured and empowered to create a meaningful, happy, congruent life. Most important, you will be the person you were meant to be. What could be more natural than playing your own role in life?

Since writing the original version of this book, *Finding Your Life Mission*, which was published in 1988, I have seen how the concept of Life Mission has struck a deep and resounding chord in people's lives. As a result, I now find myself compelled to add to that original version some important new insights and definitions, derived from the interim years of working with hundreds of people who were searching, as perhaps you are, to identify and better understand their Life Mission process—their journey of learning and service. I want to share these insights and comments with you as you begin the exciting journey to find or refine your Life Mission.

INSIGHT # 1:
LIFE MISSION IS A SPIRITUAL PROCESS

The question most often asked since I wrote the earlier version of this book is whether Life Mission has a spiritual component. Indeed, the most important message of this new edition is that Life Mission cannot be separated from its spiritual context and is, as such, key to expressing your soul's intention for this life. As I view it, spiritual means whatever pertains to the activation of connection to your spiritual base, which I call Source. Even though you may be unaware of this element at the beginning of your search, concentrating as you might be on the more practical and creative steps involved, the spiritual is nevertheless a central ingredient of the Life Mission process.

To enhance the spiritual message of this book, I use a number of words with closely aligned spiritual meanings. All play a definite role in the Life Mission process. I want to clarify the subtle distinctions between these terms: *Source, soul, spirit, intuition,* and *inner wisdom,* by offering you my working definitions. These definitions have helped me and may serve to encourage you to define your own spiritual response to these words.

Source: Each of us has a central spiritual Source. Some may call it Higher Self, some God, some Angel, some Buddha, some the Divine. Call it by these or by any other name, our Source is a spiritual foundation from which all things flow, the point of origin and return of our souls' development.

Soul: Soul is that aspect of our being most closely aligned with our Source. Soul is an individuation—a holograph, if you will—of the Source. It is that indestructible, immaterial, immutable aspect of our being that through incarnation creates the context for experiencing the life lessons and evolutionary development leading us to atunement with our Source. The soul's path is a constantly evolving one, and each lifetime, via our mission, brings new lessons, new perspectives, new levels of awareness to the soul. Our mission aligns, defines, and refines the soul's intention for this lifetime.

Spirit: Although *spirit* is often used interchangeably with *soul* in the Bible, I see spirit as the motive energy from the soul that activates the mind, behavior, and personality. Unlike the soul, the spirit can be diminished and extinguished—or conversely, restored, energized or uplifted, depending on how we are consciously connecting to our mission.

Intuition: Intuition is a conduit from our interior self that conveys immediate information on a specific matter for which we need knowledge or insight. Consider it a kind of soul emissary. Intuition can be nurtured and enhanced through meditation and quieting the mind. Intuition is the nurturing and caretaking part of us, feeding our inner wisdom with perceptions.

Inner Wisdom: The repository of whatever has been gained through intuition, experience, and our unique perspective on life, inner wisdom is fueled by our intuitive perception, and is fed in turn by the fruits of those perceptions.

In summary, Source, soul, spirit, intuition, and inner wisdom all act in creative interplay with your Life Mission. The mission process is designed to show you how these terms function and how to access them, communicate, and creatively align with them, so that you may live out your Life Mission completely and fully.

The direction you take in life, coming from your Source and purveyed by your soul—the motive and impulse for how you are to be—is defined by your Life Mission. Living your mission opens the door to the soul, activating it to operate on a material level and thus moving you ever closer to your Source.

INSIGHT #2:
LIFE MISSION IS A LIFELONG PROCESS

The discovery of your Life Mission does not culminate or terminate in some single Eureka! Life Mission is as it says: *a lifelong learning process*, ever-unfolding and weaving itself through a central theme—your soul's development in this life.

Although a Life Mission concerns one chief role you are destined to play in this lifetime, it can go through many variations. Your Life Mission is something you discover, then shape over time. A Life Mission process, therefore, is always subject to review, re-vision, redirection. Like a woodcarver slowly whittling away on works of art, you refine the pieces as you work along.

When a piece of the process is finished, there is a completion of sorts. Then you begin on the next piece, and the process goes on. It is a neverending upward spiral of continual completion within a process—as Goethe called it, permanence in change. The Life Mission process extends over your entire lifetime. Like a fine wine, it just gets better and better with age.

INSIGHT #3:
THE LIFE MISSION PROCESS REQUIRES ACTION

A TV special on the aviator Amelia Earhart asserted that Amelia spent far more time talking about flying than *actually practicing and doing it!* You can talk forever about your Life Mission, but the proof is in the pudding: you need to do it. Course corrections are fine, but you must be underway! Once insight has been achieved, there is no substitute for action. The process is not one that you put on the shelf or save for a rainy day, but is one of continuous insight and action based on those insights. To be sure, the procedure requires processing (ideas, meditation, intuitive insight, consulting our inner resources), but it must then be followed by action.

INSIGHT #4:
COMMITMENT IS NECESSARY AND
INEVITABLE FOR SUCCESS

Sooner or later, you have to commit to your love—your soul's voice—or you'll remain ineffective. Commitment begins with a working definition of your mission, however raw or fuzzy. Redefine and refine your mission as you go along. Your inner wisdom will guide you to make the appropriate changes.

Here's the good news: revisions in your discovery process automatically give you new directions and solutions for the next step, and they reaffirm that mission is not a final destination, but a journey.

INSIGHT #5:
THE LIFE MISSION PROCESS IS A PARADOX: LIVE IN
THE MOMENT EVEN IF YOU'D RATHER BE
SOMEWHERE ELSE

Everything you experience is both necessary and part of the process. Learn to work within the context of where you are. See it as right for now. Because your Life Mission is a process, there is something to be seen, learned or finished right where you are. If you choose to be in one place rather than another, it's never a waste of time. Even if you choose to stay put because of extenuating circumstances, then you are learning in some way to refocus your mission to bloom where you are planted.

The paradox is to acknowledge that you are always on the path even if it appears that you are not. You must work with the notion of this paradox. The fine line to be walked is that you always have a goal you want to reach, just like a river that heads along on its sure path. Yet, like the river, your path has occasional meanderings that seem to lead "away" from the charted course.

Thus, if the path appears to be carrying you away from your intended direction, it behooves you *nevertheless* to keep on persevering, to keep searching, seeking, and working on your goal. If you choose to ignore this paradox, either by saying, "I'm on my path, so no sweat whatever I do," or, "It's hopeless, I'll never get on track," then you're not working with the wisdom of the paradox, and stagnation can occur.

Life Mission is the road map to guide you through the maze of seeming adversity by keeping you focused on the needs of the moment as you connect to your mission. Even the "hard" times are somehow an opportunity to work things out at the time and a way to experience tremendous growth. Life Mission is not a matter of the past (although the past has led up to this point), nor is it in the future. It is actually happening NOW.

The present is the only inevitable moment we have.

CONCLUDING THOUGHTS

Another way to view Life Mission is that it represents your soul unfolding in this lifetime. When you live in ways that deny that mission, then Source, soul, spirit, intuition, and inner wisdom are blocked from giving energy and direction to your mission. Fulfilling your soul's purpose is paramount to the discovery and unfolding of your soul's path. Think of it as the soul's divine assignment, which you, via your creative gifts, are charged to fulfill in the form of a mission that you define.

You have the mandate to do so, although you can elect not to. By agreeing to use your life to carry out a specific role, you live out your destiny as it is meant to be.

Life Mission isn't the final destination or goal of our life; it's *actually the starting point.* Let's begin.

PART

One

1

Life Mission

Life is a personal mission.

You have a calling that exists only for you and that only you can fulfill. It takes courage and self-love to answer that inner voice, but being faithful to it is the only way to lead a rewarding life. It's also the most natural way to be. As the Zen master said to his student: "Zen is eating when you are eating." Life is living your personal mission.

Your first obligation is to carry out the mission you are meant for, not what your father, mother, mate, or friends say you should do. *No one can go through your life, tell you what it is or how to be it, except you.* Your mission will begin to take shape in you when you listen to your inner wisdom.

This book is all about conscious discovery of the reason for which you are living, to establish a most powerful connection between your mission and your inner voice, and thus between your mission and your soul.

We're talking about self-care here: releasing the *need to*

please others so that you take care of yourself! Every one of you has an individual mission to fulfill. Each of you has an individual part to play in that process. There are no substitutes for you, no actors standing in the wings to play your role. And there is no need, or time, to meddle in each other's roles!

Your mission is the most important gift you will ever receive and give in your life. It has only one requirement: that you follow the inner voice of your soul. You have no excuses for missing the mark because it's *your* mark.

The beauty of experiencing your Life Mission is that through it, you get in touch with that special spiritual assignment only you are qualified to fulfill.

WHAT IS LIFE MISSION?

Life Mission represents the very essence of who you are. It is your very deepest intention—the heartbeat, core, and overall theme that guides your life. It expresses what you are all about. Other words for *mission* include *calling, quest, sending, destiny, or assignment.* Mission is the specific path of your soul in this life.

Once you understand that you have a calling, you learn to connect who you are to what you are doing. Everything makes sense because you do it in the light of your mission. Every task takes on a special meaning, subsumed as it is under this highest heading of your life. A mission, then, provides the vehicle through which the purpose, shape, and direction of your soul's path is expressed.

The "I have a Dream" speech of Dr. Martin Luther King expressed his mission: namely, that different races of this country could live and play in peace with each other. Everything he did related to that mission, which was, as he put it, to be "a drum major for justice."

Likewise, your dream, whatever it may be, illuminates and enlightens your soul's path like a beacon.

WHAT IF I DON'T YET KNOW WHAT MY MISSION IS?

Some fortunate people (for example, Albert Schweitzer or Wolfgang Mozart) knew their mission at an early age and carried it out consciously. If you despair because you haven't yet completely embarked on your mission process, take heart. For many, a realized mission might not begin to blossom until mid-life. Anne Morrow Lindbergh made the transformation from poet to world explorer as a grown woman. John Kennedy achieved his goal of influencing the direction of his country in his forties. Eleanor Roosevelt moved from a subordinate role to a world figure in her later years. And look at Grandma Moses! It is never too late to embark on your mission discovery path.

The important thing here is to seek and then carry out your assignment. Awaken your own discovery process so that you can walk your own journey just as countless other courageous people have done.

WHY MISSION AND NOT CAREER?

A mission can take various forms: a career, an avocation, a hobby , a pastime, a passion, or anything in between. This book emphasizes mission rather than career, because Life Mission goes far beyond simply what you do for a living. It can be, but is not necessarily, identical with work. The term *Life Mission* refers to who you are and what you do to live out your soul's purpose in life.

A career is only part of what you do. Instead of thinking about your career as the description of who you are, think of it simply as one facet of you, which, along with your interests, hobbies, relationships, activities, and avocations helps make up your mission. Think of Life Mission as the melody, the theme of your life; career, on the other hand, is the musical instrument you play it on. Using different instruments (careers, avocations, and the like) you can express your mission in varying and interesting ways, but the melody (mission) stays the same. Thus you have infinite possibilities, infinite variations possible within one basic theme.

Put in another way, work is a description of what you do, but your Life Mission is the spiritual and holistic perspective of your life, the meaning of your life. Life Mission is therefore a fundamental reflection of who you are.

WHAT ARE SOME EXAMPLES OF LIFE MISSION?

Missions can take various forms, such as: to explore the polar ice caps, like Admiral Byrd; to protect consumers, like Ralph Nader, or to be part of a creative duo like Gertrude Stein and Alice B. Toklas.

A mission could be the greening of Los Angeles through planting trees (the goal of an urban organization called Tree People); dealing positively with the death process, as does Elisabeth Kübler-Ross; playing beautiful music on the trumpet, as does Wynton Marsalis; or sheltering injured and sick sea turtles, like Ila Loetscher. A Life Mission is, therefore, an individual role that is beneficial to all life.

Missions can be humble as well as grand. Some humble expressions of mission I have noted: to keep the floors of the local hospital sparkling, to give people the most unusual and unforgettable taxi ride they have ever had, or to make for children the most elaborate and biggest soap bubbles possible.

THE MISSIONARY SPIRIT

Every mission requires courage and commitment. People with a mission are dauntless, tenacious souls. They have answered their inner voice, taken risks, and responded when opportunity knocked. Their lives seem to say: "I know who

I am and where I want to be, and nothing is going to stand between me and my destiny. I refuse to hold back or to deprive myself of my purpose." To fulfill their calling, mission seekers may have had to battle institutions, government, society, relatives, parents, and even mates. They persevere without asking permission from others and accept responsibility for the outcome. And you can do that, too.

FROM MISSION IMPOSSIBLE TO POSSIBLE

In the old TV series called Mission Impossible, the main character always received an "impossible" assignment to perform. "Your mission, should you choose to accept it . . ." was the stock statement heard each week. The viewers knew the lead character was going to accept that mission, and there was never any doubt he would succeed. That's a good message right there. Let's compare that TV series with the concept of mission:

You Get Your Life Mission from Inside Yourself. Unlike the show's assignment, your assignment comes from within, from your soul. Your first assignment is to discover what has always been there, but needs to come into conscious awareness.

"But," you may protest, "I need to pay for my exotic cockatoo, see the kids through school, keep up my standard of living, join the country club." Anything else but "This is what I need to do." The creative web that you spin, like that of the spider, must come from within. Manifesting your Life Mission is like weaving your own special web. There's no other pattern quite like *yours.*

Your Mission is Possible. It would be the quintessential cosmic joke for you to want something you couldn't fulfill. If it's your heart's desire, you can *realize* it.

FARMER GENE

Gene, a lanky beanpole of a fellow from northern Iowa, remembered applying for management positions after leaving graduate school. Believing he should get a "real" job, he sent out applications for positions he didn't want. From the start he knew that these positions weren't his calling. Like a kid pretending to enjoy school when he'd rather be outdoors, he was just going through the motions.

The problem wasn't his qualifications. Gene had an MBA with honors from the University of Minnesota. But those positions didn't intersect properly with his Life Mission. He had plenty of clues: he enjoyed making himself feel at home with old family photos, his grandma's quilts, playing his Dad's harmonica, or taking walks in the countryside with the dog. And, every vacation he went back to the family farm, where he looked after the livestock and checked to see the condition of the soil and property. "As a child," he related, "I was really attached to the animals. I nursed many a bird's broken wing and talked to the cows during milking."

Gene was at heart a country boy. He felt about as comfortable in a business suit as a unicorn does in a water-bed store. But to please his father, he went off to the city to "make a name for himself" (that is, for his family) by taking a nine-to-five job. He was blind to his own clues.

After ten years of working indoors, Gene sought advice. It took only a short while for him to see the light. He returned to the area he loved and bought some land. Nevermind that farms were folding left and right around him. He answered his call of being a land caretaker. And his MBA came in handy.

(Nothing is ever lost.) Gene combined farming and consulting for local businesses and farmers.

For a mission to be truly yours, desire and ability need to be in harmony. Like Gene, you may con yourself into thinking you want to pursue a particular path, but that deception won't work forever. It never does. The mission search requires honesty and determination.

You Have the Choice to Accept Your Life Mission. It's yours for the taking. To be yourself is quite simple. Who else is better qualified to be you? What if someone decided to take over your role in life? Would you sit back calmly without comment? You'd probably find that person can't really be you as well as you can. It's your decision to accept your role and act according to your true nature.

Your Life Mission Is Unique. If you have been conditioned by herd thinking to be a part of the pack, to emphasize sameness and minimize the differences, it's difficult to identify the unique part of yourself.

What is unique about you? Statements such as "I'm a mother of three children,"or "I like people," or "I have an aardvark in my back yard," don't count because they refer to something external rather than a special quality in you. Focus on a characteristic that has always been inseparable from you.

When I asked Jim, a scientist, about his mission, he said he had the unique capacity to know just how things interconnected. At age seven he declared: "The bombing of Hiroshima is bad for people and it will hurt the fish, too!" For him, caring about the planet and making connections between events shaped his unique mission as an environmental caretaker.

SOMETIMES I FEEL LIKE A MISSIONLESS CHILD

Many people have neglected their mission. They remain, like the man in Kafka's parable "Before the Law," languishing at the entrance gate to their own space.

What might keep you from embracing the thing that is most yours? You may simply need the concepts and tools to gain entry to your mission. Perhaps you're just afraid. Or you might need encouragement. Maybe you feel the years lost will be too painful, that others will disapprove of your decisions, or that you'll lose what you've gained if you change course now.

But as the song lyric goes: "So how could you lose what you've never owned?" What do you profit if you've gained the whole world but lost your own mission?

Whatever has kept you off course, you can change now! Denying your destiny is the ultimate self-denial.

Remember that:

- There are clues that your mission has always been within you.

- Missed missions can—and must— be found.

- You can break through any barriers to your mission.

- Responding to a calling is the true measure of happiness.

There are no shortcuts to figuring out your life, no instant this and immediate that. Look at all the "how-to" books out there that offer easy solutions and quick fixes. The national passion for alternative ways to get high through drugs, sex, or fads is an example of trying to get to the top without doing the work. You reach your peak if you are willing to climb for it. That's why this book is not just fireside reading with popcorn and the cat, but serious business.

MISSION: GETTING DOWN TO BUSINESS

The concept of mission has long been used in business. Most corporations have a mission statement in their by-laws. Even a local golf course has a mission statement pasted onto the starter's window! The statement answers two basic questions: What benefits to humanity are we giving through our product or service? What is our responsibility to the world at large?

Whether a company produces chariots, cherries, or chimneys, or provides such services as career counseling, catering, or cleaning, it needs a clear purpose that goes beyond the product itself. Companies that fulfill their missions are immediately recognizable. Think of a shop where you like to do business. Chances are that this business is doing well and is popular with its customers because it's a place with a clearly-identified purpose.

A good example of companies with a clear mission are Celestial Seasonings, Erewhon, Reka, and Tom's of Maine. In the case of the latter, the owner, Tom Chapell, is passionate not only about manufacturing environmentally safe products and having a socially responsible business but also about involving everyone in the mission statement. In just eight years, he and his employees have developed Tom's of Maine into an 18-million-dollar company!

SELF-HELP EXERCISES FOR INITIATING YOUR LIFE MISSION SEARCH

Just because you have a Life Mission doesn't mean that it will always be self-evident. You need to do the inner work of listening to yourself, understanding who you are. You need to be very clear. Just who is the person looking for this mission?

EXERCISE: I AM

Each of us is a singular, one-of-a-kind mixture of talents, experience, and background. I like to think of it as your DNA—an unmistakable combination found only in YOU. The parts are like the warp and woof of your unique fabric. On separate pieces of paper, put I AM at the top of each page. Then list one thing, such as: I AM a daughter, student, tennis enthusiast. Now what does your particular set of ingredients tell you about yourself? For example, a sample list from a client:

I AM: woman, speaker of French, traveler, reader of autobiographies, soap opera addict, pillowcase collector, plant lover, dancer, American, golfer (in the low 80s). This person started to investigate new ideas for beautifying golf courses—in France!

By seeing yourself as unique, you can respond to your particular gift within. Your mission expresses your specific role, and your uniqueness is the particular DNA you have to carry it out.

EXERCISE: TALK TO YOUR MISSION AS A LOVER

Imagine your mission as a person you love who is sitting across from you. See it as a close relationship of yours. Feel it as an energy, a spirit, a part of you. You want to clear the air about problems in the relationship. This is the time to be candid with your partner. (For now, you don't need to know what your mission is called.)

- Tell your mission as lover everything you appreciate about it.

Address the mission as "you." For example: "I love you because you give me a feeling of power and energy whenever I do something I enjoy." "I get a rush when I know we're in sync with each other."

- Now tell your mission as lover what you expect from it. Be candid! What do you need from your mission? For example: "I want you to encourage me and let me know when I am neglecting you. Give me clues as to who you are!"

- Tell your mission in what ways your needs have not yet been met.

- What do you miss in your relationship? "I need quiet time to talk with you."

- Reverse the role now, and become your mission. (Repeat the first three steps.) As the mission, tell YOURSELF what YOU AS MISSION expect and what YOU AS MISSION are not getting. "You never spend enough time with me. You leave me last in your plans."

- Analyze this scene as if you had heard two lovers discussing their relationship. What is your assessment of their problem? How well do they get along? What's the prognosis for their relationship? If it is not so good, what does each party need to do to improve the relationship?

- Finally, write your mission a love letter. Say everything you feel. If you find you have been afraid to get too intimate with your son or daughter, put that in letter form. Do not be shy about role-playing your mission, too! It can give you a lot of insight about your relationship to it.

EXERCISE: DESCRIBE HOW YOUR LIFE MISSION
LOOKS AND FEELS

Use any metaphor, image, or analogy you can think of.
You are developing your own personal mythology. Put as
much sensory detail in it as possible. It might go something
like this: "My mission looks like a huge medieval castle on a
hill with turrets and flags waving in the summer breeze," or
"My mission feels like the actions of dedicated Persephone,
traveling back and forth between the underworld and here."

What kinds of things are evoked in you when you read
your description? For Persephone, you might write: "I am a
traveler like her, connecting the two worlds of the spiritual and
the worldly." Write your insights down in a Life Mission notebook. Add to this description from time to time. Notice if any
pattern or theme recurs. (Mine always had musical references.)

EXERCISE: IMAGINE YOU WROTE YOUR LIFE SCRIPT

You are not a victim. Start seeing your family as an
asset. By focusing on the role you played in your family,
you'll discover how your particular family configuration
enabled you to be who you are and how it helped mold
your mission.

Rewrite the script. Imagine you chose your parents.
What would have prompted you to pick them and the number of siblings you have? Why did you elect to be born at a
particular time and place in history? What can you learn
from your chosen lifestyle, relatives and family members?

Julia, a free-lance journalist, chose a family in which
there was a high degree of intellectual energy. She
got lots of things ready-made: educated parents,
intellectual stimulation, and lively conversation. But
her family had difficulty expressing feelings. When

Julia became a journalist, she found her home life gave her depth of critical analysis, the ability to think and converse. But perhaps most important was her compassion for people who avoided feelings. In therapy she worked through much of her self-expression blocks. Now she is ingenious at getting people she interviews to express themselves, knowing firsthand how difficult it was for herself to do just that.

Mike felt being gay was a disadvantage. How could he have wanted it? Then he began to look at his "liability" as an asset and discovered that his sexuality allowed him to see things from both sides of the coin. (Other minorities will understand this.) Mike's gift was the ability to solve problems. He was especially talented at coming up with alternative viewpoints—he had no trouble doing that because he was living differently from the "norm." He began to look at his sexuality not as a curse but as an opportunity. It allowed him to see things from a different perspective because his life was free of conventional choices.

In your journal, list the reasons your life circumstances required that you lived where and when you did. State why you needed each close family member for growth in your life.

CLUES TO YOUR MISSION

Everyone likes clues. They provide the most important evidence of your Life Mission throughout your life. Here are some vital tips to help get you on the right track with your mission process.

Clue #1: Passions and Enjoyments. Jean, a real-estate broker, was forever puttering in her garden and helping friends

with theirs. She would habitually stop to look at new landscape designs, and she owned a collection of books on interior
design. But hard as it is to believe, until Jean observed what
she actually liked doing—creating beauty through nature—
she didn't recognize the clues! The body always responds to
right action and right thought by giving you energy. Look for
times when you feel that energy. Most often it will be evident
when you are engaged in a passion or enjoyment. When
you're on track, you'll catch yourself feeling enthusiastic,
moved, and alive. Let's look at Brenda's example:

DRAWING ON YOUR SKILLS

A very discerning Southern woman with an
investigative bent, Brenda was heading into her forties with a sense of being totally off-base with her
mission. A native of Georgia, Brenda loved those
old Southern mansions and the sense of history in
her environment. She lamented the decay of those
buildings whenever she read about it (clue!).

Brenda knew what she was interested in, but she
spent considerable time trying to translate it into
practical terms. She constantly found reasons that
she should not pursue her mission of esthetic preservation. A French language teacher, she secretly wanted to use her artistic talents to restore and recover art.
But she insisted there was no way to express exactly
what she wanted because it was so rare.

She told me of an incident on a plane flight in
which a fellow passenger described a rather unusual passion. He made underwater drawings of
archaeological sites. "Wouldn't you love to do
that?" I asked. She literally rose up in her seat, her
eyes brightened, and she cried, "YES!" Then she
slumped back down and sighed, "But there isn't a
market for such an unusual thing." For a brief

moment, Brenda had experienced a clue of passion.
What would that "water archaeologist" be doing now if he had limited himself with such thinking? The market for your talent needs only one person— why not you?

What are *you* passionate about? What gives you energy? Include any items from the past. Pay attention to those clues that tell you what YOU want in your mission. Even if the enjoyment is for a fleeting moment, make note of it! Observe what you catch yourself enjoying (it isn't always obvious). Sometimes a passion can stare you in the face and you won't recognize it. By actively being aware of your passions, you can begin to see your mission take shape more clearly.

Get out your mission journal and write down examples. Don't stop to analyze or censor them. Just write down your passions and enjoyments as fast as you can until you can't think of any more. Add any that occur to you over time. After you have a sizable list (say 10 or 20 items), look for the clues—common threads and experiences that weave throughout your list.

Do you enjoy physical things? Mental things? Outdoor things? Solitary things? Things involving nature? Animals? Position yourself to encounter more of your passions and enjoyments by seeking out attractive environments where those feelings will be unleashed. If you like animals, for example, go to a zoo. If you like mountains, go hiking. If you like children, go to a playground!

Clue #2: Monitor Your Aches and Pains. When you fail to respond to your inner wisdom, you'll feel specific emotional and physical reactions resulting from that neglect. Your mission will nestle somewhere in your body and reveal its presence through aches and pains. Consult your body and let it tell you what the problem is.

Keep track of those aches and pains. When and where do they flare up? Identify any sad experiences you have had and where the pain was located. What were the circumstances of the experience? How did you react? What caused the pain to stop, if indeed it did?

WOOD THAT CATHERINE COULD

Catherine, recently divorced, first felt the pain when she worked on the doors of her house. The process of sanding, staining, and varnishing wood brought back memories of construction work that she had done just after high school. She had always loved woodworking, but had been talked out of it because it wasn't "ladylike" enough. If you asked her any question about wood she'd talk your ear off.

But it wasn't until she began to build the kids a tree house that her love of wood really affected her. She developed a pain in her chest, so much so that she thought the physical exertion might be causing a strain on her heart. The doctor couldn't find anything wrong. (It was precisely the opposite, of course. Neglect had caused a strain on her heart.) She began to spend as much time with wood as possible. The pain stopped when she satisfied her need to use wood for play and leisure. And she made it profitable besides: Catherine started a woodworking business designing and building children's tree- and playhouses.

Clue #3: Look For Rewards. You're never punished for pursuing your soul's path. Some form of reward will always occur. Something positive will happen. It might come in the form of a gift, such as a trip to a foreign country from a relative. Or it might be a sudden loan to continue graduate study.

I bought new stereo speakers for the first time in 17 years to encourage and support my reawakening musical self. The first time I listened to these new speakers, I experienced the rush I had felt with the first set. In the next day's mail I received a check from an unexpected source for the exact amount I had paid for the speakers. Coincidence? Or a reward?

For a three-week period focus on doing what you really like for as much time as you can possibly spare (see Clue #1 for ideas). During this time, write down every positive, unusual, or unexpected thing that happens to you. These events will be your rewards!

Nancy, an accountant, was wrestling with making some changes in her life. She decided to work on a project for the homeless and reduced her accounting practice. She also decided to pursue additional schooling, even if she didn't yet know what. During a period of three weeks, she kept a list and totaled more than 50 rewards. They included:

- a workshop flyer addressed to a previous occupant at her address, which gave Nancy the answer about a direction she should take in her schooling.

- an unexpected referral for a new account with a huge commission.

- permission from her landlady to keep a stray (homeless!) cat.

There are always rewards for carrying out your Life Mission. They may be invisible at the time, but you will get them. Move closer to your path, and you will be showered with support.

Clue #4 Analyze Your Fears. Fear is a friendly reminder that you may be running from the very thing you love. Fear often arises when you refuse to face your mission. Look at Dan:

FATHER DAN

Dan, a CEO in a large financial institution, was so terrified about dealing with his Life Mission (nurturing young people) that he actually cringed whenever

he said any word remotely connected to it. It was as
if saying the word would cause lightning to strike.
He feared what he loved. Dan was especially interested in helping kids with their financial planning.

Dan had spent twenty years escaping his desire to be
a financial nurturer for youngsters. He thought it wasn't
manly and couldn't see any way to make a living from
it. Dan resisted going to the local youth center and
offering financial advice to teenagers. He finally faced
his passion to nurture others and was rewarded with a
new job and a leadership position in a local youth club.

He volunteered his services now and then to youth
groups and his face would flush as he told me about
it. "Those kids actually thanked me for helping them
set up a budget," he said as tears welled up in his
eyes. "Maybe they'll have a future a little freer of anxiety than I did at their age."

Here's an exercise that may help you face your fear of
your mission.

- Complete the sentence: "I'm afraid of _____."
  List every fear individually, no matter how silly, triv-
  ial, or huge. "I'm afraid of coughing in movie the-
  aters" is just as important to acknowledge as "I'm
  afraid of death."

- Then on a separate page, turn those fear statements into desires by completing the words, "I
  want _____." Write, for example, "I want to
  sit through a movie quietly" or "I want to accept
  my own mortality."

- For each desire example put the result that you
  want. Such statements as "I want to go a movie
  once a week" or "I want to write my will calmly"
  might be things you would do if fear hadn't pre-

vented it for so long. Just putting your fears in written form will encourage you to address them through action and get moving in the direction you want. Now get started on one example!

Clue #5: What Do You Want To Learn? When you want to find out about something, it shows that a desire is awakened in you. What stimulates your curiosity? Get a college catalog and page through it, picking out five courses you'd take if you didn't have to be concerned about time, money, skills, or other restrictions. Write all those items down in your notebook.

Then look for clues about things you want to know more about. Some items on the list may even surprise you. One client's list included astronomy. She realized that she needed to move to a western state with wide open skies to fulfill her mission of raising people's consciousness about the gentle treatment of animals.

The teacher teaches what the teacher needs to know. Mission and learning mirror each other like reflecting pools. After all, Mozart wanted to learn more about music and Leonardo da Vinci about the human figure (and not vice versa). What you want to learn gives you clues about your mission.

GENTLE JOE

Joe, a 45-year-old politician with a tough, streetwise exterior yet gentle interior began to sense his Life Mission taking form: making the world a safer place for children. When Joe was a young boy, he would get beaten up regularly on the way to school. Later (still not knowing the reason), he decided to become a policeman. He was interested in learning about crime detection, self-defense techniques, and breaking patterns of violence in school children.

Joe became a police commissioner. It was not until 20 years later that Joe realized why he had entered law enforcement. (Remember, your Life Mission can often be staring you in the face and you won't always see it.) Joe made a further transition: studied for a degree in political science in order to continue his mission process in politics.

List up to 10 things you want to learn more about. What is it about each of them that intrigues you? Who can help you get more information or training in this field? What does your list reveal about your Life Mission?

Clue #6: Who Are Your Heroes? Think of the books you used to read as a child or the ones your parents read to you. Who are the people, fictitious or real, living or dead, whom you admired? Maybe you kept a scrapbook or clippings on your heroes. Maybe you went back to the city library again and again to reread that one story about Amelia Earhart or the first big-league African-American baseball player Jackie Robinson. They will tell you a lot about the person you want to be. The kind of people they were, the situations they found themselves in and the results they got will give you insights into your own directions.

Santa Barbara

Barbara identified with Saint Joan of Arc. She recognized that her needs to be a crusader, an activist, and a famous woman had long been languishing. Her interests were in science and writing, and her heroes included Jacques Cousteau, and Maria Sybill, known as Merian, an 18th-century German naturalist. Barbara wanted to learn more about how to write non-fiction and scientific articles creatively. She wanted to direct her crusading spirit in the service of the environment by using her scientific background and her writing ability to support her crusades in these causes.

Write down three heroes you identified with and list the qualities and deeds you admired in them. Identify those traits that YOU would like to have. In what context (setting, area, workplace, geographic location, etc.) could these qualities best be put to use?

LIFE MISSION STATEMENT

It's time for you to take the first step toward describing your Life Mission. Begin by filling in the spaces in these sentences. Use only one word per space:

I AM _____.

I am most me when I am _____

(state of being).

I enjoy _____ (interest/field)

most, and I feel it most intensely when I am

_____(environment).

I am most confident when I am _____

_____(activity).

I feel best when I use my talent of _____

_____.

I most want to learn about _____

_____.

My hero is _____.

I believe I was born into my family to experience

_____.

My mission needs the quality of _____

from me.

My mission feels/looks like _____

_____(description).

My mission is inseparable from my talent of_____

_____ .

Build from here by adding your own sentences. In the following chapters you will be encircling your Life Mission by focusing on it from different angles. In fact, the goal of every exercise in this book is to help you identify, develop, manifest, and then live the mission you are here to express. Does your mission have something to do with making people laugh? To perform plays for the disabled? Or does it involve creating beauty from cardboard, recording the lives of elephants, making life easier for people through the manufacture of rubber bands, or educating people about the beauty and ecology of the Grand Canyon? (I have culled all these examples from real sources.)

The nature of a mission can be anything. Any mission is valid so long as it expresses the talent, gift and cause you hold most dear. The important thing is that it reflects your soul's intent. Be assured that when you live your mission, you are in sync with your Source, and the world can only benefit from your contribution.

This chapter marks the beginning of an exciting and fulfilling process. Know that your mission is now within your reach. Your task is to begin this discovery process with commitment, joy, and faith.

Your Life Mission is, in the striking poem "On His Blindness," by John Milton, "that one talent which is death to hide." It's the talent you were endowed with. You have the answer to your soul's bidding within you. Make it a part of your conscious awareness. There is no better gift to give yourself—and others—than the talent you have.

2

Mission á la Mode

Are you here to to make a splash or work quietly? Do you prefer to work with people or with facts and things? Do you want to make your mark on stage or behind the scenes? Do you want to move mountains or inspire people to move them?

Check the category which describes the way you most like to do things:

___ I take charge to get things done.

___ I motivate others to get things done.

___ I cooperate with others to get things done.

___ I make sure to get things done with quality and standards.

Each of you prefers to run your life in one of four specific ways to meet your goals and needs. I'll call that your Primary Mode (PM), the process style for your mission. The one you use (called Doer, Motivator, Stabilizer, or Analyzer), is descriptive of your behavior. Life Mission expresses who you are, and PM expresses *the manner* in which you prefer to carry out that mission.

Like your mission, your PM is a "comfort zone." It should match *you,* and not the other way around. When your mission is out-of-phase with your PM, it creates tension and distress and rarely leads to productive efforts.

Your PM reflects who you are when you are acting most naturally. As soon as you recognize that you like to do things a certain way and understand how to use that knowledge appropriately, you can risk accepting the mission that matches your PM (it always will). The purpose of this chapter is to give you insight into the way you like to do things and how to make that PM work for you in the service of your mission, as well as dropping ways unsuited to your PM.

DOING WHAT COMES NATURALLY

You function better when you can be and act in self-awareness and in harmony with your PM. One person's PM is not necessarily another's. But, you say, wouldn't I naturally use my own Primary Mode? Not necessarily. We often defer to others on ways we should run our lives. My father and I, for example, had different ways of accomplishing our goals, and each way was valid in its own right. For him, sermons had to be rehearsed in the study on Thursdays from nine-to-twelve and be exactly three and a half typewritten pages in length.

For many years I used a PM more like my father's (he was an analyzer), writing out all my lecture notes and rehearsing them the night before. I knew how many pages an hour's lecture required and even practiced those lectures while walking around! I deliberated and obsessed about things. Would we discuss the Rococo Period before Spring break or after? It didn't work. I was unconsciously trying to pattern my behavior after my father's PM. (I am a Motivator/Doer.) I later realized that, to be a more effective speaker, my approach had to be more spontaneous. My mission—in *all* of its aspects (coaching, writing, composing, and speaking, for example)—had to be carried out using the Motivator PM.

Have you patterned an aspect of your mission after a parent or role model whose PM in that activity *clearly differed* from yours? Then it is time to become consciously aware of your PM. To realize your mission smoothly and successfully, it is imperative to honor your own mode of operation, that is, how you need to act to travel your soul's path most congruently.

Perhaps you, too, have patterned some of your PM after someone else's. Now is the time to learn about your style and how you must act to travel your soul's path.

WHY YOU MUST BE AWARE OF YOUR PM

In a hilarious scene in *I Love Lucy*, Lucille Ball portrayed a harried worker trying to keep up with an assembly line moving faster and faster. The conveyor belt won. Perhaps you have on occasion felt in that position. No matter what you do, life wants it done faster or differently. You feel helpless to meet others' demands. And then, like Lucy, you end up thinking any failure is your fault.

Misunderstanding your PM can cause you to negate your own behavior. The clearer you get about your own PM and the more comfortable you feel about yourself, the more you can work on a mission your way. Let's look at Alan and Marilyn:

ALAN ACCEPTS

Alan, a free-lance writer, was in a funk. His mission to inspire people to political awareness through writing was faltering. A lanky man with broad shoulders and a shock of blond hair falling into his eyes, he seemed about to fall apart as he sat in my office shuffling through his briefcase to find his portfolio. Alan's business was also in a state of chronic chaos. Unpaid bills and invoices fluttered among his written work.

Whenever Alan did proofreading, correcting, and editing of material, he felt a certain heaviness. Now Alan *thought* he was really a detail-oriented person; after all, a person who writes must be organized, right? When his feature article appeared in a magazine with the caption "General _____ arrived *uninformed* and ready for action," Alan realized he had to do something.

Awareness and acceptance of his PM helped Alan act more in sync with his mission. He had figured his frequent mistakes (like *uninformed* instead of *uniformed*) were a character flaw rather than a result of his low priorities. Frustration over his disorganization was taking away from his ability to write effectively. I suggested he set about getting a proofreader and a bookkeeper instead of knocking himself out with something he wasn't good at. Why try for excellence doing things he didn't like when others performed that service so much better? His commissions and his self-esteem increased.

MAGIC IN HOLLYWOOD

After analyzing her PM, Marilyn, a soft-spoken New Englander with an elegant demeanor, realized why she didn't like details, formal suits, working in structured ways, and "toeing the line." (She was a Doer.) Yet this was what her position in a city agency "demanded" of her. She could also no longer accept being the dutiful employee, especially since she was older than her bosses. The atmosphere at the agency was grim and devoid of humor. To vent her frustration, Marilyn would wait for the next vacation, during which she could dream of her mission (to be an urban sorcerer).

I asked Marilyn to describe how she would spend a typical work day if she could design it her way. Her PM took on an entirely different look. "In a bright Hollywood office I'd develop new ideas for designing streets that would show people a new way of experiencing their city," she recounted excitedly. She wanted to be her own boss and acknowledge the adventurer she always was. "I don't know why I didn't see this before, but I want to be a big splash, not a tiny drop." Now she is working on a city project dear to her heart, but in her own way.

Marilyn felt she was incompetent and wasting time; Alan thought he was sloppy. Marilyn realized that an esthetic, urban atmosphere of unsupervised creativity was crucial to her emotional and mental health. Alan, on the other hand, realized he needed an uncluttered environment in which to write his essays.

EXERCISE: WRITE ON

Take a pen and write your signature as if you were writing a check. Better yet, take out your checkbook and make it out to Naomi Stephan. (Just kidding!) Now take your non-preferred hand and write your signature again. Compare the two. Which one looks better? Went faster? Was easier? More efficient? The signature you wrote with your preferred hand, of course. How many times in the last hundred checks did you use your non-preferred hand? Probably never, and for good reason. Your PM, like your mission, makes life easier, gets results, works faster and looks better. Right? Why not start using it more consciously?

GETTING CONSCIOUS OF YOUR PM

Work this list horizontally and rate each of the four words in every line as to the way in which the word describes you:
4=describes me most; **3**=next highest; **2**=next to lowest; **1**=lowest.

Use all four numbers (none twice) for each row. A sample answer is: <u>3</u> strong-willed; <u>4</u> enthusiastic; <u>2</u> responsive; <u>1</u> organized.

DOER	MOTIVATOR	STABILIZER	ANALYZER
4 bold	1 generous	2 understanding	3 conventional
4 strong-willed	2 enthusiastic	1 responsive	3 organized
4 decisive	1 influential	2 agreeable	3 orderly
4 competitive	1 gullible	3 calm	2 unresponsive
4 self-assured	3 humorous	2 supportive	1 indecisive
3 tension producer	1 imaginative	4 dependable	2 exacting
1 pragmatic	2 charming	4 traditional	3 orderly
4 blunt	1 emotional	3 low key	2 restrained
1 tough	2 self-promoting	1 team player	4 critical
4 impatient	3 impulsive	1 predictable	2 disciplined
4 dominating	1 manipulative	2 loyal	3 meticulous
1 cold	1 dramatic	2 thorough	4 proper
4 action-oriented	3 trusts a lot	2 good listener	1 evaluates
4 self starter	1 high contact	3 logical person	2 works alone
4 accepts challenge	3 uses intuition	2 sticks to procedure	1 slow-paced
4 likes risks	2 likes persuasion	1 works in small groups	3 non-verbal
4 forceful	2 likes fun jobs and opinions	1 likes structure	3 business-like
3 disciplined, quick	1 likes to motivate	4 quiet in meetings	2 respects facts
3 works on hunches	4 dislikes details	1 methodical	2 problem solver
4 accepts challenges	1 visionary	2 traditional	1 likes clarity
Total 11	38	44	47

My highest score is _____ 71 _____   My PM is Doer

The next step in your PM work is for you to validate and accept your PM. See if your choice from the inventory on page 30 (and the beginning of the chapter) *feels* right to you. Some of you might have second choices which scored nearly as high as the first one. Obviously, we are combinations of all four traits, but usually we prefer to use one trait more often than the others. For the purposes of this book, concentrate on your highest score.

DESCRIPTIONS OF EACH PM

The following descriptions will give you further clarification and information on each PM. Read about yours first, then look at the others. You have scores in all categories, and you use all styles at some time or another, but for our purposes here, concentrate on identifying your PM. Remember, we're not judging actions here. Rather, we're describing ways persons of a particular mode prefer to act to meet their needs.

DOERS

Doers get things done fast. I recognize Doer clients when they ask me right off, with eyes screwed up and fingers tapping impatiently on the chair, "How long is this process going to take?" (Guess who has the greatest problems with Life Mission as process?)

Doers enjoy challenge, risk, and obstacles. They like to go out on a limb, especially when trouble is involved. Doers seek dissonance and thrive on conflict. As one put it to me: "I can't stand a job in which nothing happens. Give me a good fight, and I'm all set to go."

Doers rarely mix emotions with tasks. If people don't perform and someone has to be terminated, Doers will take care of that job without flinching. They want to tell the rest of the world what to do and take responsibility for the results. Well, some of us need to be daring enough to risk achieving what we say we are going to!

But if something demands incubation or deliberation, Doers find it difficult to wait. On the other hand, if an instant decision is needed, let the Doer handle it.

If you are a Doer, you take decisive steps when everyone else runs around wringing their hands. You probably have your own work space but are rarely in it (and it looks that way, too). In bridge, you bid first and count your points later.

Things that suit your results-oriented PM are those with heavy take-charge responsibility and fast deadlines. You like to cut through things and get down to business. You are competitors who like nothing better than to be #1 (remember Marilyn). You don't cry over spilled milk or get emotionally involved in the process. You have a strong sense of purpose, of self, and you are a person who cares about what is going on now rather than the future.

Incidentally, you might find yourself saying: "So what? I know all these things." Remember, you Doers tend to see yourselves as the model of human behavior.

DOT THE DOER

Dorothy, a stately woman of 35, had long kept herself in low-profile jobs. Seeking out a change of direction from her manufacturing sales rep position in Kansas, she had abruptly moved to Los Angeles. In a PM workshop, Dorothy "discovered" she was a classic Doer. "So what?" she quipped (quick confirmation that the analysis was right).

Dorothy was in transition and planned to have a new job in a new field (human resources) within the next two weeks. (Dorothy was always ten steps ahead of everyone.) Doers do things fast, and sure enough, Dorothy got her new job in record time. I called her and asked how it was going. "Oh," she

said, "I'm angry I have to go to work at five A.M."
"Why?" I asked. "I have to get there by six A.M. to
make sure nobody gets ahead of me!" was her reply.

I told Dorothy she could continue to leave the
house angry or realize that it was in the nature of her
PM to want to be ahead and that she could leave early
for work at peace with herself if she took responsibility for her competitive approach. Dorothy's understanding has led to better performance because now,
she arrives at work ready for action rather than being
angry and hostile. Her colleagues began to find
Dorothy easier to work with. First thing you know,
she was presenting a seminar for her company. Doers
know only one direction: forward!

You must have a high key mission. It must be a headline
edition that requires power and commands recognition. You
need to make things happen fast. You must champion a cause
and challenge complacency. You are a born rebel for the good
of humanity. To accomplish what you need, you must have a
leading position.

Friendly advice for Doers:

- Incubate ideas, (*be* more, *act* less).

- Weigh evidence more carefully.

- Listen to the advice of others.

- Inject more warmth and feeling into your relations with others.

MOTIVATORS

Motivators are the show people of the quartet. Always on stage, emotional, witty, and fast thinking, they want to be like the Pied Piper of Hamelin, inspiring people toward a common goal. If someone is needed to promote ideas or make a product or person look good. Motivators are the best choice. They are consummate salespeople and can wax poetic about toothbrushes, dog collars, table salt, or cemetery plots.

Motivators love a pleasant, esthetic, non-businesslike atmosphere. They would prefer to do their work in a local café rather than in a stuffy office. When playing bridge, they don't always have their cards arranged properly in suits, but they are creative bidders.

If you like to make speeches, be on stage, go out in public, or give presentations of any kind, you're a Motivator. You can be counted on to be friendly, charming, and enthusiastic even under the worst circumstances. Highly reactive, you are likely to flare up easily and dramatize any situation. Tremors become earthquakes when you feel vulnerable. Whereas Doers can forget painful situations fast, you Motivators can harbor the hurt long after everyone else has forgotten what the issue was.

While Doers can work alone, you Motivators depend on other people for emotional support and approval. You wither when people don't respond, and find it difficult to be critical or disciplined. You are the harmony seekers, avoiding conflict, desiring agreement.

A Motivator friend of mine gets great pleasure out of devising funny phone messages to delight his customers. An inveterate ham, he gets people to call him just to hear the latest in witty puns. As you can imagine, any phone conversation with this fellow is bound to spark a series of laughs. Motivators do things with gusto. Beware, Motivators, that in all this fun you keep focused on your mission process.

ACTIVIST ALEX

In the first session with Alex I could barely get a word in edgewise (typical with Motivators). A good-natured, jovial, winsome man, Alex had spent the last few years in the entertainment industry working as a producer in Hollywood. In this job, Alex was able to explore much of his talent for writing and communication. His marriage was stable, the future looked bright, everything on the surface looked rosy.

But he knew something wasn't right. The old fire he had felt in the 1960s as a political activist leading marches had just never surfaced again. He also longed to go back to those areas of the world in which he had traveled in his late twenties.. Now he felt stuck, stodgy, out of step with himself, and unable to find an outlet for his energy.

Alex had spent a year coming up with hundreds of ideas for himself, but he rejected each one as a pipe dream. His present job often left him feeling alone and unappreciated, and his ideas were often discounted. The pressure of the industry sapped Alex's strength for motivational work. He missed the college-age kids he used to work with and the causes he had fought for.

Alex had a pattern of doing things only halfway before going on to the next item. Like many Motivators, he thought he needed to have it all, not understanding that when he had what he wanted, he had it all. As soon as he recognized that he needed to be out there with the troops leading them on and that he needed a cause to focus on, he finally began to get a glimpse of his mission. He returned to his sixties activism self, twenty years wiser, and put it in the service of teaching.

Alex demonstrates that Motivators are masterful at creative ways to do things and use quick-thinking methods to get something done, but need help in following through.

If you are a Motivator, you need to be surrounded, loved, and nourished by people, contact, and applause. That's why you are the performer of the group. You must be visionary and instill people with enthusiasm. You are a missionary with dreams. You love to generate ideas and come up with more ways to do things than you can use in a lifetime. When no one can think of a new way to do something, or all the ideas seem stale, you get people unstuck.

Your mission needs to involve the stimulation, motivation, and inspiration of people by using your creativity and talents to the common good. You need to use your ideas for future change and to create an atmosphere of true harmony.

Friendly advice for Motivators:

•Check impulsive behavior.

•Avoid manipulating with emotions.

•Organize your priorities.

•Work on completing what you start.

STABILIZERS

Someone once said that Doers and Motivators get raises for what they *say* they do and Stabilizers and Analyzers for what they *actually* do. Stabilizers are the rocks of Gibraltar, the cool, calm, collected folks who put everyone at ease and make life bearable. Stabilizers are friendly people who prefer being around similar types, although not in such large groups as the Motivators. Stabilizers are sincere, loyal, and cooperative. They are excellent team players. They do not like to rock the boat but prefer to work in a careful, thorough way without sudden changes.

I once had a secretary who was a Stabilizer. I couldn't expect her to initiate things but when I gave directives she carried them out. She had a fantastic routine and followed through on everything I asked. I could count on giving her many things to do because she would decide the method of getting them all done. A Motivator would try to work on them all at once and a Doer secretary would last only as long as it took her to revamp the entire office.

One of my clients, Dora, refused to acknowledge that she was a Stabilizer. (Unlike Doers, Stabilizers often have trouble accepting their PM.) I asked how long she had been in her present position. "Nine years," she replied. And what was the average length of time anyone had been in her department? "Two." 'Nuf said. Stabilizers tend to stay in jobs, relationships and projects longer than is productive for them. For them, too much rushing results in pressure but too much delay in frustration.

If you are a Stabilizer, you have an even temperament, put people at ease, and make the work atmosphere relaxed by reducing conflict. You are a true bridge over troubled waters. In fact, your niceness often gets you into trouble—you heap upon yourself more work than you can manage. You put the needs of others first, and the resentment you feel gets suppressed rather than expressed. I often recommend assertiveness training for Stabilizers.

You function very well with procedures and routine. You probably have a work space with plants and pictures of your loved ones. You take in information and are supportive and dependable while radiating calm. In bridge, you bid in a traditional fashion and rarely take chances.

You like environments and processes that are traditional. You question why things should be changed just for change's sake. If a long-standing procedure changes, you are inclined to say, "Couldn't we talk about this first?" Stabilizers want things to be permanent. That is why security is a top priority for them.

You Stabilizers must have missions that concern preservation, community service, continuity, nurturing, and permanence. You must keep the world in balance and stable. You are the glue that holds things together. You Stabilizers love process—almost too much. But remember, the mission process is fluid and subject to alterations

Friendly advice for Stabilizers:

• Take the initiative.

• Say *no* more often.

• Work on flexibility and spontaneity.

• Learn to face conflict and give criticism.

ANALYZERS

Analyzers contribute a detailed, careful approach to life that enables them to deliver quality. They are the watchdogs for doing things right according to rules and regulations, collecting and analyzing data to insure accuracy and precision.

Would you want your surgeon to be a Doer? "Let's get this operation over, I've got my golf game this afternoon and I have to beat Dr. So-and-so. What? I accidentally took out the patient's appendix instead of her gall bladder? Oh well, this patient is better off without it." If you need an operation, you'll want your surgeon to be an Analyzer!

Analyzer Trish came to her first Life Mission session armed with twelve different neatly-stacked career tests in alphabetical order. She hadn't yet made up her mind about the results because she needed a little more information. I knew right away she was an Analyzer because Analyzers are the information addicts, preferring thorough, copious detail and careful analysis to get results.

If Analyzer is your PM, you like things to be rational and organized. Talking is not your favorite way of communicating. You are far more likely to use non-verbal methods more effectively.

You make decisions with difficulty because you must weigh all the evidence. You have your information ready, your credentials in order and your facts straight. You prepare a lot of questions that serve to clarify any fuzzy issue. You are not apt to let something slip through your fingers without careful scrutiny! Since you are sensitive about the way things ought to be done, it may take you longer to decide what you want, but your choices are always well-informed.

You expect punctuality, organization, and detailed agenda rather than the slapdash approach of the Doers. Chaos can get in the way of your need for clarity. You work in a neat, focused, and serious manner and could easily locate last year's memo to the neighbors about mowing too early in the morning. You often confuse process with solutions and delay making decisions because you have too much information. Watch that you avoid analysis paralysis with too much data.

You're the bridge player who knows the most obscure conventions and plays according to Hoyle. You know all the rules by heart, and you play by them. You fare best in an atmosphere of deliberation and weighing the evidence. You will not want to go with risky ventures but rather opt for the safe bet. Environments that suit you well are ones in which there are clear definitions of what is expected and slow, patient, accurate, investigative approaches are needed. You are a quality control person. Look at Laurie:

LEERY LAURIE

A quiet, deliberate woman with carefully coiffed hair and a penetrating look, Laurie came up with a creative new type of business venture involving office design. Laurie was leery of making the transition to self-employment. (Going into business for themselves alone can often be difficult for Analyzers.)

Laurie made the transition only after preparing a two-year business plan, thoroughly researching her market, seeing a marketing consultant, and taking several tests.

She was very aware of her strong points (planning, design, calculating). They enabled her to overcome a lot of personal resistance to going solo and gave her the courage to work on her lesser strengths of assertiveness and initiation. She has gotten closer to understanding her mission, which is to enhance environments, particularly interior ones.

If you are an Analyzer, your mission must incorporate safety, protection, accuracy, quality, or research and development. You complete with precision what the Doers, Motivators, Stabilizers, and Analyzers have worked on. Your mission must deal with anything which has to do with improving quality of life. You are the watchdogs of the universe, ensuring everyone that things function better with your expert help. Analyzers need to remember that the mission process has no "end" but rather a series of beginnings and endings.

Friendly advice for Analyzers:

- Learn to make decisions faster and stick with them.

- Learn when to stop gathering information.

- Avoid a rigid approach to life.

- Be willing to take more risks.

Your PM is the way you express yourself most authentically. It reflects your creative process and mission. Understanding your PM gives not only life shape and direction but also a framework within which to carry out your mission in the manner most characteristic of you. Armed with self-awareness, you can develop options and crystallize them into your quest.

Mission seekers do it *á la mode*!

3

The Creative Connection

*A cat said to a squirrel: "How wonderful it is that
you can so unerringly locate buried nuts to nurture
you through the winter!" The squirrel said: "To a
squirrel, what would be remarkable would be a
squirrel who was unable to do such things!"*

It's a myth that creativity is an elusive quality only some people
are born with. As our squirrel would say, "Nuts!" If you feel
that you must sculpt like Michelangelo, write poetry like Emily
Dickinson or compose like Beethoven in order to be creative,
wait a minute! Could Emily Dickinson paint, Michelangelo
sing, Marie Curie write poetry or Ludwig van Beethoven understand bacteria? Probably not! And it doesn't matter. What
matters is that they nurtured their own creativity.

Everyone has the ability to be creative. You have it, I
have it. The important thing is that you tap your inner
resources and express your creative capacities, whatever they
may be. As the psychologist Abraham Maslow said, "I
learned . . . that a first rate soup is more creative than a sec-
ond-rate painting and that, generally, cooking or parenthood

or making a home could be creative while poetry need not be; it could be uncreative."

The purpose of this chapter is to:

1. Help you recognize, appreciate, and develop your creativity.
2. Relate the creative process to your PM process style.
3. Put that creativity in the service of your Life Mission and your soul's path.

Strengthening the connection to your creativity will increase your self-esteem as well as affirm and enrich the inventive storehouse within you. Work on the chapter's techniques daily, and the results will truly amaze you.

CREATIVITY AND LIFE MISSION

Creativity is the link for accessing your Life Mission. Both are processes. Paul Torrance, a well known authority on creativity, defined creativity as "the process of becoming sensitive to problems, deficiencies, gaps in knowledge, missing elements, disharmonies . . . identifying the difficulty; searching for solutions . . ." In other words if you develop your creativity, you will be better able to deal with your problems and design your life as you want it to be.

Creativity connects you with your inner wisdom, from which all your ideas come. Creativity is a non-linear, non-logical method of gaining information. No amount of list making, skill identification, vocational tests, or reasoning can really explain the passion for a mission like, say, making soap (such as Dr. Bronner writes about on his soap labels).

We'll look now at what creativity is, why it's important, and how to transform stumbling blocks into building blocks for your mission.

CREATIVITY: A CLASS ACT

Creativity is fundamental to discovering your Life Mission in two important ways:

1. You find your mission by creative means.
2. You tap your creative resources within for clues to your mission.

The suppression of creativity contributes to unhappiness, dissatisfaction, and lack of productivity. Wherever innovation and exploration are discouraged, jobs become routine and boring. People then become frustrated because they are blocked from self-expression.

At the beginning of one semester, I asked the members of a class called "Women and the Creative Process" if they thought they were creative. Many doubted that they were. I asked students to bring to the last class session something imaginative they had done and share it with others. Fourteen weeks later, they brought an amazing variety of creations to that last class.

One woman read poetry about her grandmother, material she had never showed anyone. Another brought in mobiles. A third wrote some Haiku poetry in Japanese—and she was an American! One woman brought in house plans she had designed and for years kept secret from her family. Everyone had done something she was proud of. There were lots of laughs and tears that evening as these women expressed themselves openly, many for the first time.

Animals can also demonstrate for us the importance of creativity. A TV program showed a baboon sitting listlessly in a cage—until someone gave it computer paper to play with. The next scene showed the animal racing around the cage happily tossing the pages in the air, sliding on them, and having a wonderful time. The baboon had something to stimulate its brain.

And then there was the experiment with baby rats.

Every day researchers would come to the cages and give baby rats new toys. They responded positively to the stimulation and variety their toys provided and literally began lining up in front of the cages to wait for their daily "fix."

BROKEN CONNECTIONS

When your life is stimulating and full of variety, you'll react joyfully like those baboons or baby rats. But without tools for the imagination, people listlessly go through the motions of life. They have broken the connection to their creative selves. It's a common phenomenon in the late twentieth century—why?

Research suggests that much of our creativity is suppressed as early as age seven. In the 1970s, many classes in the arts were passed over in favor of such "practical" subjects as business, science, or technology. The ability to get a job, earn money, and get ahead became of primary importance. The situation continues to this day. What was the value of learning to play the piano? To draw? To write a poem? To understand Greek mythology? To understand the lessons of history? That won't pay for a house or buy a car, those "practical"-minded people claim.

If your school was like mine, as a student, you were rewarded more for regurgitating facts than for what you could dream or shape with your mind. You were encouraged to get 100% on your tests rather than inspired to use your imagination. The message was clear: creativity is a frill, icing on the cake or something to use in your spare time—or for loony artists.

Add to this the effect of the tube. Before the average person reaches the age of 21, that person will have spent a total of five years watching television. Although some educational and public television programs are excellent, chances are these are not the programs people watch. Constant input from TV, radio, and movies leave no time for inner reflection and sorting things out. Imagine what growth and insight people could gain if a total of five years were spent in cultivating their creativity!

Three major factors contribute to the decline of creativity: the inability to think, staying uninformed, and lack of imagination.

I THINK, THEREFORE I AM

Creativity depends on a willingness to keep one's mind alert, open, fertile, curious, and (above all) the ability to think. But basic thinking skills have declined. In a recent study on school children, it was found that they could easily solve problems with a calculator. When asked how many people could fit into a bus under certain conditions, children would give answers like 36.7, indicating they had failed to consider whether their answer made sense. (Would you like to be in a bus with 36.7 people?)

Technology has given people the false notion that they can *abdicate* their responsibility to think. I recall standing at a department store cash register watching the clerk struggle to add up my purchases. Finally, he turned to his calculator and exclaimed: "Thank God the machines have to think and we don't!" There certainly has to be a connection between abdication of thinking and the decline of creativity. To be sure, machines can retrieve information, calculate, and relieve much of the need for remembering things, but they do not replace the need for using our minds. Technology vies for our devotion, and our inner wisdom often goes begging as a result.

When Einstein was asked his telephone number, he said he didn't remember and didn't need to clutter up his brain with such information. For that he could use a telephone book. He wanted to use his brain for thinking. As Einstein recognized, you can use technology—instead of your head—for storing information. It leaves lots more room to use your imagination and far fewer excuses for not using it.

IGNORANCE IS NOT BLISS

Ignorance is bliss, the saying goes. (Well if that's true, why aren't more people happy?) Technology gives power to a degree never before possible in history. But power without the ability to think creatively is a deadly combination. Take the individuals in a missile site somewhere under the earth: without the ability to think they could wipe everyone off the map with one press of a button.

Information on just about anything is available. It's impossible to stick your head in the sand and say "I don't know" or "I don't have to think." Ignorance is a cop-out. You understand the effects of alcohol on your body, what cigarettes will do to your lungs, and what will happen if you choose to lie out in the sun too much. And, if you are doing drugs, you are aware (even if you might not care) that you are destroying the capacities of your brain.

Instant access to other countries through information and travel have removed any last vestiges of global ignorance through isolation. The world is a single connected unit, no longer consisting of separate countries with strange and quaint ways of doing things. Contaminated air in one part of the world will drift into another, just as the radiation from the Russian nuclear plant in Chernobyl polluted Western Europe, and rainforest devastation in Brazil affects weather patterns in North America. Likewise, ignorance in one country affects another. Burying your head in the sand won't do any longer. You have a mandate to be alert, aware, wise—and creative.

THE FUTURE ISN'T WHAT IT USED TO BE

You won't solve tomorrow's problems with yesterday's methods. Life choices used to involve such survival issues as staying alive, getting crops to grow, keeping warm, or managing with a third unwanted pregnancy.

It used to be that you would pursue the same career as your father or mother. A parent's career choices automatically became yours. No longer. Farmer? Pharmacist? Minister? Shoemaker? Even if you carry on the family tradition, you probably won't do it for life.

To make matters more difficult, career choices themselves are more complex than ever. There are likely to be, on average, from three to five career changes in a lifetime, in addition to several lateral shifts (that is, staying in the same kind of job but moving to another company). Whew!

You can't manage these rapid changes without imaginative thinking. Today, questions of a moral, ethical, and personal nature, such as "Who am I?" "How can I maximize my potential?" "What is my soul's path?" must, unlike earlier survival questions, be answered with the intuitive (right) side of the brain, which sees and processes things in a holistic manner. The foundation for supporting these changes is to live a solid mission.

BLOCKS AND CREATIVITY

"Sure, I'd love to be creative, but I find myself totally blocked!" an exasperated client said to me recently. If you are blocked, too, and are eager to "get on with it," this next section is especially for you. You can turn those stumbling blocks into building blocks. How?

Treat blocks as friendly signs for attention! They may be an indicator of something you want because they have to do with things you like. Look at a statement like "I'm blocked from doing the wash, paying the bills, or defleaing the cat!" The word *blocked* in this context is misused. *Blocked* means a chronic inability to perform a mental or creative function. Thus if you are blocked from a mission, from writing a story, or from solving a problem, it means you are separated from something creative and challenging.

It means the creative energy flow is stopped.

You get *rid* of blocks by redirecting your energy. Start swimming downstream and go with your creative flow!

EXERCISE: FOUR STEPS TO TRANSFORM BLOCKS

Be the kid on the block instead of having blocks on the kid. Transform those stumbling blocks into building blocks! You need to first understand your block, before you can transform it or move beyond it. There are four steps to this process:

1. Describe the block.
2. Identify the reason you created the block.
3. Transform your block into a positive image.
4. Relate the meaning you see in the positive image to your mission.

First, give definite shape to your block until you can identify its form. If it helps, recall the situation that has caused the block and feel how it is affecting you physically. Figuring the connection between the form and the nature of your block will clarify your own role in the process. You created that particular block. What is it telling you about yourself?

Remember, if you can create it, you can transform it. Every person's block is quite individual in appearance. Work on the most effective way of transforming the shape of your block. Now examine three cases—one in greater detail—of ways people have mastered their blocks.

Let's look at Jane and Irene:

JANE'S BLOB

Jane thought of her block as filled with some sort of slippery substance, elusive, heavy, black, and massive. When she tried to do anything with it, it would slide around, and she couldn't hold it. Unable to get rid of this blob, Jane squirmed in her seat just talking about it. In her case, shrinking or demolishing it wouldn't have been the right way to tackle her slimy blob. She literally never got a handle on things because she couldn't focus on them.

Jane had never had to make choices. At 38, she had never even signed a check for herself. Her husband decided everything. When they went out to eat, she'd habitually say, "Whatever you want." Jane rarely had an independent opinion.

Jane got in touch with her unwillingness to commit to anything. She transformed her blob into a white laser beam that directed a current of energy toward the matter she was refusing to deal with. Whenever Jane created new blobs (when she tried to avoid focusing), she redirected them into that beam and focused on her issue.

The laser beam gave her a new image of herself as direct, bold, to the point, unstoppable. (Actually, she had been that way as a youngster, she discovered.) Although she had some work ahead of her to retrieve this recovered image in reality, it gave her renewed energy and determination.

IRENE'S CHASM

Irene, a legal secretary, had for eight years been putting off a career change. Her block was a huge chasm. It was so deep and threatening that she had no way of getting across. She was stalled at the edge. She had always stopped short of following her inclination to become a lawyer and had created a huge chasm between herself and her goal.

Irene constructed fanciful ways to bridge it, taking cues from her imagination (and a vast storehouse of reading). She designed a delightful companion, Old Mother West Wind, who helped blow her over the chasm whenever it appeared. OMWW would simply furrow her brow, take a huge breath, and lift Irene gently over the gap with ease. Irene was comforted by the image of OMMW lending her help.

Actually, OMMW was the nurturing force within Irene that she was reluctant to use. Her block resulted from a feeling that she had to do everything herself. She had created the block because of her feelings of isolation. She began to see there were forces outside of herself that could help her if she first accepted responsibility for her actions.

Now we'll look at John's case, going through all four steps of the process.

John's Journey

1. Describe the block.

John had a block that looked like a huge concrete wall. There was no way to jump over, go under, or penetrate it. It was unlike anything he had ever seen in reality. Even the Empire State Building paled in comparison. He was both afraid of and intimidated by his block.

2. Identify the reason you created the block.

A frail man with intense eyes and a wan smile, John had reluctantly followed his father's footsteps by managing a retail store in a large city. He realized why he had made the wall so imposing. Since he felt he could not be strong and big, he created something he'd never be able to get over—or so he thought. Getting in touch with his feelings of powerlessness and worthlessness, John felt too puny to climb over that big wall. When he talked about it, he would actually shrink back in the chair and close off his body.

3. Transform your block into a positive image.

First, John stood up and imagined that he was a kind of Terminator, endowed with superior powers to transform anything. Then he actually visited a construction site where a crew was demolishing an old office building. Finally, he imagined himself demolishing buildings. Skyscrapers disappeared before his very eyes. Then he practiced doing the same thing to his own block, the wall. While demolishing it, John practiced transforming the wall's energy, feeling it course through his body where he felt weakest: in his chest, arms, and hands.

4. Relate the meaning you see in the positive image to your Mission.

It was a revelation for John to see himself as strong and powerful as a Terminator. During his entire career he had been holding himself back in weak and insignificant positions. Whenever thoughts of helplessness in his career emerged, John practiced this demolition method. Slowly, John began to transform this wall into his *mission*, because he now knew that he was his own source of strength.

As long as you have creativity, blocks will be present. It's part of the process. The good news is each time one appears and you deal with it, the transformation gets easier. Then you can move through the block and beyond.

ON YOUR PATH

You can also use guided imagery to further help you transform your block. Record the following suggestions onto a tape for yourself, or have someone read them to you slowly.

Prepare for this guided tour of the mind by sitting in a relaxed position with legs uncrossed. Take a deep breath and let it out slowly. Close your eyes, and allow the images in your mind's eye to follow whatever the voice tells you. Don't feel obligated to create everything slavishly. Simply go with what comes to you. (If you have problems visualizing, consult Chapter 10.)

Imagine that you are taking a walk on a beautiful summer day. You're in the country, heading down a path. Pay attention to the smells, sights, and sounds around you. PAUSE. As you approach a fork in the road, you notice two signs—one pointing to the right and one to the left. Make note of what you see on the signs, and pick one fork to continue on.

As you proceed, you come to a barrier. Stop, take a close look at this barrier, and pass by it with the greatest of ease. PAUSE.

In the distance you see a house. Look at the house carefully, observing its style and size. No one is home, yet it feels as if you are expected and that you should go in. The door is open, and you go in, moving from room to room, savoring all the things you see. Observe the furniture, the windows, the decor of this house. PAUSE. Now go up the stairs to the second floor where there is a long hallway with light shining from a room.

You head down the hall towards this room, and upon entering, you see a young child playing quietly amid toys and other objects. You join the child in play. PAUSE. After awhile, the child selects one of the toys, and hands it to you, saying, "This is a gift to you from me." You thank the child and leave the room quietly, treasuring your object as you return downstairs. Go out the front door with your object and resume your walk. Return with your object to the space you are in.

Use the following questions as discussion guides with a friend or counselor, since many of the insights become clearer with dialogue. Put the answers in your notebook for reference.

1. What were you wearing and how did you feel during your walk?

2. What did the path and surroundings look like?

3. What path did you take at the fork? What was written on the signs?

4. Describe the path after the fork.

5. What did the barrier look like? The barrier is akin to the block you put in your path. Did you have any trouble getting by it? How did it feel when you did? How did you transform it?

6. Describe the house itself. What kind of house did you choose? Cottage? Lodge? Colonial? Ranch? The house is often a symbol of the self. It reflects much of what you see in yourself. Did you feel you could move around with ease? Was it open and inviting or dark and closed?

7. Describe the interior of the house. Was it big, small, bright, airy, dark, full of objects, deserted? Were there lots of windows or few?

8. Describe the experience with the child in the room. What did the child look like? What was the child

playing when you entered the room? What kind of playing did you do with the child? Did the child have any difficulty in selecting an object for you? What object did the child give you, and how did it affect you? Were you surprised to receive it? Did you feel okay about taking it with you and keeping it? How did this object affect you emotionally? What does it mean to you?

PLAY AND YOUR CREATIVE CHILD WITHIN

Play is absolutely essential, because it helps remove blocks and release creativity. But play is often associated with children. Being the child is a marvelous way to enjoy, fantasize, and laugh. The adult world rarely encourages play. Often, adults permit themselves to play only in the context of sports. How long has it been since you have allowed yourself to be a child again? to be silly, clown at work, or play children's games?

In a corporate workshop, I played a music cassette and asked the participants to doodle, finger paint, or draw whatever they pleased while listening to the music. Soon they began to have fun right within those company walls! When we discussed the exercise later, participants said they had gotten in touch with grade-school experiences and sensory memories (smells, sights, sounds) from that time. While finger painting, one participant exclaimed, "I haven't allowed myself to do this in years. I feel like I'm back in third grade!"

Creative children frequently daydream, fidget, or act impatient in school. They are likely to hear "Toe the line! Be like the others! Memorize the facts to get good grades! Pay attention to the teacher! Don't daydream!" It's little wonder that our inner creative child is so elusive. It takes courage to reconnect to that child.

Dana told me a personal story that almost exactly matched

an example I had been using for two years in workshops!

"When I was in the third grade, we were asked to draw trees in art class. The teacher hadn't told us what the tree was to look like, but when she came around to my desk, she frowned and said: 'THAT'S not the way a tree is supposed to look. Draw it this way.' She drew the kind of tree you see in children's books. It didn't match my version. That moment froze vividly in my memory, and from then on I never dared be creative. I just did what I was told." Suddenly, Dana had parted with her creative self and learned the "accepted" way of doing things.

Dana was truly blocked from finding creative solutions to her career needs by a "minor" incident in her childhood. If you're having trouble with blocks, access your inner child by going to a playground, visiting a children's theater, making something a child would make or just plain PLAYING awhile (no fair taking a child along—you have to go by yourself).

Your answers in this visualization have a lot to do with the way you envision your path, what your barriers look like, and what you might give yourself for a gift. Your path is also a way of looking at your mission. The word *career* means "vehicle," from the Middle Latin word *carraria* (from which our words *car* and *carriage* are derived). You can think of a career as the vehicle you use to travel your path of life.

JEALOUSY AND ENVY: TWO FRIENDLY BLOCKS

Certain kinds of blocks can be friendly clues about what you are neglecting. Remember when you were really jealous about something? If you're like me, you tried to tell yourself it wasn't "right" to have those feelings, but you had them anyway. Well, here's a way to make jealousy work for you.

When Gloria Steinem came to town to promote her latest book, I saw the announcement in the paper and felt jealous. Mind you, I wouldn't get envious about a famous stock market analyst autographing a book. But feeling my envy of Gloria

Steinem awakened my consciousness that I needed to be writing and promoting a book and that part of my mission is to be a respected writer and communicator.

I was blocked in several areas and used my jealousies to help determine which one to work on first. (If prioritizing is one of your blocks, you'll profit doubly with this example.) List the person who triggered your jealousy and the circumstances in which the jealousy was aroused. Here's my example:

PERSON INVOLVED	CIRCUMSTANCE OF TRIGGER	LESSON TO BE LEARNED
(a) Steinem	Booksigning parties	Start a novel Buy a computer
(b) Rodgers and Hammerstein	TV feature on their careers	Take song-writing course Start composing
(c) Music professor	Seeing all his electronic music equipment	Read about electronic music Buy a synthesizer Increase income
(d) A friend	Visiting high-tech office	Be better organized Upgrade office equipment

Which is your greatest jealousy, and what do you need to get going on? Compare your jealousy of the person listed in each set of letters:

a vs b   *a*   a vs d   *a*   b vs d   *b*
a vs c   *a*   b vs c   *c*   c vs d   *c*

My highest score was for **a** (three times), which shows that I was most envious of Steinem. Conclusion? The book was the most important thing for me to be working on. (Surprise!)

You can use this method for any kind of prioritizing. Restrict yourself to a maximum of 6 items or fewer (or you'll be spending nights wading through your list instead of working on the winner). Begin with your greatest block, and chip away at others over time.

TEN BUILDING BLOCKS TO A CREATIVE
LIFE MISSION

Here are ten ideas about creativity that you can apply to your mission search.

Creativity is novelty. Using your creativity means that you bring something into being that did not exist in that form before. The important thing is that it is new for you. But there is a difference between repeating what someone else has already created (reinventing the wheel) and doing something new and insightful. If 487 other people have already discovered what you did, it makes your effort no less creative. What counts is the intention. You wanted to explore and create.

The distinction is important. Many people feel that everything has already been done, so why bother?—it wouldn't be creative. But why does the tenth recording of Beethoven's Fifth Symphony, old song favorites, or another Italian cookbook get released? Because there are always new ways of looking at everything. Creativity is personal expression. There are no rules of right and wrong. It's important to explore, investigate, risk, and look at things in new ways—like writing a novel in verse form.

Likewise, your mission is unique, singular, and without parallel to anyone else's because it's coming from you (unless you have a clone somewhere). So don't say it's been done before. The world needs your version—your input—and your output!

Creativity is upsetting the status quo. Challenge the way things are done, turn things around or upside down or inside out. There are aspects to creativity which have their painful side. When you create something, you are ending, possibly destroying, something else. Galileo showed that the earth was no longer the center of the universe, thus making people recognize their dependence on the sun and challenging theological teachings. That was upsetting, but it was part of his mission of scientific exploration and finding the truth.

Your mission, too, is going to upset the apple cart in some way. Or don't you want your pebble to make waves?

Creativity is taking risks. Taking risks can be coining a new word, making people laugh when they are ill or refusing to go along with the way everybody else does something. It's trying something you've never done before without knowing the outcome. Members of the German resistance group called the White Rose risked their lives by spreading clandestine leaflets in Nazi Germany, and the Expressionists painted faces green instead of flesh-colored, thus risking the disapproval of their contemporaries.

Creative risks can cause rifts, enlighten, rattle at the cages of the mind, infuriate, or elevate. Keep in mind that your mission might cause trouble among your friends. The greatest risk of all, making changes in yourself, can be threatening to your loved ones, because you are breaking the rules they are used to.

Creativity is making new connections. Some of the most common inventions came about because somebody combined two things or ideas together. Men's jockey shorts, for instance, were a direct result of connecting their design to that of baby diapers. What do you get when you link motorcars and hotels? Motels! The list is endless. You'll find that the things you love can be connected in new ways (commonly called a mission). Combine anatomical research, painting, and interest in hydraulics, and you get some of the main ingredients of Leonoardo da Vinci's mission.

Creativity is following through on your curiosity. You may wonder about something, ask a "what if " question, and leave it at that, or you may decide to go farther. Someone might say "I had that idea way back in 1985." Sure, it was there, but what happened after that? Creativity without follow-through is like leaving flour on the shelf forever. It's of little good unless it's used. When you were a child, you dreamed—perhaps about being a princess, a knight, a firefighter or a clown. You gave yourself permission to let go. As an adult, you have the luxury of fantasizing and fulfilling the dream. A dancer once commented that all the other kids dreamed of being a dancer, and she became one. She wanted to know more about it. Explore your curiosity!

Creativity is being different. Conditioning might be okay for your hair—it keeps everything in its place—but it's not healthy for creativity. Being creative means moving outside the pack, altering the rules and thinking independently. In a *Los Angeles Times* interview Jacques Cousteau said, "I don't look at other people's films. I don't have time. I'm not interested in what other people are doing, because we are doing it differently. . . . A movie maker has his own personality and sees things differently. . . . I make my films to be different. It will be my way of looking at things. I am convinced that [a] world where people enjoy themselves the proper way—in creation, creating anything—and thinking only about the creation they are doing is a better world than a world in which people preach. . . ."

Unless you want to live a carbon-copy life, get used to being different. Your mission can be different only if you are.

Creativity is surrender to process. The most important factor is the path that leads to a goal. The steps to this book began with my interest in the arts in college, followed by counseling students as a professor, starting my own business, and then designing creativity seminars. Eventually, that work led to the design of a bookmark, and the bookmark provided the chapters of this book. It was a process that my inner wisdom already knew at the time! I simply surrendered to it. Creativity means process before product—not a popular notion today. You must let your mission become all it needs to without constant control and squelching.

Creativity is sharing your gifts. Some people have trouble sharing their gifts with others. Leonardo da Vinci held on to the *Mona Lisa* for 20 years, constantly making changes and "improvements."

On the other hand, some people are unwilling to give of their creativity to certain groups. Bach never shared his musical teachings with his daughters. Artur Rubenstein was unwilling to perform in Germany, and Thomas Mann couldn't return to live there anymore.

Some people have problems parting with their creations. Emily Dickinson put her poems in a drawer.

A chilling story by E.T.A. Hoffmann called "The Golden Pot," which takes place in Paris at the time of Louis the Fourteenth, illustrates an artist's inability to separate from his creation and thus share it with the world.

In this story, an eccentric but highly-talented goldsmith makes the most fabulous jewelry in all of Paris. Over a period of time a series of murders of aristocratic women occurs, and no one can figure out who the murderer is. A lengthy investigation reveals that all the victims had commissioned jewelry from a certain goldsmith. The artist, as it turns out, had an uncontrollable need to kill his victims because he was unable to part with any of his creations. The story shows the horrible effects of addictive attachment to one's creations.

Your mission is a gift, and a gift by definition is both received and given. Let go of your gift and release it for the world to have. A part of you goes with it but never gets lost. To be creative, you must surrender yourself to the process of giving and receiving. You can't have one without the other. If you block either direction, you will deny the world or yourself the joy of your contribution.

Creativity is accepting yourself. To resist BEING WHO YOU ARE is the greatest hindrance to your creativity. When you resist most you feel the greatest pain, and it impedes expression by stifling the self. It's a constant paradox: whatever happens needs to, yet you must do the work necessary for it to take place. You are both creator/created, potter/pot, sender/receiver. Seeing a mission as surrender and as a calling places you in the position of hearing your inner voice and responding to it. To head off on the wrong path without listening to that inner voice is to turn a deaf ear to your mission.

Your creativity is a message from your soul. The way you express your creativity can tell you a lot about your soul's intention for this life. What kind of creativity do you enjoy? I like puzzles, spy stories, and mysteries. Working to help people uncover clues to their mission is like solving a mystery. It's like being Sherlock Holmes (whom I admire)!

Creativity requires you to give up old patterns to which you have become accustomed. It requires abandonment of all but yourself as source and resource, beginning and end. Your creativity shows you the voice of your soul, and the way to your mission. The mission in turn expresses your true essence.

The subsequent chapters, forming the acronym CREATIVITY, represent a different turn of the kaleidoscope. They will show you how to activate your individual Life Mission process. They will help you get in tune with your Source and maximize your potential.

It's time now to unleash the self that has been awaiting your call. Creative expression is shared self-love in action. Connect with the talent that is most divinely yours. All aboard!

PART

Two

4

Clear Your Mind

Imagine an attic filled with old albums and letters, trunks with clothes never again to be worn, discarded furniture, and tons of cobwebs. Like that attic, your brain is often filled to the top with chatter, criticism, old business, anxious thoughts, and incessant dialogue. It needs, as Norman Cousins phrased it, "the blessing of silence."

You can think three times as fast as you talk or listen. Your mind races constantly. Try this: look up from this page and time yourself. For one minute, try to think of nothing. When you are done, estimate how many thoughts you had. If you had none, skip this chapter and go on.

For most people, the mind conjures up thousands of thoughts a day. Here's how the opening paragraph might actually sound in your mind when you read it or someone reads it to you:

Imagine an attic, *I don't have an attic, I live in a*

condo, filled with old albums and letters, *Did I remember to leave a note for Madge to mail those letters?* trunks with clothes never again to be worn, *Isn't that a quaint way of putting it?* discarded furniture, and tons of cobwebs, *I bet Harry will never get around to cleaning out his car.*

The italicized sentences show examples of an intruding mind. You can't get much done in this muddled state.

LET ME MAKE THIS PERFECTLY CLEAR

The word *clear* actually means both *clear in sound* and *to cry out.* You must have a clear mental space to promote sound thinking. You can't think in a mental room crammed to the ceiling. Clean out your attic so that brain of yours has an uncluttered room. By weeding and sorting out the clutter from your mind, you can get organized, focus on your goals, and make connection with your mission. Your mission is crying out to be heard. Give it room!

In this chapter you will learn how to reduce outside interference, cut down on the garbage you feed your mind, and use an eight-step program which I call Clear Your Mind (CYM) to rest and recharge your brain on a daily basis. The objective is to keep your mind open and free of obstruction so that you can zero in on your mission and commit to your soul's intentions.

Here's a quick checklist for telling whether your mind is clear:

___ Does *The Who* suggest hardness of hearing or a rock group?

___ Do you usually play the radio when you drive?

__ Do you have the TV on when you converse?

__ Do you avoid periods of silence (30 minutes or longer)?

__ Do you usually notice music in stores?

__ Do you jog with head phones? (Or walk listening to a cassette tape?)

__ Do you play background music in your home?

__ Do you like to do several things at once (eat and read, watch TV and write letters)?

__ Do you find it difficult to go several minutes without thinking a thought?

__ Do you watch more than two hours of TV a day (three hours if it's PBS or C-SPAN)?

__ Do you avoid quiet places, like libraries?

__ Do you take a radio or TV on vacation?

__ Do you eat in restaurants even with loud music playing?

__ Do you answer the phone even during times when you are concentrating on something?

__ Do you talk only when you need to?

__ Do you constantly rehash the past or anticipate the future in your thoughts?

If you answered even half of the above with "yes" or "I don't know," your mind is crammed. You need to get rid of mental litter, admit only the information you can really use, and ignore the rest. The most popular part of the TV program "CBS Sunday Morning" is the two or three minute end segment showing beautiful and peaceful scenes from nature without commentary. At a local health club, I noticed that the executive locker room is quiet; it has none of the junk music piped in to the regular locker area. At heart, a lot of people know the value of silence and serenity.

MINDING YOUR BRAIN

Your brain is a storehouse of information, a place for memories and a think tank. It would take four minutes to write a number equal to all the neutrinos (the smallest particle in the universe). But at the same pace you'd need ninety years to write the number of synapses in the human brain.

The brain comprises only about two and a half to three per cent of the body weight, but it takes about twenty-two per cent of the body's energy to fuel it. If you took out your brain and spread it out on the floor, you'd have a circumference of more than two and a half feet (and an unwrinkled brain). That organ upstairs is built for action and power, but you must take care of it before it can perform well.

A well-tuned brain enables you to make choices, take chances, be creative, and above all to think. The world needs your intelligence operating at full strength, and you need that intelligence to realize your Life Mission.

COGITO, ERGO SUM: I THINK, THEREFORE I AM

Thinking is an underdeveloped skill. You probably didn't learn it in school. But the inability to think is pervasive. Ask a phone company about its rate structure, ask a company about its mission, listen to a TV talk show or a presidential press conference: if you're lucky, you'll get coherent statements fifty per cent of the time.

When I taught creativity workshops in corporations, management often asked me what benefits the participants could expect from creativity workshops. I said: "The ability to think." They responded by saying, "Well, when we have time, we'll give it some consideration. But first we need to tackle more important issues. We'll look into it when all our basic (!) training courses are completed." No amount of training will help if an employee is uncreative. The only nice thing about not thinking is that you never suffer from loneliness. Creativity is basic because it opens the mind. It informs.

BODY VS. MIND

People spend hours working on their bodies, but rarely do they have a program specifically for their minds. They spend more time sorting out their laundry than their thoughts. It's indicative of present culture that there are few workout programs for stretching the imagination, exercising the brain, and lifting the spirits. The late twentieth century version of the song Body and Soul might be: "I'm all for you body and . . . body."

High school SAT scores have consistently gone down over the years, creativity scores are lower and illiteracy is on the rise. The brain drain, folks, is going on right before (or rather behind) our eyes.

I FEEL, THEREFORE I KNOW

A disastrous effect of a cluttered brain is that feelings get blocked from giving valuable information. Like cream, feelings will rise to the top, but only when you stop pushing them down and listen to yourself. Take the example of Claudia.

"I DIDN'T KNOW I FELT THAT"

Claudia was a 44-year-old ranchwoman. She had acted in a couple of high school plays, but after graduating she had gone on to "better and more serious" things. She reasoned that acting was "just a phase everybody went through in school." (Claudia invoked the word "everybody" to rationalize her choice.)

Never mind that she had taken English literature courses, especially Shakespeare, in college. Never mind that after moving to a rural Western town, Claudia would drive two hours to the next large city just to see a new play. Since college, Claudia had married, raised four children, volunteered for numerous organizations—including a project for a local amateur theater group—and raised funds for the new high school (making sure it had a good theater).

She forgot her love for the theater, she realized, by overloading her brain with things to think and do. As supermom, she had little time to connect to dormant dreams. Claudia never took the time to reflect on the way her life was going, even though the pain of a missed calling took the forms of headaches, angry outbursts, and arguments. Claudia always ended up having "better things to do" than her mission.

I encouraged her to practice Clear your Mind (CYM) by taking walks and reflecting and by sitting quietly at night listening to her inner voice. No kids, no television, no activities, just Claudia with Claudia. The message that came to her during these quiet times was unmistakable: to "do something for herself away from the kids." She visited New York, saw her former high school acting teacher in a play, and was reminded of his encouraging words many years back: "If you don't choose it, you'll lose it." Claudia knew it was now or never.

She decided to resume acting and move the family to Los Angeles. She gave her husband an ultimatum: "Either accept my new direction, or you'll be playing both father and mother to our three children still at home." (Her acting ability came in handy here.) Luckily for Claudia's husband, he decided to go along with her plan. The relationship was actually saved. Now Claudia is taking drama courses at a local college and preparing for a theater major. Claudia accessed her true self by removing the barriers that had clouded her thinking and blocked her creativity. Then she could hear and respond to her mission of self-expression through theater.

Many people, like Claudia, are blocked from their mission because their thinking and feelings are cluttered. CYM gets you in touch with that mission by giving you clarity, focus, and purpose. Once you feel your mission, your deepest wishes, desires, and passions will radiate outward again. When you have rekindled the flame, any sadness will diminish.

THE INFORMATION AGE: GARBAGE IN

Now we'll take a closer look at the what's causing cluttered, unclear minds, and at what you can do to clear your own mind. You can't have a mission with a brain in remission. Going into remission, however, is the brain's way of protecting itself from the ravages of information.

This is an age governed by information—getting it, giving it, and processing it. Much of the time it is junk, or unsolicited, or both. We humans are bombarded daily with ads, radio, TV, Muzak, car radios, signs, computers and telephones. Garbage in. We may have conquered space but not our surrounding air space.

The other day I went to a small café and had to endure a radio talk show as my "entertainment." Restaurants and bars frequently have a TV set blaring. (Don't leave home without it.) Every department store has its own sound system. Movie houses advertise before the show (remember when that didn't happen?), and main thoroughfares and superhighways are draped with billboards.

It's getting tougher to escape this intrusion. You even get

mindless ads over the phone when you're trapped on hold. Or you're subjected to music that I hope you never listen to otherwise. Computers with prerecorded telephone messages intrude upon your life, as well as car alarms and beepers.

Even worse is the juxtaposition of mindless TV ads with serious programming. A visiting professor from France once told me he got up to watch TV in the early morning and was delighted to find a lecture on Voltaire. "Suddenly," he said, "this gorilla began to move forward toward me on the screen, and I couldn't for the life of me make the connection to Voltaire." Welcome to American commercial breaks. A local classical radio station ended a beautiful violin sonata and followed it with a jarring ad for a steak house. Is it any wonder people have trouble connecting one idea to another?

Instant accessibility has made it almost impossible for people to be unreachable. Cars and airplanes have phones, faxes, and even TVs. People carrying beepers are everywhere. Our society truly suffers from excess access. The only way to guarantee silence is to subpoena government and military officials to testify before a Congressional committee. And then there are the people who like to give you a piece of their mind. They're generous and like to dish up a big piece, too. Friends, relatives, and partners can be relentless in their advice and chatter. Sometimes it's easier to turn off a radio than get rid of another person's meddling.

DECISIONS, DECISIONS, DECISIONS

Because intrusive information is so abundant, your brain is in a constant state of stimulation. Try to make a decision in this overloaded state: it's like thinking in a shop with ten TVs blaring.

Now add to this mess the types of decisions you are required to make. Buy anything, and you're inundated with choices. Checks with or without telephone number? In color or plain? Lined or with pictures? With carbon or stubs? Designer motifs or a personal message? Beginning with what number?

Or take buying a car. Henry Ford once said, "You can have any color car you want, just so long as it's black." Were it only so now, Henry! Besides the color, you have to choose the model, the style (stick or automatic?), the type of tires, paint (metallic or not?), and what kind of glass (tinted or plain?). The choices go on. Air conditioning? Power steering? Digital radio with or without tape deck? Alarm system? Extended warranty? And then there's the insurance. No wonder buying a car—or anything else for that matter, is so traumatic.

To say it's all hopeless and life is too difficult is not the solution. In spite of today's complexities, if decision making is too much trouble, too difficult, or results in paralysis, you've got a thinking problem. Your brain is no doubt on overload.

To stay clear-headed, you must remove yourself from any outside stimuli that fail to contribute to your growth and mission. You are responsible for reducing the outside clutter in your life. How would you react if someone suddenly dumped a sackload of garbage on your lawn or in your living room? Or if someone blew smoke in your face? But intrusions into our minds occur almost daily in the form of blaring radios, TVs, traffic, and leaf blowers.

Here are ten guidelines to reduce outside stimulation and give your brain the rest it needs to function at highest capacity:

1. Play radios, TV, etc., only when you are actually listening to them.

2. Do one thing at a time, such as listening to TV or radio.

3. Focus entirely on what you are doing. (This helps you with #2.)

4. Speak only when you have something to say.
   (Needless talk is like outside clutter.)
5. Avoid noise, distractions, and cluttered environments.
6. Avoid contributing to the noise pollution of others.
7. Commit to 30 minutes of quiet time per day (unless
   you're a Carmelite monk).
8. Agree on some silent time when you are with others.
9. Spend a certain period of time each day alone.
10. Find peaceful places to visit in your environment.

SOUNDING OFF FOR SILENCE

Living your mission consciously is possible only when you
can reflect on it clearly and quietly. You can do something
about outside interference yourself. Sometimes removing
yourself physically is the only thing you can do. But before
you resort to that, look at some alternative action you can
take. One woman in a nearby community collected signa-
tures against leaf blowers because the noise upset people.
Result: leaf blowers were banned.

Let companies know you dislike any music in offices or
when you are held hostage on hold. Tell restaurants to turn
off the awful stuff they play; and notify the police about
noisy neighbors. Tell the theater manager the movie is too
loud. I hate to think what shape most people's ears will be
in when they permit that kind of volume. A couple of years
back I sat in a dentist's office waiting to have a tooth pulled.
The receptionist was playing rock music loudly enough to
jangle my nerves. In spite of my urgent need to have the
tooth extracted, I told the receptionist either to turn the
noise off or have the dentist forget my appointment.

On the positive side, when someone plays decent music
(at a decent sound level) or provides a quiet environment, tell
the person in charge you appreciate it. Give supportive feedback for efforts to keep your environment safe and sane.

The point is to take positive action and silence the racket going on around you. Don't sit back and allow yourself to become a garbage dump for noise. Most communities now have noise control departments. Call them! Silence is golden. You deserve it, and your brain needs it.

INFORMATION AGE: GARBAGE FROM WITHIN

There may be a lot of noise coming from outside, but you contribute even more noise from inside you. It's no wonder you are paralyzed in making simple choices. But here's the opportunity to really begin to do something about this nuisance. The only thing you want to be able to hear loud and clear is the wisdom from within.

Get rid of everything else vying for your attention! Even talking to yourself prevents listening to yourself. Those internal tapes—thoughts about how you are doing, comments on your productivity (often, the lack thereof), planning and scheduling, reliving the past, obsessing about other people, rehearsing what to say, fearing the future—contribute little to your peace of mind. No wonder we have trouble thinking! Our brain hasn't been given a chance.

CREATE A SANCTUARY OF THE MIND

For healthy thinking, design your surroundings to include a quiet space. I call it a sanctuary of the mind. A sanctuary is a haven, a place of safety and refuge. Information overload results when people don't permit themselves the gift of sanctuary. The excuses are varied, but the result is the same: "I don't take time for me because I don't deserve it." "I don't have time to take time." "I'll take time after April 15th." And on it goes.

But your mission can make itself heard only in an atmosphere of trust, quiet, and repose. It must have your undivided attention, love, and commitment. Your mission must feel that it can communicate to you safely without inside or outside interference.

LESS IS MORE

The sole (soul!) purpose of your sanctuary is for doing nothing. Caution! You have to practice such a delicious notion actively. The solution to clear thinking lies in doing less, not more. But this is exactly what you have had drilled into you since childhood: doing something, ANYTHING, is better than doing nothing.

Doing nothing is felt by many either to be sinful, lazy, or procrastinating. Society encourages action, movement, speed and results. And although these are good things, it's a mistake to think you've got to be in endless motion to achieve. Take Winnie the Pooh. No program, no agenda, no notches on a stick for him. Pooh just was.

LA DONNA MOBILE

At age 51, Donna had given her entire life to an insurance agency. An Analyzer, she spent her entire day making lists, inspecting reports, returning phone calls, and checking data. The times she took off even five minutes from work to relax were almost legendary. She was expected to get things done fast. There was no time to think, just do, do, do. Donna felt compelled to carry out her work in a manner incompatible with her Analyzer style.

I suggested that she take a couple of weeks off from work. An unthinkable idea! "How would they survive without me?" she complained. After some struggle, she relented, and made plans for her two week vacation. She made endless lists of activities including cleaning the house, none of which included time for reflection.

She returned to work tired, resentful and angry. No wonder she had prepared and revised lists forever and planned to the hilt but never gotten around to giving herself space and quiet. It was difficult for Donna to think clearly. The "time off" period showed that even when she had the time, she was unable to take advantage of it. Donna had to do some serious attitude readjustment. She needed rest in order to recharge her mind before going into action, and she needed to spend more time alone in quiet meditation.

I now insisted she cut down on work, take nothing home, and make her weekends absolutely unstructured. Above all, she was to come first before anything—husband, dog, children, house, or friends. Every day she created a sanctuary of the mind in a space she carefully appropriated for herself in the den.

Soon Donna began to clean out those mental cobwebs. She could see clearly that the first thing to do was to reassess her frenetic pace and continue her program of CYM. Donna's mission began to take shape after her fog lifted: to provide an atmosphere of medical security for people. Six weeks later she was on the road to a new job expressing this phase of her rediscovered mission.

EXERCISE: GARBAGE IN(SIDE) OUT!

Here are five guidelines for getting rid of garbage from within. To use them best, create a special sanctuary space for yourself and actually go to it. The emphasis is on quiet and refuge.

1. **Observe when your mind wanders and why.** Find a word to get yourself back on track (like focus). Avoid situations that entice you into wandering thoughts.

2. **Allow any critical inner voices to speak but do not act on their advice.** Reacting to the critic will be like reacting to children who want to get your attention. Listen, then say politely, "Have a nice day," and go on with your meditation.

3. **Pick a definite time of day to address your worries.** Instead of fretting in the middle of the night or during work hours or during your sanctuary time, agree with yourself that you will take all your cares under advisement (say between three and five P.M. on Thursdays). You will be amazed at how many of them have disappeared by then.

4. **Spend at least 15 minutes a day on a right brain activity.** You could draw, play music, write with your non-preferred hand, practice yoga, or do whatever will take you out of the verbal into your non-verbal mode.

5. **Identify the place where your negative thoughts are lodged in your body.** When you say, "my boss is a pain in the neck," you've located the body area where the strain of your boss, or whatever else bothers you, is located. Whenever negative thoughts appear, stop, breathe deeply and imagine that you are breathing through that area. If your neck is tense, breathe into it until your muscles relax.

TURNING ON TO TUNING OUT—BUT NOT FOREVER!

Any method carried to excess, even CYM, is ineffective. Staring at the wall for two days is not what I'm talking about. CYM is a way station, a clearing of the forest to see your way. It's preparation for action as well as relaxation. And it is the means to an end.

While CYM is an important step in the process, it is not the end point. But you need this step to root out whatever is blocking you or to revive and energize yourself. Think of CYM as creating calm and averting storms. In this chapter we're talking about balance. A good recipe is just the right amount of reflection and action. So although we are emphasizing CYM, beware of staying in this comfort zone too long!

WITNESS JIM: OHM, OHM ON THE RANGE

A student of metaphysics and yoga, Jim was seduced by eternal calm. He lived in some sort of perpetual somnambulance. He made lists, spent time on long walks lost in thought, meditated, chanted, and daydreamed. Now these are all good things. But Jim became obsessed with his praying mantra lifestyle, and he was so laid back and "tuned out" that he was unable to translate his preparation into results. Jim was like a person who owned a car but never drove it, or like a plane standing on the runway that never took off. All systems were go except the one in him.

EXERCISE: YOU HAVE THE RIGHT TO REMAIN SILENT—YOUR EIGHT-STEP CYM PROGRAM

After reducing information overload from without and within, take time each day to strengthen and maintain this uncluttered state of mind effectively with this eight-step program:

1. **Prepare.** Select a time when you can rid your environment of distractions and be silent. Tell those you live with to respect your need for quiet. Children must understand that frequently you need to be alone. You don't have to have moral qualms about whether you should pull the plugs. Do it!

Unhook the phone or put on the answering machine. Go to the quietest room of the house, allowing from 15 minutes to an hour for you to stay there.

2. **Relax.** Sit down, get comfortable, and begin by deep breathing and focusing on your breath. Keep your upper torso relaxed and still. Begin the exercise when your breathing is steady and deep. Now imagine you are breathing through your feet, then move slowly up through your body, telling each area to "relax." Continue the exercise, breathing mentally through your ankles, continuing on through your lower leg, knees, thighs, buttocks, pelvis, chest, arms, shoulders, neck, face, forehead, and finally the crown of your head.

3. **Drain.** Imagine that all that internal pollution is draining slowly out of you through your limbs. When you have finished, feel a glow of inspiration washing down over your crown and all through your body. All tiredness and tensions flow out through your feet and into the floor. Your mind is now free to focus on a specific concern.

Continue your session, and when a thought occurs to you, gently push it aside, as you might do with tender saplings as you walk along a forest path in the spring. Spend at least ten minutes without thinking about anything. Your mind is now free to focus on a specific concern.

4. **Meditate Actively.** The purpose of active meditation at this point is to center on a concern. Sit in a chair or on the floor with legs uncrossed, or lie on the floor. Do not meditate in bed, because you might fall asleep. Practice without listening to music and with your eyes closed.

Imagine the question you want to address now

moving forward into your consciousness, unobstructed and uncluttered. Wait quietly for guidance. Listen to what you are telling you, and disregard any critical voice. Maybe nothing will come to you just now. That's okay; the more you practice CYM, the more it will come to you. The main thing is to practice this technique regularly. You will be paid back with greater ease in dealing with your mission.

Let's see how John used this active meditation. He asked himself what quality was so much a part of him that if he lost it he'd be a stranger to himself.

Spiritual Moves

John, a former clergyman, felt that his unique quality was compassion. He discovered in meditation that he couldn't bear to see his housekeeper exploited by a car dealer, and although he wasn't a lawyer, he handled her case personally by negotiating with the dealer. John also worked on projects for the poor and the homeless. He was incensed over a professor who refused to allow him to make up a test because a project for the poor had conflicted with the exam date (John needed compassion, too).

As he thought about a transition from the clergy into the film industry, he wondered if compassion were the quality needed in films. But as he discovered, there was a way to use his compassion and spirituality on a much broader scale in documentaries and educational films. His first documentary was about care for people with AIDS. John's capacity for compassion was the key to the success of that film and a central quality of his Life Mission.

5. Use Quick Flicks. What is your special quality and where could you begin to use it more effectively in the service of your Life Mission? You can use this active meditation with great effectiveness for even brief periods of time throughout the day. Let's suppose that you work in a busy office with lots of activity, noise, stress, and ringing phones. You have just about reached your limit when Mr. Frazzle comes in announcing the latest crisis.

This is precisely the time to take from one to three minutes for a quick flick, as I call it. You can mentally paint the most beautifully serene spot on earth. We'll call it your secret paradise. Put yourself in it and stay as long as you can. If you have to run out to your car or sit on the toilet or go outside to find a spot to meditate, do so. This will serve as a test of whether you can give yourself permission to meditate at a time when (or where) it seems inappropriate. Quick flicks can be just as effective as long sessions. Frequent use of these small chunks of time gives you a shot in the arm for creative action.

6. Read. Now for at least five minutes, turn to some inspirational reading for the day. You can simply open a book at random and read a page. You will find that something on that page will be information you need that very day. For ideas about what books to read, please check the bibliography.

7. Affirm. An affirmation is a short, positive sentence in the present tense, first person, and describes a quality you want to develop or something you want to have manifested. "I will not be afraid" is an example of how *not* to write an affirmation. Reword that sentence into something positive: "I practice my courage daily," or "I am courageous." An affirmation for this chapter might be "I think easily, and my mind is clear," or "I am a serene person." A thought held in the mind is a thought manifested.

At first you may find it hard to believe what you are saying. Exercise trust in your inner wisdom, the part of you that knows and reveals what you desire. Affirmations set things in motion from the moment you speak them. Solidify your session by affirming that the solution you have reached or the advice you have heard is manifesting itself now. What you desire will transpire!

8. **Act.** The goal of steps 1-7 is to recharge and prepare yourself in a positive way for the day, as well as to organize and focus your energy. Now move directly thereafter into something active. Perhaps you might work on your latest book, dream up ideas for a project you're working on, or plan your day. You are most creative at this time. The important thing is ultimately to translate your meditative wisdom into ACTION.

Although there are eight parts to the CYM program, you need not do all eight in one sitting. It is better to have a looser format than a compulsive, structured one, because then you can use whatever seems right for the particular day. Having a number of possibilities to choose from also gives variety to your meditation. And you can also add your own variations. You might for instance feel like skipping the hour altogether or going for a walk, that's okay, too. Or you might want to chant, sing a favorite song, or dance to music for a few minutes. Use whatever works, whatever gets you in tune with yourself, activated and positively charged for the day. Soon you will develop your own routine, one that works for you. The main thing is to do your CYM program regularly, and be sure that each session includes some quiet time with absolutely no agenda.

As Goethe writes in his poem, *In the Forest:*

I walked in the woods, just for me.
I focused on seeking nothing.

Do CYM "just for you." Make room for yourself and listen to yourself. Armed with the advice you get from within, you can move forward with confidence. That's the subject of the next chapter.

5

Risk Daily

Life is a risk. The first steps you took as a child were just that. Did you know what to expect? You could have fallen down and hurt yourself (risk does mean incurring possible injury) but something urged you on, and you did it. You wanted to walk, and you did. Recover that adventurous child within you to get what you really desire. As Raymond Loewy, the famous designer, once said, "I sought to surprise. I sought excitement and taking chances. I was all ready to fail in order to achieve something grand."

Take the risk toward living your mission instead of waiting for something to happen.

RISK AND LIFE MISSION

Risk means venturing into unknown and untested arenas, moving out of acceptable patterns—and most important—*achieving illumination on your unique mission.* Life Mission is a risk? you ask. How come? Isn't it the very thing that is uniquely mine? Yes, and that's the mandate: dare to make what is yours, yours!

Many people are not comfortable doing something just for themselves. They prefer to be like parents who speak up for their child but never express anything on their own behalf. And the pursuit of your mission may alienate you from those who want to squeeze you into their mold. There is enormous seduction in staying with the messages—and agendas—you get from others.

LIFE MISSION: TAKING IT PERSONALLY

The path to discovering your Life Mission is an intensely *personal* process. No one can fulfill your soul's purpose but you. You have the option to respond to your calling or not. Yes, intentionally taking on an assignment *by yourself* can feel risky. You might feel like first-time swimmers do, standing at the water's edge watching others swim. You feel safe where you are. Testing the water seems so scary. After all, you might drown. You first have to master swimming by a form of surrender—learning to float. Almost in defiance of common sense, you have to trust that the water will support you. And the same is true of the Life Mission process.

To follow your Life Mission means you allow yourself to surrender to the support of your Source (the same as you do with the water). When you cross the threshold of absolute trust and shake the feeling that nothing will be there to take its place, you will learn that you will be held up by your Source.

RISK: TAKING A CHANCE ON MISSION

Learn from the old song title: "Taking a Chance on Love." What does the title mean? Well, simply, when I take a chance on love, I am willing to embrace love in my life. Similarly, when you take a chance on your Life Mission you are saying, I am willing to take the risk of loving and pursuing my mission rather than staying the person I am not. The only way to achieve my mission is to rely on my Source, from which I am and to which I return, as the unabiding foundation of my being."

Taking a chance on your mission validates your support of yourself. But here's the paradox: you risk *everything* by not being yourself! You can fulfill your soul's purpose only to the degree that you are willing to take a chance on fulfilling your own mission.

THE MEANING OF RISK

To risk means to move out of the familiar into the unfamiliar. It means leaving your safety zone and stretching on to the edge of new possibilities. If you're feeling secure, you'll be less motivated to try something new. When you are willing to forsake certainty for growth, you benefit.

As an executive said astutely: "You have to recognize that every out-front maneuver you make is going to be lonely. But if you feel entirely comfortable, then you are not far enough ahead to do any good. That warm sense of everything going well is usually the body temperature at the center of the herd. Warm fuzzies and risk do not mix." This chapter invites you to slip into something less comfortable and learn how to risk so that you can "achieve something grand," as Loewy put it.

REWARDS OF RISK

The payoff of daring to be who you are is enormous. Risk gives you a heightened sense of self, enabling you to explore and validate your authentic needs. *Remember that every time you risk, it demonstrates that you are worth the effort.* What you gain is growth, development, and transformation.

Risk can make you fearful because it sets in motion an evolutionary process that moves you inevitably toward transformation, including death. Only with the acceptance of death and transformation can you face life squarely.

Risk puts you in touch with your strengths. You realize that the comfort of living others' plans for you is an illusion and begin to live your own agenda. You'll increase your self-love and self-esteem by opting for authenticity (being who you are) and identify more of what you need. Finally, you'll learn how to risk living a life that gives you what you want. (Would you risk getting something you didn't want?)

FIRST STEPS

Learning how to take risks is an ongoing venture. There is no better antidote to depression and inertia in your Life Mission process than taking those first steps of risk. Sometimes the whole matter might look too overwhelming and huge to manage. One way to approach risk is to take the process apart and break it down into small chunks.

SALLY'S TRIP

A silver-haired woman of 63, Sally wanted to take a trip by herself and had never dared to do so. A widow with two dogs, she had not traveled for ten years—since her husband died. She spent her time sitting home depressed, hardly venturing out. Her husband had always done the planning, so she was terrified at the prospect of traveling on her own. I asked her to make a list of everything she feared about taking a trip.

Her list:

• Being alone and away from home overnight.

• Deciding where to go.

• Being without my animals.

• Finding my destination spot on the map.

• Going to a library to read up on the location.

- Calling up the travel agent.

- Looking at my checkbook to see if I can afford it.

- Buying luggage.

- Deciding how I want to get there (car, van, plane, train).

- Identifying the special things I need, such as pills, shots, special equipment.

- Investigating kennels for the dogs.

I asked Sally to identify the scariest item on her list. To her surprise, she realized that her fears centered around leaving the animals. No one could take care of them; a kennel would be unthinkable. "Caging them up like that would be terrible," she insisted. Sally had allowed her animals to tie her down. She resolved to face her fears: she investigated alternative ways to have the animals cared for and found a kennel where her dogs could run and exercise.

Sally's fear of travel had to do with that imaginary list she was carrying around with her, as you can see. Each item in itself was manageable (some more than others, of course). But by tackling the "worst" one on the list she got the ball rolling. By daring to risk, she finally visited a brother whom she had not seen for five years, continuing on from his Minnesota home to New York to visit a friend. Upon her return home, she vowed to herself that she would travel once a month. Her health and her emotional vitality improved.

EXERCISE: BREAKING DOWN YOUR RISK FACTORS

It's easier and less imposing to begin with one aspect of the risk process. Like Sally, identify something you are afraid of risking. Then break down the project or activity into its component parts, selecting the key item you are having difficulty with.

1. **Look at the one item you want to master.** What bothers you about it? Identify the steps you can take to overcome your fear of this item. For Sally it was how to cope without her animals. The solution: Sally took her dogs to a neighbor for a day.

2. **Break your risk down into stages.** If, for example, you are afraid to take a course at the university, you could spend an afternoon walking around the campus, read a book on the subject, attend a lecture, talk to a professor, or audit the course. Sally went on a day trip by herself without her animals.

3. **Make attitude changes.** If you picked something that you simply don't like to do, how can you change your attitude toward it? For instance, if the details of a trip are a drag, like negotiating with the travel agent, or doing research, can you persuade a friend to help you with some of it?

4. **Examine how the risk is going to benefit you.** Sally realized two things. First, she hadn't considered what she would do if she was hospitalized. Thinking about her risk item made her aware of the need to have an alternate care plan for her animals. Second, she could see her brother, whom she missed.

What do you feel about your risk now? Is it so bad? I'll wager it looks halfway good.

RISK IS IN THE EYE OF THE BEHOLDER

Often people assume something is a risk when it isn't. I quit a tenured position at a university, having waited much longer than necessary because I feared the consequences of that risk. There was no job to replace it and none in sight. Looking back on it now, I wondered what all the fuss was about. My assumption was that it was a risk to leave a secure job, whereas the real risk was to continue teaching at the university.

Valparaiso, Indiana, the town in which the university is located, is a quiet, sleepy little conservative place that looked forward to the big event of the year: a popcorn festival. My life at the university consisted of preparing for classes, planning next year's courses, and—for relief—going on vacation. Without vacations I couldn't have faced the semester. It was, as St. Augustine said, my way of backing myself away from hell to get to heaven.

Today, I see my discontent and depression as clear clues I needed to leave, whereas I thought I feared leaving a disappointing situation! And yet by labeling my departure a risk I had kept myself in fear of leaving for a good five years. It took three years to make the transition away from Valparaiso, but it worked because I dared to follow the vision of becoming who I already was instead of staying who I was not. I began to see that leaving was the only way to mental and emotional health. Above all, I saw that in order to get in sync with my Life Mission, I had to resign from my position as professor. At that point of realization, leaving no longer seemed a risk.

RISK AND YOUR PM

Some PMs will feel more comfortable with risk than others. Doers prefer risk (but not emotional risk), because they want to maintain power. Motivators avoid taking concrete action. Stabilizers fear change and sudden moves, hence they are reluctant to initiate. Analyzers do things only when they are sure they will be right, so decisions are risky for them.

Think about a risk you're reluctant to take. Is it on an emotional level? Saying a kind word to a boss you can't stand? Crying in front of one of your children or a mate? Showing your loving self? Saying what you really feel to someone you love or dislike? Exposing a vulnerable part of yourself? Or is it perhaps making a mistake at work, taking the initiative where others have always made the decisions, or just sitting back and listening when you know the answers already? Risk is a new behavior, but in the newness and the change you will invite growth.

EXERCISE : YOUR RISK QUOTIENT

Rate yourself on the way you respond to the following statements, circling the appropriate number. If you agree strongly with a statement, circle #1; #2 if you agree; #3 if you are neutral; #4 if you disagree; and # 5 if you disagree strongly. Add up the total.

agree<—>disagree

	agree				disagree
1. I have to ask myself permission before I risk anything.	1	2	3	4	(5)
2. I take risks only after everything else has failed.	1	2	3	(4)	5
3. I risk only when I've done the same kind of thing before.	1	2	3	4	(5)
4. I investigate things thoroughly before doing them.	1	2	3	4	(5)
5. I am not an impulsive risk-taker.	1	2	3	4	(5)
6. I risk only when absolutely necessary.	1	2	3	4	(5)
7. My parents or guardians tended to make safe decisions.	1	2	(3)	4	5
8. I tend to do things in predictable ways.	1	2	3	(4)	5
9. I don't laugh at myself much.	1	2	3	(4)	5
10. I care more about being right than taking action.	1	2	3	4	(5)
11. I don't like to structure my day a lot.	1	2	(3)	4	5
12. I try to fit in wherever I am.	1	2	(3)	4	5
13. I make a big deal out of little things.	1	2	3	4	(5)
14. I follow instructions and procedures easily.	1	2	3	4	(5)
15. I tend to accept the status quo.	1	2	3	(4)	5
16. I tend to go along with the group.	1	2	(3)	4	5
17. Questionnaires like this make me feel uncomfortable.	1	2	3	(4)	5
18. Change scares me a great deal.	1	2	3	(4)	5
19. I discourage others from taking risks.	1	2	3	(4)	5
20. I like to know what I'm getting into before I do it.	1	2	3	4	(5)

total: _____

What Your Score Means:
20–30 You're probably scared to leave the womb.
31–40 You leave the womb, but not the house.
41–50 You always take an umbrella with you, except perhaps to Palm Springs.
51–60 You haven't checked your spare tire in a while.

61–70 You plan your vacation while on it.
71–80 You often bet on dark horses.
> 81–90 You never venture anything too soon.
91–100 You notice the cliff after you've jumped off.

Seriously though, if you score below 40, you might consider taking an assertiveness class in addition to the exercises below. If your score was between 40-60, the self-help methods that follow should help you increase your score. If you score between 60-80, you will want to examine any aspects of your life where you have not yet risked and give them attention, and if you scored more than 80, you'll want to assess whether you take risks without first incubating your ideas.

RISK-TAKING AND ASSERTIVENESS

Risk-taking and assertiveness go hand in hand. A healthy approach is to protect and claim your own space. When you do, you're saying, "My behavior indicates I think as much of my space as others do." Here's how passive, assertive, and aggressive behavior look:

The circle represents the relationship between two individuals. Each is responsible for her or his own 100 percent (saying 50 percent would be more "logical," but does not carry the import of full responsibility).

Aggressive behavior invades the other person's space. Passive behavior, on the other hand, allows the aggressor to enter the other half of the space. Assertive behavior says: "I am responsible for my 100 percent but not your half. I may be responsive *to* your half, but I am not responsible *for* it and I choose not to enter it." Risk means claiming your space without encroaching upon another's.

You'll need this preparation for claiming a space of your own (your Life Mission).

To B. or Not to B.

Evelyn B., a quiet, shy secretary, illustrates how using assertiveness helps in taking risks for a Life Mission. In the follow-up session to a workshop series, participants reported what things they had risked doing in the intervening months.

Evelyn had changed her work process. Working in a small medical office, she decided to computerize her office's files even before she knew how to use the program. Previously, when she thought of doing anything new, she killed the idea by telling herself the company wouldn't allow it or she wouldn't allow it. She felt the frustration of files of information piling up in the office and knew there had to be a better way.

Evelyn literally decided to assert her space, which was difficult since she was a Stabilizer. Evelyn said she had asked her boss for reduced time at the office in order to set up the system. This meant going out on a limb in a big way for her.

Begrudgingly, her boss gave her only a few hours off a week and little emotional support. The threat of being fired "for taking so much time" loomed over her head constantly. She kept her stance, "worked on her half of the circle," and came up with a positive solution to the office problem.

Now Evelyn's co-workers save valuable time in looking up and updating files by accessing the information quickly. She was willing to take a leap in a manner she had not done before. Her private risk was to tell herself she could initiate a project at work. Her decision to take responsibility for her own space gave her confidence and opened her up to a Life Mission involving ways to improve communication and organization. The next step was easy!

HOW-TO'S FOR TAKING RISKS

It's never too late to explore taking risks and going out on your own personal limb. (After all, that's where the tree bears fruit). The object is to get comfortable with risks. Increase your risk-taking as far as you feel safe (but not TOO safe!) Here are some suggestions:

Review your risk process. Think back to the last time you risked something. What were the circumstances? What were you risking? What were your expectations? How did it turn out? What did you learn from the event? Would you risk in the same way again? Have you ever risked this way in your career?

Know what you want from your risk. So often something seems risky because you haven't the foggiest notion of the results you want. Be clear about your purpose in doing something, and take time to think it out first (especially good advice for Doers and Motivators). If you are unsure as to what results you want, list the worst and best outcomes possible. Probably what you want is somewhere in between. Write out the specific objectives, using the information you have, and visualize yourself actually reaching them. Evelyn's example points up an important factor in risk-taking.

Too often, people tend to stop themselves in mid-course by interrupting a spontaneous risk-taking impulse. But if you know what you want out of a particular situation, you can risk more intelligently and minimize the likelihood of stopping in mid-stream. Remember when you were on the road taking wrong turns because you had no road map? With your Life Mission, you have that road map, a clearly defined need is your goal, and risk is the fuel to get you there.

Take a private risk. I suggest a private risk because the risk level is usually low and has a good chance of turning out in your favor. A private risk is something you alone know you are taking. Here's an example: in one class the participants shared their private risks. One participant reported that she went for an entire Saturday afternoon without a single agenda. Normally, she would fill up each minute with scheduled activities. For her it was outrageous, *but no one knew about it.* Here's another example: a workshop participant said he had never before dared to wear a red tie to work! For him, a private risk might be to start wearing a brighter tie and work himself up to a red one.

Rehearse your risk. Rehearsal is vital to Stabilizers and Analyzers, who like to do things thoroughly, whereas Doers and Motivators need a run-through because they rarely prepare anything.

Pick a situation in which you want to improve the outcome. Let's say, for example, that you bought a microwave that turned out to be defective or not what you wanted. Review what you did about that situation which failed to meet your need. Maybe you simply lived with your purchase or took it back and got angry in the process.

Redo the scene as you want it to turn out. Practice this mentally until it becomes comfortable. The next time a similar situation occurs—say, a washing machine doesn't perform as guaranteed—rehearse what you are going to say. Be sure that you have the desired result in mind before you begin. Try it out with a partner and role-play it, if you like. Get some feedback on how you're doing. That will help defuse the sense of anxiety and give you confidence. Then go and carry through what you rehearsed. You'll put some steam in your self-esteem!

Encourage yourself. Boost your risk-taking ability by telling yourself all the things you admire about yourself. Practice doing it in front of a mirror. (That in itself is a risk!) Maybe one of your sterling qualities is your empathic skill. By using it perhaps you can persuade the clerk to take back that defective item mentioned in the example above. Or perhaps you're funny. (You Motivators will tune into this.) You can risk telling a joke to colleagues. For each risk that you take and get what you want, treat yourself to something as a reward. At all times be kind and gentle to yourself.

Share your fears. Risk can be a lonely venture. Talk over with yourself any feelings of isolation you are experiencing. Give yourself space to experience any anxieties or worries, and discuss them with yourself. Admit to any fear so that you can work through it.

Accept failure as part of the process. Risk demands that we accept possible mistakes along the way. As one client put it, "If you've failed somewhere, you must be doing something right!"

If you stop taking risks because you fear failure, consider Jane. She was paralyzed by the thought of any kind of failure. The irony was that she had "failed" numerous times along the way! Among other things, she had flunked a certification exam, been fired from two jobs, and had a divorce. (She didn't yet realize that she needed to experience these failures to be free.) Naturally, I had to ask her why she was afraid of failure, seeing as she was so good at it. After all, successful people experience setbacks. Edison catalogued scores of separate failures before inventing the light bulb.

Ask if it's really a risk. Take a long hard look at the risk you're considering. Is it really a risk? Who says so? You or someone else? If you *didn't* quit that job, for example, how would your health be? If something is a risk, what are the alternatives of not carrying through with it? (Remember my example from Valparaiso.)

Take a risk with others. You don't have to risk everything alone. Clue others in on your risky ventures. Get their support and feedback. Ask people about the risks they have taken. Read autobiographies of adventurers, explorers, pioneers, and risk-takers. Find out how they did it and the process of trial and error they went through. Their stories will give you encouragement. Paste pictures of your heroes on your wall and scan the newspaper for stories of people you can emulate and respect who have taken bold steps in their lives.

Recognize the risks you have already taken. Turn a piece of paper on its side, draw a horizontal line and put hatchmarks for every five years you have lived. Above the line, write at least four major decisions you've made at the time in your life you decided them. Below the line, write what you would have done had you not made this decision.

EXERCISE: IMPORTANT DECISIONS I MADE

Draw a chart that looks like this:

5	10	15	20	25	30	35	40	45	50	55	60

The numbers refer to the age you were when you made a life-changing decision. Write the important decisions you made and when you made them. Underneath the chart write what would have happened if you hadn't made those decisions.

Here is the way I completed the exercise:

IMPORTANT DECISIONS I MADE

learned to ride bike	moved to Europe	quit my university job	started writing and composing

5 ▼	10	15 ▼	20	25	30	35 ▼	40	45 ▼	50	55	60

RESULT HAD I NOT MADE THOSE DECISIONS

would have had fewer friends	would not have been fluent in German	would have ended relationship	would have continued seminars and avoided creative expression

This exercise lets you see the risks you have taken in the choices you have made. Compare the person you chose to be (the top of the line) with the person you elected not to be (below the line).

Were you surprised at how many risks you took?

Give the exercise to a friend and ask that friend to describe both persons. What differences did you discover about the person you risked being (the one above the line)? Who was responsible for the person you decided to be? Where would you be now if you hadn't taken the paths you did? Congratulate yourself for every decision. Each one shows that:

1. You were in control of your life.
2. You chose who you wanted to be.
3. You made some good choices.
4. You had definite reasons for doing what you did.
5. You took many risks!

Examine your past for risk takers. If you think you can't risk, look at your family history for examples of courage. Most of you who live in the United States are in this country because your ancestors braved new frontiers and followed their destiny, or, they were forced to come here against their will and risked their lives.

All of us can find a tale of heroism and risk-taking in our heritage somewhere. Look for the pioneers, immigrants, adventurers, or captives in your past and the risks they took! Ask your parents, grandparents, or relatives to tell you stories of bravery in their memory. Get together with friends and share tales of courage from your respective family histories. These accounts will give you an added boost, instill you with pride, and demonstrate the positive effects of taking risks.

Give yourself this day your daily risk. It is your staff of life, your source of power, growth, uniqueness, and authenticity. The more you risk, the more you'll say to your Life Mission: "I embrace you."

6

Eliminate Negative Thinking

If you say you can or you can't, you're right.

Negative thinkers are people who get up in the morning, see a molehill, and turn it into a mountain by nightfall. These nay-sayers get a lot of encouragement because negative thinking (N.T.) is pervasive in our society. It's very difficult, for example, to find anything positive in the news or on TV. Media executives are candid in admitting that disaster sells better than the "soft" (that is, more optimistic) human interest stories.

If you are blocked in your mission search, it could be that you're damming everything up with negative energy. N.T. keeps you from trying for the career you always wanted, daring your dreams, and realizing your Life Mission. Positive thinking enables body, mind, and spirit to give you the affirming confidence and faith in yourself that you need for your Life Mission.

The goal of this chapter is to help you eliminate the debilitating effects of N.T. and replace it with positive, proactive thinking. You'll learn the causes for N.T., how to kick the N.T. habit, and how to take charge of your thoughts. Remember, the way you think is a self-fulfilling prophecy for every event in your life. If you say you can or you can't, you're right!

COMPARING POSITIVE WITH NEGATIVE THOUGHTS

Thoughts are things. They create energy fields. When you give thought a certain kind of energy, you attract that same kind of energy back to you. You receive exactly what you send out. Put another way, what you wish for affects what you fish for—and the kind of fish you catch. Notice how you respond emotionally and physically to a positive story in the newspaper. It can actually make you feel better. Norman Cousins discovered the healing effects on the body when he induced laughter in himself during a severe illness. Comedians Bob Hope and George Burns have demonstrated the positive relationship between humor and longevity.

The same equation is true of negative thoughts. If you see everything as negative, you will reap negative results. Thinking of things in terms of disaster diminishes and drains your energy. N.T. is every bit as destructive as poison.

You can demonstrate for yourself the debilitating effects of negative thinking on your body with the following experiment.

EXERCISE: YOU'VE GOT ME UNDER YOUR SKIN

Get a friend who has not read this part of the book (in other words, a friend who has not yet bought this book). Write down three sentences you are going to say mentally to this friend. Pick one negative and two positive sentences (or vice-versa) and the order in which you are going to say them. Example: (1) "Jane couldn't do anything right if she tried," (2) "Jane is the most wonderful person on earth," and (3) "Jane can be anything she wants to." Do not show these sentences to your friend.

Ask the friend now to hold one arm straight out to the side and to resist any downward pressure you apply to it with the second and third fingers of your hands. Then apply the downward pressure to test the friend's resistance. The friend's arm should stay firm. Tell your friend you are now going to press downward three more times, as you did in the practice attempt, prefacing each mental message by saying "one, two," and pressing down after you say "three."

Mentally say each sentence with your fingers resting on the subject's arm, and give the preparatory count. After saying "three," apply downward pressure as practiced. Watch for the difference in the resistance of your friend's arm between the time you thought the negative sentence and the time you thought the positive one. Immediately after you think the negative sentence, your friend's arm muscle will invariably weaken, and you will push it down easily!

If you can make a person's muscles grow limp with a mental N.T., imagine what a constant mental *and verbal* bombardment of such negativity can create over a period of time in you and in others. Even worse, imagine what your N.T. will do to *you* in your mission search!

Let's return to the discussion of our exercise. If you revert to thinking the positive sentence (without giving away your secret) your friend's arm will once again bounce back with strength, thus affirming your thought!

N.T.: THE SUGAR-COATED PILL

Why is negative thinking so widespread? Why in the world would you want something that blocks you from your goals? Here are some reasons.

N.T. often gives a false payoff (sometimes known as secondary gain). If, for example, you got sick as a child, maybe you were subconsciously looking for your parents' attention. But there's the rub: the payoff might seem positive, but in order to get that attention, you have to diminish your capacities (get sick).

N.T. gives a cushion and protection from admitting you are wrong. If something you predict as "wrong" turns out that way, you won't have to blame yourself for being wrong! Your assumption that it was wrong all along, after all, becomes correct. Some people even unconsciously need the negative outcome in order to confirm their prediction. With this philosophy, you "win" when your negative prediction is negative. After all, you were right. Some victory!

If all of this seems a bit obscure, just apply it to an everyday situation. You're on the golf green. You tell yourself you are going to screw up ("I know I won't make this putt"). And *Voila!* you miss the putt! You may not like the results, but at least you were astute enough to predict them (I knew it all along!).

Negativity sounds so authoritative. N.T. frequently connotes realism, wisdom, clarity, and authority. For many, being realistic is proof of intelligence and sanity! It also seems so mature! After all didn't you learn N.T. more or less as an adult?

Positive thinking is associated with the child-like naïveté. It is practiced by the gullible, dreamers, those in denial, hedonists, or the slightly loony. Pollyanna is the word often used to describe an unrealistic, optimistic person. Yuck!

WAYS TO ELIMINATE N.T.

Give your positive self the respect and attention it deserves! GET THE N.T. OUT! You're aiming for one result: to remove any barriers, blocks and obstacles created by N.T. that keep you from finding your Life Mission.

Acknowledge N.T. as an addiction. In spite of the harmful side effects of N.T., it can have a stranglehold on you because it is just like alcohol, drugs, or other addictive substances. An addiction is a compulsive habit, like downer thoughts, predictions of disaster, or finding fault. Negative thinkers grow dependent on them, much as the substance abuser does with chemicals.

The unconscious works with the material you give it, accommodating your interpretation without objection. If you believe the letter you just got from the I.R.S. is a sure summons for an audit, your muscles will tense, your heart will pound, and adrenalin will race into your bloodstream.

Addictive N.T. throws up a giant wall between you and your goals, because each event is (pre)judged and diminishes your performance. (Try doing something productive in a physical and emotional state when you think the I.R.S. is after you.) If, on the other hand, you open that letter without assuming anything, you'll be able to deal calmly with whatever the content is. It's all how you choose to apprehend the situation.

John's Stalled Self

John had built up a neat N.T. defense system to keep him from his passion for motorcycles. He was a small-town Kentucky boy who had made it in the big city. An account executive for 25 years, he had left his job and was looking for another one with similar pay (over $100,000 a year). John had yearnings for the outdoors, race cars, and a different life.

But his negative thinking critic went something like this: "Your constant need to tinker with machines, your fond memories of having driven a tractor at age ten on the farm, and your passion for racing are unbecoming to a grown man."

There was no breaking through the wall of doom

around John's desire. "If I do what I love to do, it will mean that I am selling out to something hokey. Anyway, my hobby is not going to earn me money, and if I did what I liked, I'd go bankrupt." John preferred to be negative about what he loved so as to avoid embracing it. John truly "just said no" to his mission.

Kick the N.T. habit. Eliminating N.T. is a process of transformation. You can change N.T. into something that will work for you by learning to redirect your energy into something constructive. It's like harnessing an electrical current, in and of itself neutral, for something that can be used effectively. (So go fly a kite, already.)

Kicking the N.T. habit begins with becoming aware of how dependent you are on negative thoughts racing through your head. Jot down some of your habitual mental tapes. Review them, and ask yourself what you would do if they suddenly stopped. What new behaviors would you have to engage in if your daily fix of N.T. were missing? Which N.T. have you been addicted to most?

BIOLOGY (CLASS) IS DESTINY

A true N.T. addict, Glen was miserable if he didn't have his daily fix of N.T.. Literally tied up in "nots," he could hardly say a sentence without a negative in it. Although his college work demonstrated a promising career in biology, Glen was convinced that for the rest of his life he was "doomed" to a high-school teaching job showing students how to dissect frogs or collect butterflies.

But he was getting exactly what he wanted. Glen was like a fellow in a rainstorm standing with a pole to attract lightning to himself. He had put all his energy into dreading the high-school job, the location, even what his miserable room would look like: outdated microscopes, dirty walls, lackluster textbooks, etc. He had in fact attracted just the kind of job he was focused on. (What you resist persists.)

Glen monitored his negative tapes for several weeks and realized how dependent he was on them. Getting a job more to his liking meant he would have to assume more responsibility for his thoughts. Since fear resulted in negative thoughts, he began to shift his focus to what he wanted rather than what he feared.

Today, you'll find Glen working happily in a research firm. "The only butterflies I have to put up with now are the ones I experience before a research report is due." For the first time, Glen has a sense of fulfilling his mission of improving the immune system through biological research.

Believe positive thinking will work (pre-event approach). Beliefs are powerful agents. They help construct the reality you experience. You accomplish something only by truly and honestly believing it is possible. In order to stop N.T., you must have faith in what you are telling yourself. I call it "using the #5 iron":

STRIKE WHILE THE (#5) IRON IS HOT

Annie, an avid golfer, once used her #3 iron at a driving range. Up to then she never believed she could hit the ball well with this iron. One day, she thought she was using her her favorite club, a #5 iron. Suddenly she noticed that she was actually using the #3 iron. Her good performance with that #3 iron happened because she believed she was using her trusty #5, with which she could do no wrong.

When I hear clients tell me exactly why a situation will turn out badly for them, I ask them why they are so sure, so fervent, about predicting unfavorable results. I always urge them to use the same passionate belief to achieve positive results!

Use detached involvement. Who knows if it's good or bad? (post-event approach). People use N.T. to anticipate an event not only proactively, as in the example of the #5 iron, but also *reactively,* to judge an event after it is experienced. While the proactive approach is to think positively about upcoming events, the challenge in a post-event situation is *not to react at all* but to see what can be learned so that the next event can be approached positively. I call this detached involvement. You play to win (**pre-even**t) but are not attached to the outcome (**post-event**).

There's an old Zen story that illustrates this detached involvement beautifully. When a man lost his horse, he responded, "Who knows if it's good or bad?" Shortly thereafter the horse returned with a mare. Now the man had two horses. His son rode the horse, was thrown from it, and injured his back. The man once again said, "Who knows if it's good or bad?" Soldiers of the local army came through the man's property, recruiting men for battle. The son could not go because of his injury. The father said, "Who knows if it's good or bad?" And on the story goes.

Take any event that you reactively labelled negative at the time. But looking at it with hindsight, what did you learn from this situation? Many clients have interpreted a firing, job transfer, lay-off or a similar change as the universe's way of dropping not-so-subtle hints. But sixty to seventy percent of the people polled on their careers after such a change felt they went on to a better job after being fired. The word *fired* in itself is neutral. To be fired (up), for instance, is positive!

Learn to see events which have happened in a detached, neutral way. "Who knows if it's good or bad?"

JOVIAL JOAN

Joan was a 45-year-old businesswoman in the midst of a relationship break-up. Her successful greeting card business had stalled, and she was up to her neck in personal debts. Tired of her old business, she didn't know what to move into. But something about Joan's attitude and demeanor was different. Always smartly dressed right down to eyeshadow that matched her blouse, her eyes sparkled with a refreshing zest for living, although she could have found dozens of reasons for doom and disaster thinking.

Joan had a glowing, positive attitude about things. She knew her experience was for the good, knew things would turn out all right. Everything she did was in the context of her mission, to brighten people's lives through creativity and humor. She had the greatest faith in herself, even if she didn't know exactly which way to go at the time.

She was stuck as a problem-solver, yet not mired in N.T. As she reviewed the reasons for her situation (she is a Motivator), she realized she had been too isolated in the past, needed to get out in the world, be more visible, and use her verbal skills to promote a cause. (Detached involvement!) I told her to worry less about the specific outcome for now and concentrate on seeing just what turned her on.

Now, a year later, Joan is negotiating a contract with a philanthropic organization for a project in which she can combine her skills as a businesswoman, art lover, and designer.

Does Joan have some access to a secret formula concocted by the ancients? Positive thinking did not prevent her from having "setbacks." But it was her attitude towards the events and her undying belief that everything was going to turn out just as it must, that pulled her through. She believed in the ultimate wisdom of each event. It was the unshakable nature of her belief system that helped her shut out N.T..

Accepting the process: aim where you hit. Acceptance enables you to say "aim where you hit." The spot where your arrow landed was the one you had intended all along. That's neither fatalistic nor defeatist. On the contrary, it affirms the rightness of any situation and the conviction that you will discover the wisdom of your experience.

If your car breaks down, and you have a negative reaction, then what are you telling yourself? My car (unlike any other car) ought not to break down. Things of this sort are unfair and do not fit my universal law #1, namely, "Nothing inconvenient or difficult should ever happen to me." Instead, consider the reason why your car broke down and why you needed car trouble at *precisely* the time it occurred. Then you can approach the next situation positively with greater insight.

This discussion also pertains to traumatic events. A former colleague of mine, Mary Louise Poor, is a flutist who suffered a near-fatal automobile accident resulting in severe injuries, including a collapsed lung and lacerations to her mouth and face. She spent 13 weeks in a hospital, three months in a body cast, and another six months on crutches. When she resumed playing, she had to restructure the way she played and used a special mouthpiece. "Playing is not just my occupation and my life's work . . . it's my being . . . it's part of my soul." The mission process goes on even when circumstances change drastically. Mary Louise Poor was able to carry on her mission in another form. She revised and redeveloped her skills, and she has let her mission evolve into helping musicians who have suffered similar injuries.

No matter how terrible or devastating the situation might seem, reflect what you can learn from it. But do it without beating up on yourself by saying it's your fault. (N.T.) There is a difference between acceptance of events and the belief that you deserved them or are being punished for them. When you insist on seeing yourself as victim, you abdicate the control you have over your life.

FRIENDLY PERSUASION

Although most of the emphasis in this book is on individual work, N.T is so pervasive that you can use supportive help from others. Because it is an addictive habit, a local Alcoholics Anonymous (AA), Al-Anon, Emotions Anonymous, Overeaters Anonymous (OA), or Adult Children of Alcoholics (ACA) would be an ideal support group for you if you habitually use N.T. You could learn how others overcome addictions through the 12- Step Program and apply it to N.T..

You can also form your own network of people willing to work on encouraging positive thinking. (You could call it AINT—Anonymous Inveterate Negative Thinkers.) Here are some ways a group can be especially effective. Each person lists pet negative phrases, and then the group finds original or humorous alternatives to them. When you catch yourself saying your pet phrase, use the replacement suggested by the group. Group members can be supportive by reminding you if they hear you slip into your pet phrase—or any kind of N.T..

You can further discuss with the group the context in which you tend to use this negative phrase. Again, feedback from the group can help you realize how your N.T. is triggered. Finally, the group can also brainstorm to devise its own techniques and exercises for transforming N.T. into positive action.

EXERCISE: FLUSHING OUT YOUR NEGATIVITY

Write down all your negative equations surrounding a particular issue:

work	=	drudgery (not fun)
drudgery	=	good pay
pay	=	what I get for pain and suffering

Now rewrite the list in the most positive way you can. For example:

work	=	passion
passion	=	money
money	=	freedom
freedom	=	achieving my mission

Remember, you don't have to believe the list (yet), just jot it down and put it on your refrigerator! Now to the flushing part. Write down everything you feel negative about. Get all of those feelings OUT! Don't spare anything. If you dislike your kids, are negative about your mate or hate the dog, ADMIT it on paper. Then get rid of the list! You could (a) burn it, (b) tear it to shreds, or (c) flush it down the toilet (if you've written it on toilet paper).

Be creative and invent your own way! One client eliminated his N.T. list by saying it aloud and expelling it in huge breaths after each item. You can imagine yourself releasing your N.T. items like balloons drifting into the stratosphere. See them fade forever from view. They'll return from time to time, but you'll find that they diminish in strength or frequency of appearance. How would you like to keep showing up at a person's place where you are not wanted?

Each time you get new negative thoughts, gather them up as before and dispose of them in your favorite manner. Remember, this is a *constant* process. Just expelling the negative will in itself accomplish little if you fail to replace it with positive. Now that you are releasing your negativity regularly (isn't it nice to be regular?), you will find space opening up for the positive.

If you looked for red GM pickup trucks this week, you will start to see them everywhere because you directed your attention to them. What you look for is what you get. Apply this phenomenon to positive thoughts, and anticipate them in your life! Look actively for good fortune to happen in your life. Every time it does, affirm that the universe has rewarded you for right action.

Get rid of ugly N.T. in just 30 Days. N.T. should be thought of as crystallized thought patterns (and you know how hard a crystal is). It will come as no surprise that habitual behavior resists change rather vigorously. This exercise will help you get rid of ugly N.T. by means of a 30-day program using a different way of thinking.

Any crystallized N.T. must be transformed by a fresh, vital, energetic, and softened mental system charged with a positive outlook. It will neutralize the acerbic and acidic effects of N.T..

EXERCISE: AROUND NEGATIVITY IN THIRTY DAYS

First, decide what N.T. issue you wish to transform. Perhaps you need to learn how to keep your home free of clutter, begin an exercise program, or improve your time management. State in a short, positive phrase exactly what you want. (You can identify important issues with the help of your most prevalent negative thought: "I can't ever seem to find anything." Change it to: "I need to organize my closets, files, or desk.")

Now write a second sentence that states the results you want. Make the statement short, to the point, in the present tense, and without any negations. "I want to be happier," or "I want some time to do what I wish," are vague and give your subconscious little to go on. If you say "happier" or "some time," how do you know when you have reached your goal? Effective examples might be: "I want to reduce my cholesterol count by 20 percent" or "I want to have one hour of leisure time daily to write in my diary." These sentences state your desired outcomes clearly. Be sure you are detached from the outcome. This is what you want without any strings attached. A results-oriented sentence for your clutter issue might be: "I want to find anything I need in my closet, files, or desk within one minute."

Say your statement silently (or aloud, if you prefer), each morning and night for a period of thirty days. If possible, devote five to ten minutes on each session. Make a contract with yourself to do the program daily. If you forget and skip a day, devote twice as much time to your issue the next day. If you skip two days, you must start over, because the program is effective only on a continuous basis. For effective results, you wouldn't diet or take antibiotic pills every other day, would you?

You may feel a certain amount of resistance, especially in the first few days, but don't give in to it. Stick to your program! You will in time begin to feel results, if you believe in what you are affirming.

EXERCISE: A LITTLE HELP FROM YOUR FRIENDS

Here's a final exercise that shows how to maximize your mission positively:

1. Write down the major things you intend to accomplish in your lifetime. As guidelines you can use such categories as creative, financial, personal, material, spiritual, educational, or professional.

2. Ask three friends to make the same list about you without having seen your version.

3. Now compare your list with theirs. What things did the friends think *you were capable* of that you did not?

Perhaps your self-assessment is merely a matter of degree, like Jenny. She was shocked to find out her friends thought she should go into politics and be a charismatic leader. "But I'm terrified to get up and speak in front of more than ten people!" she insisted. But then Jenny began to remember all those civil rights and Viet Nam marches in which she had participated and the big rally she organized for the ERA. She was up in front of people talking to them with no trouble! "I can't believe I convinced myself for so long that I couldn't do this," she exclaimed, fighting back tears.

    4. Now take one ability, talent, or achievement your friend(s) know you are capable of. It does not matter if the ability is big or small. Just get it down on paper! Then complete the following:

        As my friend has recognized, I am able to _____ _____ (friend's words). Yes, the truth is, I am very capable of _____ (put in your own words). I am therefore going to give positive energy to achieving _____ _____ (what you intend to do with this ability).

Affirm You 30-day program daily. No matter how major or minor your statement is, resolve to make your statement materialize. Be passionately involved in the success of your goals! When you go through this program of eliminating addictive N.T., of affirming the positive, of believing in and watching for the positive to transpire in your life, you can expect the riches of the universe that are rightly yours. Surprising things will happen!

Your Life Mission will become a reality when you say "I can."

7

Anticipate the Unusual

Surprise!!!   When you hear that word, you know something enjoyable or unexpected is going to happen. That's why science fiction, whodunits, fantasy films, clever jokes, and dreams are so popular—they all contain unusual, weird or bizarre events.

Real life, however, is another matter. Many people have days so characterized by routine and predictability that you know exactly what they're going to be doing at three P.M. Even worse, three P.M.for them seems about the same as three A.M. They're here today—and here tomorrow.

If you are one of those who is bored with what you are doing but can't get out of the rut, if you feel you've had about as much of yourself as you can take, if you think you are boring yourself, then this chapter is for you.

We'll discuss the ways to be the architect of a vibrant and thrilling mission by injecting more of the surprising, the off-beat, and the amazing into your life. This chapter will be especially valuable for Analyzers (who look for rules) and

Stabilizers (who look for precedent), but also for Doers (who are too much in a rush) and Motivators (who are the most comfortable with the unusual).

"WHAT'LL YOU HAVE?" "OH, THE USUAL. . . ."

People often have dull existences, dreary jobs and relationships because they anticipate the usual—in fact, they actually expect it. If life is nothing special, then it is difficult to view a Life Mission as special. A humdrum existence does not foster an exciting life.

Viewing things as "business as usual," stops the flow of process and prevents you from experiencing life in its variety and richness. Life becomes one-sided, monotonous, and lacking in options. You learn nothing from sameness.

We'll turn now to a discussion of three detractors from the unusual: conformity, the commonplace, and control, and to its three attractors: change, creativity, and context. The former will show how you build up barriers against the unusual. The later will offer ways to remove those obstacles.

DETRACTOR #1: CONFORMITY

The problem with a "usual" life is that you must follow all the rules and conform to prescriptions. That kind of living will ensure that nothing unusual happens. The results are as sure as betting on rain in Seattle. Conformists expend a lot of energy maintaining and protecting their beliefs, thereby shutting out change and variety. They pursue the straight and narrow to the point of exhaustion. Conformity demands sameness without exceptions, while the unusual is by definition an exception to the rule. A belief system that tries to conform on all levels is an illusion.

By adhering to unbending points of view, conformists unwittingly contradict other beliefs they hold. Example:

"Long hair in women is okay but not in men—" while a picture of Jesus (with long hair) hangs on the their wall. Or "It's okay for someone to be gay as long as they don't actually talk about it" while at the same time they believe that "it's a sin to tell a lie."

And on the contradictions go. Rigid beliefs clash with each other like bumper cars at the local fair. The usual feeds on conformity, rules, rigidity, whereas nonconformity doesn't like confining "rules" (which don't mesh with each other anyway).

DETRACTOR #2: CONTROL

In her book, *When Society Becomes an Addict*, Anne Wilson Schaef talks of the pervasive illusion of control in our society. "We feel as if we must control, because we do not have inside ourselves what we need." The need to control affects a Life Mission adversely in every way! If you've got it all mapped out, why bother to go through the process?

Control prescribes rather than describes events. It's like the coach who tells the team: "I expect you to win. And here's how you are to do it. In the third quarter, Smith will pass to Jones at exactly 3:52 into that quarter, and Jones will cross the goal line at a spot three yards and 10 centimeters from the edge of the playing field." Sound ridiculous? Sure, but it is no less exact than the statements of some of my clients, who prescribe for sure how something is going to happen just the way they program it—even before they've tried it!

You can't control how a child, a vacation or life is going to turn out, so stop trying to do it! Concentrate rather on letting what is inside you unfold and let yourself be surprised!

DETRACTOR #3: THE COMMONPLACE

Familiar things are the antithesis of the unusual. Such symbols as McDonald's arches or the Campbell's soup label are popular because you know what you are getting—a similar, if not the same, experience. (Andy Warhol played upon this sameness in his Campbell soup paintings.)

The commonplace rarely affords you the opportunity of encountering something different. It's like using English abroad rather than trying a few phrases in a foreign language. Will it be McDonald's or that cute little café where they speak only Flemish?

On the other hand, when you eschew the commonplace, you welcome change. "I don't know what I am getting, and that's okay." Growth comes from experiencing differences. Sameness begets only itself.

THE COMMON PATH TO ROUTINE AND RUTS

Familiarity breeds content! With the same route to work, food for lunch (McDonald's anyone?), radio station, work pattern at the office, you don't really have to think, because everything happens on automatic pilot. No wonder, then, that you're reluctant to explore when routine and sameness are so enticing. And, of course, doing things in a routine way saves you from experiencing *yourself* in another context.

Missions suffer from much the same miring in ruts and routine as do everyday activities. Many clients complain of their lives and jobs being too predictable, too boring, and too much of the same, all of which indicates a need for stimulation. But people continue to stay in what they know (the rut) rather than dealing with what they do not know (the unusual).

Routine is not always bad. Certain activities lend themselves to a ritualistic approach, such as cleaning out the bird cage, shifting gears, and brushing teeth. The only problem with routine is when it goes unchallenged. Useful as a means to an end, routine must nevertheless be re-examined from time to time. Ever driven to work and wondered how you got there? Hoped you hadn't run someone over without even noticing? Routine is a compulsive, unconscious habit that needs monitoring because it can dull your Life Mission search and rob you of experiencing the present directly.

ROUTINE WAYS TO THE UNUSUAL

Ironically, routine is the starting point for getting out of ruts and anticipating the unusual. The following exercise will give you the opportunity to change things you are very familiar with and don't think much about.

EXERCISE: THERE'S GOTTA BE ANOTHER WAY

Take any daily activity and figure out another way to perform it. Start simple and mundane. Maybe it's the way you shop in a supermarket, swing your tennis racquet, or fry eggs. If you practice your tennis serve for ten minutes with your non-serving hand, you'll discover all sorts of things about your PM that you didn't realize. (And your serve will improve.)

You can also redesign an ordinary object in another way. I once asked workshop participants to analyze a common desk calendar. How did the calendar interpret time? What, for example, was important, daytime or night? Weekdays or weekends? Was it work- or pleasure-oriented? Was it present- or future-oriented?

Participants then were to design a calendar that expressed their own concept of time. One person reduced weekdays to one-fourth the size of the weekends; another gave each day a different color; a third changed the days to the size of a postage stamp while giving the evenings a larger space. One woman made her days all gray and narrow and realized that her job depression was due to a feeling of restriction and imprisonment. She needed greater expansiveness and excitement in her life. An unusual calendar made the oblivious obvious.

ATTRACTOR #1: CHANGE

If you can do just one thing out of the ordinary today, you will experience the benefit of change. Change involves risk, growth, adventure, exploration, and newness; all are fertile ingredients for nurturing the unusual. Where there is conformity, change is stifled. Anticipating the unusual comes from the willingness to consciously alter old patterns.

Change helps break ordinary patterns—those that we all fall into from time to time. When you say: "I can't do anything about it," that means you feel it's impossible to break the pattern of sameness. That's just the problem. People fear change and think they have no power to effect it.

Dreams are also proof that you have the innate capacity to imagine and engineer new and extraordinary things. I've never had—or heard of—a dull dream.

ATTRACTOR #2: CREATIVITY

Anticipating the unusual is a creative act and must be practiced continuously. If you wait for the unusual to happen instead of creating an environment for the unusual, you'll be unprepared for dealing with a truly unusual situation. Waiting until you are in the throes of an unusual event is too late. Your creative self looks better when you are prepared.

But how can you program yourself in advance to respond to something unusual? By being loose and flexible. Like a tennis player, in order to hit the ball you need to be prepared to move in any direction. That's why players stay light and bouncy on their feet, ready to go a number of ways. But if you program yourself to go only to the right—in other words stay fixed, rather than being creative in your response—you will not master an unusual play. Creativity is the means to respond to the unusual.

We need new ways to perceive and respond to situations. Responses cannot be pre-programmed, only practiced and anticipated. What so often happens in crises is that people react with routine, patterned and repetitious responses. Being able to handle the unexpected in a situation has to do with the intention and ability to recognize the unusual in everything. Only then can you generate options rapidly and easily when they arise.

The paradox is that the unusual must be an everyday event, yet will always be unique. Bertolt Brecht created situations in his dramas that forced the audience to remember they were in a theater. He attempted to destroy illusion with his so-called *"Verfremdungseffekt"* (alienation effect). The theatergoer was, for example, invited to "sit back and smoke" (well, now they just sit back, thank heavens). Actors talked to the audience directly, and banners announced what was going to happen. Brecht wanted to jolt people out of the lethargy of the "four walls" of the theater, in which they "lose" themselves in the play. In the same way, we need to see the theater of our own lives with the same alert, conscious awareness.

EXERCISE: STALKING THE STRANGE

1. Make up your own mind games that force you to see things from another (and therefore unusual) perspective. Put one noun each on a slip of paper, put them into a hat, and draw out three slips at a time. Invent a story with the three words, and establish a connection between them. (Authors practice this method when they take three characters and weave them into a plot.) For now, use the words *hat, string* and *baby rattle* to create a story.

2. Be on the alert for the strange in any situation. An unusual feature in the Iran Contra Hearings of 1987 was that most of the participants wore ties in various shades of red. Now this color has become

routine for politicians—and broadcasters, too (especially those who want to become politicians). Keep a log of unusual things you see and read. Observe how your ability to see and attract offbeat things increases.

3. Get books with exercises and mind puzzles. Devote a period of time each day to work on them. Make up your own games and try them out on others.

4. Observe how cartoonists feed on the unusual to make you laugh. Practice writing new captions for their cartoons. (Don't peek at the cartoonist's version.)

5. Do anything you can to force a change of perspective on an issue. If you are in agreement with someone, you learn very little that is new or unusual. If you are in favor of amnesty for aliens, take the other side and defend that position. Or pretend you are Dracula being asked to promote blood donations to the Red Cross.

6. Record your dreams as examples of your own built-in fantasy factory. The unusual is usually there if you look for it!

ATTRACTOR #3: CONTEXTS

You can wake up knowing something refreshingly different is going to happen by deciding to make it happen. Even your dreams can become more fantastic. You shape and define a situation by the way you see things. The event occurs according to the situation you are in. That's a context.

Life is not meant to be lived in a boring context. The unusual thrives on your willingness to step out of a comfort zone (something I talked about in Chapter 5). It's up to you to create suitable contexts in which the unexpected can thrive.

People love to travel so much because it allows for surprise, often of the humorous variety. One day I was frying an egg in my dormitory kitchen in Germany. I was well aware that Germans prefer to eat eggs only sunny-side-up. As I turned the egg over, the German student cooking next to me announced in shock, "You just turned your egg over!" The student had never seen a fried egg over easy.

SHAPING CONTEXTS

The successful handling of your mission depends upon the context you create. Here's an example of the way you might do it. In a drama class, we were given an exercise to pick an emotion and then look for it in everything we saw, felt, or experienced for the next ten minutes. My choice was humor. Looking around the room, I began to see all kinds of odd things that had escaped my attention: the strange way people sat, funny props backstage, humorous conversations people were having. After a while even my own body seemed comical to me. I found myself repeating the same word (tuna) over and over until it became hilarious.

Other people in the class picked very different emotions, and although they had the same surroundings they experienced things in the way they had programmed them. Some responded to their context with tears, others with anger, still others with depressing silence. Thus a setting that was funny for one person may be interpreted by another as angry or depressing.

The variations one can generate are endless. But sadly, most people opt for unchanging and closed-ended contexts. If you stay within defined boundaries, unaware of your fenced-in approach, you create a dull life. Your mission will follow suit.

Look in the mirror, steam it, and trace the outline of your head. You might have assumed both your real and "mirror" heads were the same size (unless you've done this little exercise before). Surprise! You'll discover the mirror version is about half the size of your "real" head. But how could you become aware of that on your own? Only by looking for the out-of-the-ordinary, by taking nothing for granted (nothing as expected). Everything depends on how you choose to view it. Anticipating the unusual requires an expectancy that surprise is everywhere to be found.

EXPECTANCY VS. EXPECTATIONS

Think about the meaning of "You get what you expect." It's used almost exclusively to refer to negative or unfavorable outcomes, and it functions much like watching a videotape of a sporting event. If you know the outcome of the game, there are no surprises. Expectations by definition deny the possibility of the unexpected. With expectations you assume you are in the driver's seat and that you know what the best solution is for every situation.

I remember the first time I visited Los Angeles. I expected the city to be tacky, smoggy, and full of traffic. I believed, as W. C. Fields remarked, the only thing which belonged in L.A. was an orange. I didn't want to be that orange. I could taste, feel, and see smog everywhere. (Where else do you get the luxury of seeing what you're breathing?) But I found out later that pollution levels had been relatively low in Los Angeles when I was there in December. In fact, there had been no unusual smog activity for the dates of my visit. But I expected the negative stuff, and I got what I bargained for. I coughed and gasped in reaction to my expectations.

EXPECTANCY: GETTING WHAT YOU DON'T EXPECT!

Expectancy differs from expectations in that you are open to outcomes rather than controlling them. The latter focuses on products and results, whereas expectancy focuses on surrender to the unfolding process. You plant seeds, set the stage, and allow (release) your work to happen in its own way. You achieve expectancy by injecting surprise and wonder at what will transpire.

Expectancy makes life exciting and easy because you can replace pushing with pulling and attracting what you want. Expectancy approaches life with an anticipatory rather than a controlling attitude. Of course, it's important to prepare for what you want and to do your groundwork (context!). If you want corn you plant corn, but you leave the maturation process to nature.

When you expect something, you define the outcome, or push to make your outcome happen just the way you want it to be. You may be disappointed in the results, especially if they do not match your expectations (which is often the case). In the case of expectancy, the key is *surrender.* You do the leg-work needed, and then watch the outcome unfold as an observer. If you don't try to control the results, you are more likely to get the results that you need.

GOING APE

I tested out my theory of expectancies in a creativity work-shop. Participants were asked to go "APE," that is, to develop the **A**ttitude of **P**oised **E**xpectancy. The method went as fol-lows: people selected a word, subject, or object of their choice to focus on. Their selection had to be possible, reasonable, and quantifiable. (Seeing a Martian would be too fantastic, five wart hogs too unrealistic, and Beethoven in the form of a cloud somewhat hard to prove.)

Then, they were to observe how often this item occurred in their everyday lives. They were to await its occurrence without expectations, but with poised expectancy. They visualized *what* was to occur, not *how* it was to occur. In other words, simply to *await* the results they had focused on without *programming* those results.

This is the way APE worked for one workshop participant: he picked the town of Philadelphia. (We eliminated Philadelphia Cream Cheese as off limits.) He reported that he began to notice the name occurring in conversations, newspaper articles, on a license place, in the news, and even at a fast food stand.

Another participant decided to see how many nickels she would find in one week. Easy choice, you say? Well, she excluded the ones in common places in her house (dresser, coin jar, kitchen table). She began to find them on the street, in her file cabinet, and even in her toilet bowl! The amazing thing was, she casually told her niece about the project in a long-distance call, and her niece began finding nickels everywhere, too!

A nice bonus to all this: At the office this person also found things for which she had been looking more than six months! (Remember what I said about rewards?)

I went APE over finding playing cards on the street and told the group I would bring in the results the following week. After that class I found four outside my car in the company parking lot, and the next week I found eleven on the street at once (precisely the correct number for a tarot reading—which I happened to be interested in at the time).

The importance of the exercise is not to force Philadelphia into conversations, make coins appear magically, or put some hex on playing cards. The real lesson is a paradox: things that you express a desire for happen because you believe they will happen (trust), because you give them energy (focus), and because you then release control (surrender), and unconditionally await manifestation (expectancy).

Discovery is possible only when you least expect it, when you surrender to the process instead of programming the results. This same process is true for the discovery of your mission.

Exercise: WISHING WELL

1. Identify what you want without guilt or hesitation. "This is my desire, and I own it."
2. Trust that your choice is appropriate and that you will release doubt.
3. Stick to what you have selected, refusing to let yourself get sidetracked or tempted to give up on your goal.
4. Relinquish your impulse to work on the issue by controlling the outcome in any way.
5. Invoke the law of expectancy. Watch, rather than control, the outcome. It's akin to bearing a child: you initiate the process, but you don't know exactly how the child will develop.

Let's look at the way Andy applied expectancy to finding his Life Mission.

Andy's Angst

An executive in the direct-mail business, Andy stumbled into that field after going through a number of jobs, all of which he "fell into." A rather brash and cocky guy, Andy assumed things would come his way whenever he wanted to make changes. But somehow the magic he hoped for never materialized. Of course, since the direction he had taken in business had little to do with his mission, how could there be that magic?

Andy had always secretly wanted to promote personal growth through sports, yet he was convinced his mission was too "weird." He felt he was past the age of being an athlete. That stemmed from his "logical" (rut) thinking.

Andy needed to release seeing his sports mission as "strange." First, he went APE over anything that crossed his path combining sports and personal growth, and during that process he completed the exercises below. (We'll come back later to the outcome of Andy's story.)

EXERCISE: FROM FAMILIAR TO STRANGE

1. Open a newspaper and look at an action photo until it becomes strange, silly, or weird. Furnish a new caption or scenario for the picture—one that describes your new viewpoint.

2. Exaggerate "fixed" things. Victor Borge has done this with his inflated language. In this language, a tuba becomes a "fourba" and *forget* becomes "nineget".

   In the same vein, imagine what it would be like if everybody had more than the "usual" number of fingers on one hand—say seven. Or three heads. Or think of variations you could use for parts of the body in old songs: "You Go to My Heads," "I've Got You Under My Armor," "Moonlight and You in My Tendrils". Have fun—surprise yourself with your inventiveness!

3. Devise novel ways to transform a familiar object into an unusual one. Your coffee cup for instance. What else could it be? (A giant's earring.)

4. Look at things as if you were a member of the other sex. How would you express yourself, walk, or gesture? What secret things would you do that you don't do now—and what things could you do after this exercise that you resisted doing because of your expectations? In the privacy of your own

home practice walking around, talking, or gesturing in the manner you described. (If your loved ones begin to react strangely to your antics, you could say that you were rehearsing for a local theater adaptation of the film *Mrs. Doubtfire.*)

5. Look for unusual combinations that you don't normally associate with each other: the elderly and day care (there are now day care centers for seniors). Find examples that capitalize on creative combos of unusual or humorous combinations. Advertising is a particularly rich source for inventive, strange—and often deceptive—combinations. (The smoking Joe Camel ad, through its absurdity, cleverly disassociates people from smoking by using an animal.)

6. Now think about a familiar career and see if you can describe it in a bizarre, humorous or unusual way. Example: A computer programmer could be a person who organizes and controls how people move their fingers across little square keys to get information.

EXERCISE: . . . AND BACK

In addition to sprucing up the ordinary, we need to occasionally demystify the exotic. We'll reverse the process and go from the uncommon to the common. This part is especially useful for those of you who, like Andy, can't accept their mission because it's too strange or too far out for words. Get rid of equations and categorized thinking. "Weird" is in the eye of the beholder. Look at your mission with a new vision, accepting it first on its own terms for what it is, as just there. You can accept what's there as possible, right? (The only one who couldn't was Gertrude Stein, who felt there was no *there* there.)

1. Look at something quite strange, and turn it into something ordinary. You can fantasize why creatures created by Gary Larson might think of themselves as quite ordinary. This is in fact part of the humor Larson uses—his odd creatures are just folks. Creatures from outer space might think we're weird, since we lack three eyes, tentacles, pear-shaped head(s), and so on. Use comic strips as a daily exercise to see the strange as ordinary.

2. Identify something about your family that is actually a bit uncommon although you always thought it was normal. Observe how often people talk about "strange" things in their families. (In one client's case, his father stayed at home, and his mother worked outside the home. This was in the late 1940s. He was in for a surprise when he went to school and found out almost everyone thought this situation was weird.)

3. Take what you think is an "offbeat" career, one you might have even fantasized about, and describe it as "ordinary." (Artist: shrinks people and things by putting a whole landscape onto a piece of canvas.)

4. Read about "weird" missions people have, and make them ordinary. Some from my scrapbook include: knowing everything about the potato, manufacturing soap while preaching religion, collecting obscene words in every language, and chasing violent storms.

Perhaps, in the example of the computer programmer, the purpose gives a sense of the power to provide people with access to information. With the artist, on the other hand, the process is perhaps not so mysterious as you might think.

Remember Andy the athlete? Soon after completing the exercises outlined above, a friend came to him with an idea for starting hiking and exercise workshops for adults who were recovering from illness or surgery. Now he could accept something he would previously have thought weird, and it awakened his slumbering mission. And now, of course, he was using the mail-order experience to promote his new endeavor.

Whatever you come up with to describe a mission in a different way furnishes a fresh view. Doris felt she was an "ordinary" secretary. What mission was there in that?

Doris Directs

Doris was a woman of unbelievably positive energy and organizational talent. A Doer/Motivator, she had whipped her office into shape after only one week on the job. She got away from her commonplace view of being a secretary by describing her job in a creative way. She painted a colorful scene, seeing herself as a combination of traffic cop, air controller, and railway station engineer. Everyone had to stop in front of her desk; nothing could really move forward until she gave the signal. Doris switched one person to another on the phone, sent out and received information from near and far, facilitated traffic flow, determined (with a call) who was to arrive and when.

"I'm a giant mood motivator," she quipped. The cheery tone she set affected the office, as if she had slipped the staff pills in their morning brew to influence how she wanted the office to behave. She realized her enormous power for motivating people. She also felt much better about her contributions in her job and began to appreciate how much she was needed. After this exercise she asked for a raise and got it! She began to recognize that her calling involved being a kind of human relations theater manager/set designer who prepared the stage for maximum performance.

To recap: if your life needs sprucing up, if it's "just like everything else and nothing special," rewrite the script into something more fantastic, unique, or inventive! You are responsible for co-creating that script. It does not happen on its own.

Adding the unusual to life makes it spicier, richer, and more stimulating. Life is not meant to be dull and drab, so give it drama and excitement! In order for life to have twists, you must change the way you approach it. Surprise yourself daily with your own creative additions and ingredients. Invite, await, anticipate, be expectant of a marvellous life!

Yeast your mission with novelty, humor, and growth.

8

Tolerate Ambiguity

Hamlet: Do you see yonder cloud that's almost in
          shape of a camel?
Polonius: By the mass, and 'tis like a camel, indeed.
Hamlet: Me thinks it is like a weasel.
Polonius: It is backed like a weasel.
Hamlet: Or like a whale.
Polonius: Very like a whale.

—SHAKESPEARE, *HAMLET*

Nature allots time for things to take shape before a process is complete. It is a period of time for an entity, not yet fully formed or shaped, to develop. Take butterflies, for example. During their cocoon stage, they are actually liquid for a while.

Ambiguity is like that fluid period. Just like the butterfly, you too, must traverse a formative, ambiguous phase of a process to reach mental clarity in your mission search. The goal is to be centered and focused for your mission. The way to certainty requires that for your thoughts to take shape, you first tolerate any ambiguity required in the process.

By accepting ambiguity, you can look at a situation honestly and without prejudgment, before it is complete. Ambiguity operates on its own terms and permits your imagination to open up to new possibilities. It allows time for play and creativity, when you can fool around, speculate, maybe change your mind, or just toss ideas back and forth. As Hamlet and Polonius said to each other: camel, weasel, or whale? It really doesn't matter at first. It's fun to play with possibilities!

An ambiguous phase can be scary, because it's fuzzy, loose, elusive, slippery—even confusing or chaotic. It's like a jigsaw puzzle. At first the pieces lie scattered helter–skelter. They don't fall into place immediately. But gradually the picture emerges.

The same process is true of your mission. You take things in, without judgment or comment, rearrange the pieces this way or that, until you see a picture emerging.

In this chapter, you'll learn how to tolerate ambiguity by developing flexible thinking, suspending assumptions and prejudgments (which block desires and restrict options). Your goal is to clarify your present mission path.

AMBIGUITY AND YOUR PM

The word ambiguity means "going on both sides." Put another way, it means not taking sides *for the moment.* Doers and Analyzers are the most uncomfortable with that notion. They find it difficult to release control. Those who tolerate ambiguity agree that *not* getting there immediately is part of the fun (very appealing to Motivators). They need to take that delicious opportunity to be flexible, to explore and discover by refraining temporarily from making decisions.

Analyzers and Stabilizers have difficulty with ambiguity because of their preference for predictability. Analyzers have the greatest need for clearly defined answers. For Stabilizers, procedure and logic are all-important. They represent the methodical approach to life. Doers head straight for fastest results (witness Lois' story, next) and tend to bypass any nebulous phase. (Many Doers I know would have preferred to skip the womb and enter life full-blown out of the head of Zeus.) Motivators appreciate ambiguity, but they need practice moving beyond it and on to clarity.

BEING CLEAR ABOUT TOLERATING AMBIGUITY

Ambiguity enables you to create possibilities. There is a professor at a California university who offers a course in fuzzy thinking. Imagine! Encouraging chaos and ambiguity before designing a high-rise!

Philip Davis and David Park in their book *No Way: The Nature of the Impossible,* point out that "a major task in becoming a physician is to accept the impossibility of ever being sure." Tolerating ambiguity means being comfortable with the assurance you don't yet know it all.

The more you operate with foregone conclusions without allowing for any other approach, the more one-dimensional your Life Mission will be. Those who cannot tolerate ambiguity have everything figured out in advance. They remind me of the man standing in front of me at the movies, talking about the film he was going to see: "Whatever it's about, I'm certain I won't like it." His mind was made up.

In the previous chapter, I discussed the difference between expectations and expectancy. Ambiguity is a kind of expectancy. It puts emphasis on process, development, and surrender. Expectations are like a parent saying: "This is the way it's going to be, and that's that!"

LOIS CLOSES

Lois is a good example of closing off her mission options out of fear of ambiguity. Strong, high-spirited and independent-minded, she resembled a cross between Eleanor Roosevelt and the German tennis player Steffi Graf, with a pinch of Italian opera flair thrown in. A chip off the old block, she went about life in the same tough-minded way as her father, a naval officer. A Doer, Lois preferred getting on with things rather than mulling them over.

Lois had always had in mind a mission path that she wanted to follow, but she used up all her marvelous energy by carrying around a clear list of reasons (assumptions) her calling wouldn't work. At 29 she was, not surprisingly, headed for boredom and burnout. "But," she declared, "I'll stay with my nursing job, the 'correct' thing to do for a woman, because the passion I have for the ocean means going back to school, loss of income, and stiff competition." The only way she got close to water was by being over her head with rationalizations—none of which was rational.

She knew for certain she was going nowhere and also knew "for certain" that where she wanted to go was impossible. Unlike St. George, Lois preferred to generate dragons rather than conquer them. Her mission was omission—she couldn't tolerate ambiguity. She wanted her life neatly wrapped, clear-cut and absolutely defined. Lois didn't have two sides to go on; she really had none.

A WAY STATION TO CLARITY

Seekers of the truth know there are way stations along any continuum—all the points between A and Z. Tolerating ambiguity allows you to tarry at those way stations for observation, reflection, and eventual clarity. Part of the fun is the whimsical and unstructured period of the process. Let me make this perfectly clear: *premature closure can reduce options or restrict choices*. The path to certainty is often cloudy and needs time for focusing. Ambiguity allows a temporarily blurred picture to work in your favor by making the right choice apparent on its own.

OBSTACLES TO AMBIGUITY

Fear and rigidity are two major barriers that prevent people from tolerating ambiguity. Fear of ambiguity results from an inability to release control or to suspend the need for clarity. It often creates anxiety because ambiguity requires you to defer for now the wisdom that will come later. When you are in quicksand, the temptation is to struggle, when in fact the best thing to do is to release control temporarily.

It would be absurd to preface looking at clouds by saying: "I know exactly what I'm going to see," or "There's no use doing this because I'm not going to see anything anyway." Yet many people use similar controlling statements about their Life Mission. No fuzzy clouds, please.

Exercises with the greatest ambiguity have the most anxiety-producing effect on those whose thinking is rigid. Such people usually ask, "What's the purpose?" "What's this leading to?" "How am I supposed to do it?" These questions reveal a rigid, prescribed way of thinking. The Life Mission process is not a granite block, immutable and unmovable. It combines a solid base (achieved only by clarity). Mastering the changes, evolution, and transformation a basic mission will undergo requires pliable thinking.

Martha, like Lois, illustrates the pitfalls of defining everything rigidly. She showed a high degree of artistic interest, but because she had little practical experience in the arts, she felt that admitting these interests "doomed" her to becoming a poet, painter, or potter. And these stereotypes were fixed in her mind.

MARTHA'S MADE-UP MIND

A prosperous and impeccably dressed suburban-ite in her late forties, Martha was struggling with a nameless hankering, a sense of boredom or ennui, in spite of her beautiful home in Malibu and her two scholastic-minded teenagers. She had not felt the need to generate her own income because her husband had a high-ranking position in a large downtown law firm.

Like many of her suburban friends, she had served enthusiastically in a number of volunteer capacities at art shows and local library fundraisers, but all this community service was wearing thin. Martha's testing indicated that she was attracted to art, but when she thought of the word *artist* she had all sorts of preconceived definitions. I asked her to list what *artist* meant for her. (Before you read on, do the following exercise):

EXERCISE: MY EQUATIONS

Make your own list of what the word *artist* means to *you* (type of work, age, environment, financial situation, location, ethnic background, political leanings, and so on). Then compare your list with Martha's. Hers included:

eccentric
male
painter
living in loft
pitiful
small, disheveled apartment
poor
dedicated
in poor health
alone
apolitical

Martha had kept her artistic interests neatly suppressed. She found it difficult even to fantasize about being an artist. Her view of an artist's life was rigid. For her, that lifestyle meant starvation, a lonely existence in a drafty loft apartment, with no chance for obtaining a dream house or feeding his child. (You see, her artist was male, to boot—not much chance of her becoming that, either!). She was sure beyond all ambiguity about the exact components of that profession, and, armed with this immutable information, she rejected any possibility of pursuing anything connected to art.

WAYS TO CHANGE RIGID THINKING

Being in the state of ambiguity enables your imagination to develop options, as it did for Hamlet and Polonius. The following exercise will help you develop those fantasy skills:

EXERCISE: CUTTING UP

1. Cut into irregular shapes some pictures from magazine ads. First look at your shapes  without trying to define them. Then give each shape at least three names.

    Practice by "seeing" different objects and things in the above shape.

2. Now look at the following picture. What or whom do you see? Focus your eyes on the dot in the middle of the picture. Some answers will appear later. (But don't peek yet!)

In the first example, people have identified such things as a boat, a person sleeping in a tent with their feet hanging out, a rainfall, and part of a rainbow. In the second example, did you see both the old and the young woman? They are both there! What else could you identify? Some people have seen a gorilla or an eagle.

By practicing this way of looking at things, you are strengthening your ability to view things kaleidoscopically. That is, you'll encourage yourself to see shapes in a variety of ways. Even if an item seems obvious, for the sake of practice suspend your need to see it only that way.

ASSUMPTIONS

Assumption comes from the Latin word *sumptus*: to take charge of, to take by choice, and *adsumere*: to take to oneself, to borrow. In other words, assumptions are thoughts which we have taken to ourselves, which become our perception, but not necessarily the truth. So, before hastily "taking a thought to yourself," give yourself time to assess the situation.

If, for example, the driver ahead of you does something you disapprove of, try to think of creative reasons he or she is driving that way. If you observe someone driving very slowly, maybe they are on the way to the vet with a sick parakeet on board. Some guy speeding may be transferring Mafia funds to another account before the authorities catch up. Consider both sides in your mind (not with your car, of course!) before you judge too quickly.

The greatest deterrent to ambiguity is the unconscious use of assumptions in your belief system. Unreflected assumptions slam the door on your storehouse of divergent ideas and exclude information needed for a more complete picture. Unconscious assumptions (also called prejudice) are sometimes so subtle that they can escape attention.

One example from a newspaper headline:

Arabs Release 8 Women and 5 Blacks

The assumption? That the women are white and blacks are male. The norm is white males, who don't require special identification. Language supports a similar assumption that doctors are male unless proved otherwise. If doctors who are female are called *women doctors*, who are the doctors? (You guessed it.) Is it any wonder that fewer women aspire to be doctors? (The opposite is also true for the word *nurse*.)

The only occupations restricted as to sex are sperm donor and wet nurse. Carol Mosely Braun didn't let herself be stopped from running for Senator of Illinois because she was an African-American woman. Unconscious assumptions narrow conclusions, block possibilities, and perpetuate rigid approaches. Don't restrict your mission dreams prematurely! The only limitations to your calling are the ones you impose on your own mind. Witness the leading percussionist of the world, Evelyn Glennie, whose calling includes performing only as a solist—almost an unheard-of feat for percussion players. The amazing part is: she's deaf.

AMBIGUITY: CATCHING YOURSELF WITH YOUR ASSUMPTIONS DOWN

To ASSUME anything unconsciously makes an ASS out of U and ME. Dropping assumptions allows you to "go on both sides" before coming to a conclusion.

You can't suspend something that is not in your consciousness! Being conscious of your assumptions gives you the flexibility and vulnerability to allow for alterations, revisions, and changes. One-way thinking begets only the same. The sequence of the ambiguous process is:

starting position > conscious suspension of assumptions > ambiguity > generating options > making choices > conscious selection of position > conscious assumption being admitted.

In a workshop, Eduard de Bono told of a juvenile locked in a local jail who wanted to spend the evening in town, and engineered an elaborate escape by climbing over the walls, using sheets as ropes. Upon his return, the boy discovered that the front door was unlocked! He had assumed he needed to break out the hard way. (This is not, however, a recommended method for dealing with prison sentences.)

CONSCIOUSLY GETTING RID OF ASSUMPTIONS

Of course, any belief or action has a point of view. The trick is to be consciously aware of your assumption, because it functions like an equation: If I do X, Y will result. And usually those equations tend to be negative, particularly regarding careers. Let's look at what Roger, a young CPA by day and a clarinetist by night, came up with:

Roger's Assumptions About Work:

work	=	paid activity
paid activity	=	pain, drag
pain	=	work
play	=	I do "off hours" (music)
off-hours activity	=	poor pay
poor pay	=	poverty
leaving career	=	significant decrease in income
decrease in income	=	loss of lifestyle
loss of lifestyle	=	unhappiness

His conclusion?

work	=	pain
play	=	poverty
leaving career	=	unhappiness

For Roger, fulfilling his dreams of performing clearly meant that he would be poor, unhappy, and leading an unstable life. With that kind of rigid thinking, there was no way out. How can Roger find an enjoyable career when he predicts it would mean unhappiness, abandoning a lifestyle, and emotional deprivation? Moreover, the CPA job was clear-cut, though without a goal.

Roger's other issue was that he was unsure of exactly what his music meant to him and what he wanted to do with it. One thing was sure: his feelings were always better when he was playing clarinet. He was caught in a Catch-22 situation: if he pursued the music, he'd be poor, and if he stayed with the CPA job, it would make him miserable.

GENERATING OPTIONS

Roger had to alter his concept of work. Just for an exercise, I asked him to view it differently from the way he had in his usual equations. He was to float with new work ideas (ambiguity), and let them take shape over a period of about two to three weeks. In other words, he was to to confront his tendency to make rigid assumptions with premature conclusions. To get ideas, I suggested he look at people he admired, people in professions he liked, or friends.

Why are many people so envious of football players, TV stars, or comedians? Because they get paid for having fun. A local announcer recently commented on his talk show: "I get paid every day for playing." Roger needed to see that there were people like that in the world.

Not surprisingly, Roger realized that work is not necessarily the painful activity he assumed it to be. Here's what his new work list contained:

Issue: Work Associations
interest
talent
music

joy
physical health
happiness
energy
achievement
fulfillment
satisfaction

The conclusion now? Work (that is, music) can bring fulfillment, joy, satisfaction and good health. Roger had previously assumed that music brought poverty and disappointment. That's why he wanted to give it up. He needed to see music as a part of his mission. The CPA job was to serve his life mission music by keeping Roger financially stable in order to also concentrate on music. The path to a healthy point of view began with Roger's willingness to suspend his entrenched thoughts about work and be open to (temporary) ambiguity.

Roger started immediately on his new set of associations with an action plan. He listed everything he could do that very day to get started on the positive road to fulfilling his musical dreams.

Roger's Action Plan:

- List all the ways being a CPA can serve my mission.

- List what I enjoy about music.

- Find intersection points between being a CPA and my love for music(such as CPA for music company).

- Audition for more gigs.

- Investigate a short leave of absence or reduced work hours so I can to devote more time to music.

- Enjoy the combination of CPA and musician!

Roger had changed his assumption from "It's impossible to be happy as a CPA", to understanding that "Being both a CPA and a musician is possible, advantageous, and somehow part of my Life Mission." He began to investigate becoming an accountant for free-lance musicians, thus moving one step closer to integrating music into his day work. Now Roger's present expression of his Life Mission has changed from ambiguity to clarity—reviving the popularity of the Clarinet in contemporary pop music.

EXERCISE: TAKING ISSUE WITH YOUR ISSUE

Take an assumption that might be holding you back from your mission. Maybe, like Roger, it has to do with combining talents. Follow the exercise through these four stages:

1. Getting the Issue Out

Issue:_____

My unambiguous (inflexible) assumptions:

(and so on)

Now allow yourself to float with your equations awhile and let your associations become fluid, flexible, fantastic, funny, humorous, silly, even bizarre. Somewhere in all of this the answer you need will emerge. It might take a day or a week, but allow enough time between stages one and two to drift like a cloud.

2. Free-Associate

Issue _____   Associations:

_____ = _____
_____ = _____
_____ = _____

(and so on)

What changed for you specifically? Examine the areas of difference between stages one and two. What can you do to stay out of the mire of the first? For Roger, it was to reduce the time he spent at his job from five days to four.

Make an action plan from your associations. Include one thing you can do today to get started on any aspect of your action plan.

My Action Plan:

_____

_____

_____

3. Learn and Listen about Others

Read inspirational stories, biographies, and autobiographies of people who have believed in themselves and said yes to their dreams. Success stories help counteract fixed assumptions about what is possible. Betty Ford has survived a mastectomy and drug dependency and built a clinic to help others. Auguste Renoir kept on his artistic mission after his right hand became disabled. Beethoven continued with his mission even after he lost his hearing.

MARY, MARY, QUITE CONTRARY

For Mary, a young bright woman with an entrepreneurial spirit, red hair, and temperament to match, life was completely settled and unambiguous. She was fiercely sure, for instance, that only other people were lucky. She had trouble admitting that her life could take any kind of different direction.

Mary once had big dreams to use her scientific skills in the service of children. But how? She had "only" a B.S. in Mathematics. "And besides," she declared, "everyone knows you can't make money with children." Mary was living a life contrary to the real facts: namely, that you can make things happen if they are your soul's desire, you believe you can, and you're willing to do the footwork to get what you want.

Mary needed to read inspiring examples of the ways others pursue their dreams. She agreed finally, to float awhile. She went to a local library and ran across an article about Candy Lightner, the woman who had single-handedly founded MADD (Mothers Against Drunk Driving). She saw what one person could do if she put her mind to it! That article changed her way of making assumptions. Rather than boxing herself in with unambiguous, fixed, and self-defeating equations, she remained flexible and allowed ideas to come to her.

One result of her new approach is that she has initiated children's projects at a girl's club in which the youngsters can explore and develop an appreciation for math by making scientific displays.

4. The Baby and the Bathwater

Fixed thinking leads many people to get rid of an entire idea once they have rejected it. But that can be like throwing the baby out with the bathwater. When you eliminate things from your life, there will frequently be a recycling of past experience, knowledge, and skills. Parts of what you wanted to eliminate will actually need to be kept.

The following exercise will help you determine what you want to retain (the baby) or eliminate (the bathwater). Your mission will become clearer when you know what stays and what goes.

Here's how this exercise worked for me. I no longer wanted to teach German at the university, and I thought that this meant giving up all forms of teaching. I found out to my surprise that I wanted to keep some aspects of teaching:

Bathwater:	*Baby:*
employee status	flexibility
grading papers	speeches
meetings	art/culture/music
committees	flexible schedule
fixed schedules	ideas
grading papers	lectures, speeches
German grammar/lit.	counseling
student population only	university setting

I wanted to leave the specific environment I had been in as well as some peripheral aspects of the work: my particular university, setting, meetings, committees, teaching German, grading papers, being an employee, and the semester system. I wanted to *continue* teaching, giving speeches, having a flexible schedule, counseling, and traveling (for the first time, travel became possible in October, and not, as I had assumed, only in the summer). What would the new combination add up to? I took the parts that remained, mixed the pieces, adding some new elements, and came up with my new mix:

be my own boss

music (composing, singing)

perform, (composing, singing)

write a book

private practice in self-improvement

designing motivational programs

The "cloud" or "jigsaw pieces" turned specific: I began to design creativity workshops and seminars, do Life Mission coaching, public speaking and performing. In other words, I recycled what I had done previously and came out with something new.

EXERCISE: SAVING THE BABY

Now do the same, using a career or issue you are struggling with:

1. Give the list a title, and jot down all the component parts.

2. As in a smorgasbord, select the items you want to keep and separate them from the ones you want to eliminate.

3. Look at your "baby" and see what these words suggest to you. Add anything you want to keep, if applicable.

4. Put each word on a slip of paper and the slips into a hat. Take any three slips and place them side by side. Ask yourself what each combination suggests. Remain open and flexible. Work with this list as much as you want to, developing combinations for at least several weeks.

5. Now see what new picture emerges, and do what it takes to manifest it.

SUMMARY

Row, Row, Row, Your Boat: Flowing with Ambiguity

In ambiguity you suspend certainty in order to find it. The round "Row, Row, Row Your Boat" is a metaphor for that paradox.

Row, row, row your boat
Gently down the stream.
Merrily, merrily, merrily, merrily,
Life is but a dream.

The river knows which way it is going; it has a sense of

purpose. The song invites you to go with the flow—the river's flow. Row down the river GENTLY, following its path, capitalizing on its energy, knowing that it will guide you to your destination. The trip takes shape along the way naturally.

A river has a bed and two banks. Without them, it would be a delta without definition or direction. Ambiguity provides an opportunity to flow and drift within the overall framework of direction. Ambiguity makes life wiggly and interesting. Imagine a straight river—no bends, ox-bows, or twist—how boring! The same is true of life. The choice is yours. Look at the clouds and enjoy the show! Willingness to tolerate ambiguity is your admission ticket.

Now we'll move on to an arena where your ideas take place.

9

Ideate, Then Incubate

Can you imagine that, instead of saying "Let there be light," God said, "Golly, I'm stuck. I want to do something, but what?" Without ideas, nothing happens. The same is true of your Life Mission: to realize it you must learn to generate ideas—lots of them.

Ideas are your imaginative thoughts and responses to situations in the moment. They are the expressive ingredients of your inner wisdom. Here are some examples of ideas: an inventive way to prepare an old recipe, putting two things together into something new, taking a piece of piping and a hub cap and making a table out of it, finding a new use for something—like turning an old porcelain sink into a birdbath, or converting those five hundred ping-pong balls from an unsuccessful garage sale into soundproofing for your daughter's percussion room.

Ideas stimulate and spark more ideas. By allowing you to solve problems, they provide you with the options and the freedom to pursue your desired goals. The creative mission

seeker (what you're learning to be in this book) must be a ver-
itable idea factory.

This chapter therefore shows you:

1. What ideas are.

2. Where and how to come up with them.

3. How to transform your idea-killers into positive action.

4. The value of incubation.

The goal is to pinpoint your life mission accurately by
generating abundant ideas.

EDUCATION AND IDEATION AT ODDS

Ideation is nothing new. It simply means the formation of ideas,
a talent you've had ever since childhood. Perhaps you turned
piles of sand into castles, invented interesting creatures to talk to,
or devised fantastic ways to get to the moon. (NASA certainly
had nothing on that fantasy—children were going to the moon
long before astronauts actually got there.)

At some point, sadly, kids learn the difference between
fantasy and reality and realize they aren't being rewarded for
transforming things into something they were "not." To stay
safe or avoid criticism children learn linear, logical thought
patterns and shut down their creativity. The system often
forces them to abandon their ideational talents. Fact, not fantasy, is demanded. When was the battle of Waterloo? (fact)
instead of what might have happened to the course of history
if Napoleon had won? (fantasy)

HIT 'EM AGAIN, HIT 'EM AGAIN, HARDER! HARDER!—THE
IDEA KILLERS' SCHOOL CHEER

The adult version of the process begun in childhood is the
onset of idea killers. Idea killers are phrases or statements
which prevent you from considering an option. They have a

devastating effect on your ability to pursue your mission.

In an exercise, participants tackled a problem by generating ideas. They were unaware of the fact that all groups but one had a negative stooge, whose purpose it was to kill every suggestion proposed. One lone group contained a person who greeted each new item with encouragement (without being too obvious—after all, such behavior can arouse suspicion!). That one group with the supportive "plant" generated more ideas than all the rest! The negative stooges had put severe restraints on each of the other group's performances.

Of course, you can perform the same "ideacide" by yourself.

Here are some idea killers a writer friend of mine generated about a planned book:

- No one will read it.
- The market is already glutted with similar topics.
- I haven't anything new to say.
- It will never sell.
- I haven't got the talent.
- It's not worth the time.
- I don't have a publisher.
- Who needs it?
- I haven't the expertise to do this.
- I can't afford the time away from generating income to write.
- I won't earn anything from it.

A depressing list! Those phrases can literally knock the energy right out of you. Try surfing or balancing on a beam and then saying the words "I can't make it, I'm going to fall." See how long you stay upright!

Daniel, a young professor of sociology, told the story of his student entrance exam for college. There was a physical part to the test, consisting of climbing a rope to the ceiling of a room.

Daniel had been up rather late the night before and arrived for the test fairly groggy. Before he realized it, he had climbed up to the top with one hand. As he descended, he was told he had to go back up and touch his nose to the ceiling (part of the requirement), and as he began to think about how impossible this would be, he was unable to perform with two hands the same thing he had done with *one* a minute before.

All Daniel heard was his inner voice saying "can't," even after he had just performed that task successfully! Remember, if you say you can or you can't, you're right!

YOU CAN GET AWAY WITH MURDER (OF IDEA KILLERS)

All right, all you pistol-packing mamas (and papas), here are two ways to blow away your idea killers and get away with it. Get rid of your anti-mission mafia!

Activate the child within you. When you were young and dreamed of becoming a sea captain or queen of the universe, your critical self didn't come along and say, "CAMAAAAN, do you really think you're going to do that?" A child's fantasy doesn't include such sophisticated deterrents. Do childlike things: observe how children are free to think in ways you may have forgotten. Allow yourself to daydream as you once did as a child. Play with possibilities. Read children's books demonstrating that anything is possible (such as *The Little Engine That Could*). Whenever imagination is valued and taken seriously, your critic doesn't have a chance.

Become "irrational." Allow yourself to fantasize, even if the process doesn't "add up"! Generating "irrational" and crazy ideas is the stuff of which exciting missions are made possible. Even if you don't eventually carry through on everything, the first step is to fantasize.

That humans can fly is an age-old "irrational" idea. The Greek myth tells of Icarus, who attempted to escape from the island of Crete by using wings of wax and feathers. He flew so high that the sun melted his wings and he fell to his death into the sea. Leonardo da Vinci explored aerodynamics—but in sketches—wisely waiting for future generations to carry out his ideas. When the time was right, Orville and Wilbur Wright had the same dream and finally made it happen.

We'll never know how many great ideas never come into being because they were unable to be imagined first. Is the time right for your fantasy?

EXERCISE: TRANSFORM YOUR IDEA-KILLER LIST

After making a thorough idea-killer list of your own, replace each item with statements as boldly positive as the negative ones you had. The writer replaced "Who needs it?" on the list with: "This book is as important for the world to have as a square meal."

After finishing your idea killer list, destroy it and keep only your positive statements. Each time idea-killers emerge, repeat the process. Post your new statements in a prominent place in your house.

Destroying lists offers no guarantees by itself. The value of this exercise is to keep those idea-killers out of your consciousness. It's like emptying your closets: there is no guarantee that you'll not go back to cluttering them. But, by the physical act of removing things, you are making a statement: "I want only positive ideas in my mind, those uncluttered by idea-killers."

PRACTICE MAKES PERFECT

Practice leads to improved performance, whether it be in memorizing, typewriting, piano playing, or ideation. Take piano scales. You might practice them for years when finally, the payoff arrives: you've reached a stage where you can do them automatically. By knowing how to play those scales, you can then more easily master a Bach fugue. The scales suddenly sound like music because you have done the practice work!

Likewise, generating ideas comes through practice. Ideation needs practice before it can be automatic. And like scales, ideas are a tool to get you where you want to go.

EXERCISE: COOKING ON ALL BURNERS— YOUR EMOTIONAL WARM SPOT

We'll concentrate on ways to generate and evoke ideas within you. To bear fruit, ideas need a nourishing environment. We'll use an exercise in which we identify the Emotional Warm Spot (EWS) and learn how to create that space. By EWS, I mean a place in or around your childhood home where you went to feel safe, where you could be most at one with yourself, where you could be you. It's a location with very special sensory association (seeing, smelling, etc.). These associations function much as soil and nutrients do for plant growth. Arousing those sensory elements helps prepare the brain for ideation, much the way a good stage setting enhances the success of a play. Let's examine the way Jack and Frances came to their senses through EWS.

JACK O' LANTERN

Jack was a mechanical engineer experiencing classic symptoms of mid-life job burnout. Much of his problem was environmental. He was a creative man working in an aerospace firm in a busy, wide-open modular office with glaring neon lights. Jack knew his thinking had become unclear, he felt pressured, and his creativity had diminished.

The location of Jack's EWS was his childhood bedroom, which he kept like a dark retreat. He loved to hole up there and spend hours alone reading by a small lamp and dreaming up new things to invent. He especially remembered the smell of the lamp. Is it any wonder he experienced emotional discomfort with his job?

Jack related that during the workshop he had rejected the EWS notion almost totally. While driving home he mentally argued with me, but when he turned into his driveway he suddenly realized the EWS made sense. (Guess what Jack could see from his car.)

Without even knowing it, Jack had sought out the same EWS in his ranch-style adult home. For his best ideas he always went to the den, where he enjoyed a combination of darkness, one lamp burning, silence, a hideaway, and the feeling of having time out from everything. When he went there, his wife felt hurt. After he told her about the EWS exercise, she finally understood that Jack needed a retreat that involved silence, the smell of the lamp, the darkness and a childhood feeling, not a refuge to escape from her. After talking with his wife, Jack felt better about his need to withdraw to his den.

TAKING TIME TO SMELL THE TREES

As a child, Frances had spent hours in a tree house perched in an apple grove in her parents' back yard. An active girl, she climbed every inch of that tree and inspected every blade of grass under it. For ideas, Frances found that she absolutely HAD to go outdoors to a nearby park. Now a nurse manager in a large psychiatric ward, for years she felt guilty about leaving her windowless office at the hospital to get out and reflect. I told her she was doing precisely the right thing.

I suggested she take time before ideation to smell the grass, feel a tree, or even climb it if she felt comfortable doing so (and, perhaps, think about getting a position with an office window looking out onto trees and grass). Frances' guilt about "sneaking out" diminished.

LOFTY FEELINGS

My EWS was on the third floor of our tudor-style house, looking out over the lawn and the meadow across the street. To this day, I like lofts for creative work. In college I felt miserable living for a semester in a basement apartment. As a student in Germany I experienced similar uncomfortable feelings in a basement pad, but I failed to understand the reason until years later. I especially missed the feeling of literally being on top of things in my perch away from the emotional storms of life. Wherever I live, a loft or upper balcony will be important.

EXERCISE: EWS, EWS, EWS, I'M IN LOVE WITH EWS, EWS, EWS

Locate your childhood EWS in or around your childhood home. If you had many homes or an unhappy childhood (many of us did), pick the one where the EWS is strongest or clearest in your mind, even if you could treasure it for only a short moment. Think about feeling safe and at one with yourself. Where did you go and what did you do? Were you alone or with someone? Recall any sights, smells, sounds, tastes, and tactile sensations that you can.

On a sheet of paper, write EWS, and then environment, location, and sensory connectors. Describe the general environment of your EWS, where you were within this environment (as precisely as you can), and finally, any sensory connections to this location. Here is my own EWS, as an example:

EWS

Environment

Loft, slanted ceiling, big window, wide view, away from everyone, quiet of morning

Location

At desk, perpendicular to window, wood ceilings, big wooden desk, next to radiator

Sensory Connectors

Daytime, preferably mornings, dew on grass, sycamore trees, pictures on wall, chimes from bell tower, smell of coffee

When you're done writing about your EWS:

1. Write down a minor concern for which you have not found a solution, and set that paper aside.

2. Immediately thereafter, recreate a space or place that most closely approximates your EWS. Use that space for this exercise. (It's also an ideal place to practice all the other exercises in this book.) You may be able only to approximate this space for now. Be creative! If you can't find an apple tree, another kind of tree will do (or a picture of a tree). If you haven't got a back yard, maybe you can use your balcony, a courtyard at work, or rent a space somewhere.

3. After you have created your EWS, go into your space for five minutes a day for the next week, reliving all the sensations and images of your childhood EWS that you can.

4. Work on the concern you identified.

5. Each day, write down as many ideas as come to you and then sort them out to pick one as a solution.

MORE WAYS TO INCREASE YOUR RECEPTIVITY TO IDEAS

Think back to the last creative ideas you have had. When did they occur? Just after taking a shower? After taking a walk? Upon finishing a meditation? Or after a quiet period?

Chances are, it was after time of solitude or reflection.

Begin ideation with a quiet period. Turn off everything, especially your thoughts and agenda. For your brain, rest is a battery charge. Your goal for fostering imaginative thinking is to establish an open, receptive mental and emotional state.

Edison actually put a sofa into his laboratory so that he could take a half hour nap, after which he felt extraordinarily creative. Mozart received his musical themes in dreams. W. Clement Stone took several ten-minute naps during the day to allow intuition to flourish. Some people prepare best by exercising, such as jogging or walking, before they tackle an issue of the day. Pick what works for you.

EIGHT WAYS TO GET IDEAS

Now that you have set the stage with relaxation and your EWS, use this seven-step program to generate your ideas more effectively. Your objective is to gain some insight about your mission by triggering new ideas in the form of questions, each of which reflects a different perspective on the issue. It's like turning the kaleidoscope a bit to see a new pattern—ideas will form as soon as you do that. We'll use two basic approaches: asking questions in a new way, and making new associations.

EXERCISE: PART ONE: ASKING QUESTIONS WITH "WHAT IF . . ."

Select a problem you wish to solve. For now, don't worry about whether it relates to your mission. This is a practice session designed to increase your ideational skills. Let's say your problem has to do with commuting to work. Pose it as a question, using *What if . . .* as a starting point. The *What if . . .* method will shed light on the real issue and will suggest solutions. How can I solve the problem of driving a long distance to work?

Change the perspective of the problem. Change *driving* to *not driving.* What if someone else did the driving? The questions could be: What if I stopped driving? What if I took a helicopter to work? What if I hired a chauffeur to drive me? Went in a van pool? And so on. Use the "I" form in asking the questions.

Change the focus to another part of the question, by turning it around. *I go to work* becomes *work comes to me.* What if you didn't need to commute at all? Examples: *What if* the job were located where I live? *What if* I took up residence in the organization for which I work? Or, *What if* I worked in my own home?

Replace part or all of the question with something else. *Work* becomes *Somewhere else.* Maybe your commuting question has to do with the place you are going to instead of how much time you need to get there. *What if* I were going to a golf course for eight hours? To a resort? A park? (Forget for a moment whether you can afford this or not, the point is to get used to seeing the question from different angles.) How does the idea of a longer commute seem now?

Exaggerate the question. Sometimes you can change the degree of the question. Change *work* to *something else. What if* . . . I had the most delightful job on earth? Suddenly, that hour or forty-five minutes might not look so bad! If it still looks awful, then you know it has to do in part with the commute.

Make your question silly or fanciful. Freeze-dried coffee came about from a water-logged ship loaded with coffee. Then somebody suggested: *"What if* we froze these soggy coffee beans?" It was decided to save the coffee by freezing it. The solution came from the willingness to consider a crazy question. Don't exclude wild and woolly questions like: What if my workplace were in my back yard?! What if you bought the building in which you work and had it transported to your backyard? You'd certainly eliminate your commute!

Does sleeping in your office, plopping huge buildings in your back yard, or flying helicopters seem a bit far-fetched?

They are alternatives, albeit somewhat outrageous ones. Yet within these alternatives are kernel ideas for solutions. Helicopters were used to commute after the 1994 earthquake in California. And the building in your back yard might suggest that you would like a home office or studio behind the house so you could go into business for yourself.

By turning the problem into various "*What if . . .*" situations (exaggerate it, turn the question around, or make it silly) you highlight many facets to the problem: the workplace, driving location, time, distance, type of work, and so on. The list is endless, but those five tips (above) will get you started. Each can give you new insight into the problem and an idea for a solution.

***Here are possible solutions to the commute problem as suggested by* "What if . . ."**

- Begin working out of your neighbor's home.

- Get the boss to move the company near you.

- Eliminate the job.

- Move to a rural area which requires less commuting.

- Quit your job. (Perish the thought!)

- Win a lottery ticket and buy out the business.

- Communicate by telephone, E-Mail, fax, or computer.

- Engineer a friendly takeover.

- Get a wing transplant from an angel. (Just kidding!).

Practice now by choosing a concern of your own, and pick several ways to approach it with "*What if . . .*" questions. The object is to stimulate new ideas. Allow yourself to be fanciful, creative, humorous and imaginative.

Make any revisions on the way you stated your concern. What method worked best for you? Review the options you have generated and for now, put your work away.

EXERCISE, PART TWO: NEW ASSOCIATIONS

A frequent quagmire in ideation is that options and solutions tend to follow the same patterns. To escape from them, use random items. They give the brain fresh material to work with, associations that help avoid using your logical left brain. You're looking for alternate perspectives in order to get out of thinking ruts.

The next part of the exercise gives you further methods for generating ideas, this time using words, objects, and forms as mental triggers to get away from the problem.

Open a dictionary to a random page. Pick out a word randomly. Now force-fit that word to your problem. Suppose the word was "rock." How can the word "rock" give you insight about your problem—say, driving a long distance to work? You might come up with a rocky path or rock music. You may feel that the rat-race is making you as hard as a rock and no longer human to the rest of those around you. Or maybe you should play rock music while commuting. The process:

word > association > force-fit to problem > insight

Familiar objects are heavily laden with remembrances, such as where they were bought, who was with you when you bought them, what you were feeling then, the person who gave them to you, or what you were doing at the time.

A frequent quagmire in ideation is that options and solutions tend to follow the same patterns. To avoid this trap, use random items. They give the brain fresh material to work with, associations that help avoid using your logical left brain. You're looking for alternate perspectives in order to get out of thinking ruts.

Here are some further methods to generate ideas, this time using words, objects, and forms as mental triggers to get insight on the problem.

Take any ordinary object in your immediate vicinity. List the attributes of this object on a sheet of paper. What is its size, shape, volume, length, color(s), texture, material? Select one of the attributes, and see what you free associate with that attribute. For example, if you picked "paper clip," and selected the attribute "wire," what things could you associate with that word? Put the object out of view, and free associate your attribute ("wire") with the question. The object you select and the word you come up with seem random, but they are linked in some way, however remote it might seem. The sequence is as follows :

object > attribute > association > insight

Here's the way it can help. Workshop participants, all nurses, wanted to improve their relationships with physicians. How could they do it? They divided into several groups, each one with a different object. One group received a bottle of body oil. They picked the attribute "oil" and the word "rub" as their word association. That word produced "rub the wrong way," "lubricate," "there's the rub," "rub-a-dub-dub, three men in a tub," among others. Then they worked on discovering the connection and decided that the physicians rubbed them the wrong way, which was no surprise. But how to use the rub as part of the solution?

After some discussion, the nurses realized they needed more support—emotional rubbing and stroking. Since the solution is part of the problem, and vice-versa, I suggested that perhaps the physicians wanted recognition—like rubbing and stroking. "How could this be?" they sniffed.

I asked the nurses if they gave the doctors any praise on their work. "Well, no," they admitted, "the physicians don't need that anyway, because they are already convinced of their superiority." I suggested it might improve things if the nurses started rubbing the physicians the right way, too!

Suggestions began to flow: an exercise class together; massaging problems in a team meeting; easing "rusty" communication with the oil of skilled negotiation; a soft touch of support on the arm, and so on. All of this insight from a simple bottle of body oil! They realized that rubbing the right way goes both ways and can smooth relations.

To get new insights about an issue, change its form.

Select the part of the question that lends itself to transformation. In the commuting example, for instance, either "time," "commute," or "job" can be transformed. You can shorten, elongate, freeze (remember the coffee), squeeze, magnify, shrink, turn upside down, elongate or liquefy that part. Pick what you want to work with. Add your own transformations.

Associate the part with the form you selected. For example, let's say you selected "commute" as the part of the question and you decided to change its form and "liquefy" it. You could find ways to travel on waterways, ski or travel by boat.

To take another example, if "writer's block" is the part (still using "liquefy"), you could take a squirt gun and splash words on a huge sheet of paper, or have a good cry before writing.

If you changed the form to electricity (still using "writer's block"), you could communicate in neon lights or make words into electrical pulses. The object of the exercise is to gain insight, generate creative ideas, but not necessarily be practical at this point.

Here's the sequence again:

object > transformation > association > insight

TERRY THE PTERODACTYL

I used a variation of the last example in a group exercise called "Terry the Pterodactyl." In this process, an object served as trigger for associations and insights about a problem some managers were having at work.

Prior to the exercise the group identified an issue that it wished to address. Somehow the secretaries were not performing in the efficient manner the managers wanted. What was the reason for this lack of productivity?

I passed out some chunks of clay (object) to each person. Each participant was to mold the clay into anything they wanted. As the pieces of clay began to take shape (transformation) I started a fairy tale, using one participant's object as a point of departure. The object looked like a prehistoric Pterodactyl, whom I dubbed Terry. Terry (I began the story) was a secretary at this organization and wanted to fly far away.

Then the participants took over and continued the tale, using their object as trigger (association) for the fairy tale plot. Then each person passed the object, adding to the growing collage of their predecessors, and on the fairy tale went around the table.

The emerging story was about a female secretary who felt oppressed and burdened by lack of direction from her boss. She never wanted to return because she was never able to do anything right, and life had become unbearable and frustrating at work. Terry was an overworked person who was thought of as brainless. It was a no-win situation. Tahiti was just the place where she could escape the complexity and confusion of the office.

In the discussion afterward, questions emerged. Why did Terry want to fly away? Why did she have half a brain? Why was management giving poor leadership? Many insights followed. The managers recognized that they were contributing to productivity problems by sabotaging their own secretaries. The method was simple: give unclear directions and expect fast, perfect work but assume their "Terrys" didn't have the intelligence to complete it— a sure way to reinforce feelings of the manager's superiority. (Why can't she ever get it right?)

The managers were stunned by what they learned. Rather than coming up with a method to "get those secretaries in line" they had discovered their own complicity in the problem. Changing the form of the tale allowed them to avoid objective, hence threatening, references to "real" people. The solution to their management problems? Clarify objectives,

communicate tasks and results more clearly to their secretaries, and above all be more supportive. (Most of these men
were Doers who were used to getting results but not used to
giving emotional encouragement.) The sequence for this
problem solving method:

problem > object > transformation > association > insights
>solution to problem

CREATIVE CONNECTIONS TO YOUR MISSION

Discoveries often occur in unintended or accidental ways when
you link things together "randomly." Remember, anything can
be connected to anything else. Clarence Birdseye ended up marketing frozen fish by asking a simple "What if. . . " question.

On an expedition in the Arctic, Birdseye saw a fish frozen
in the ice. He wondered if he could do the same with vegetables and package the result for the general public. He took
one object (frozen fish) and creatively connected it to another
(vegetables) and asked, "What if I froze vegetables and sold
them in stores?"

Take a fresh sheet of paper and at the top, write down a
specific problem you would like to work on. State it in the
form of a question. For example, "How can I work fewer
hours and still pay my bills?" Now brainstorm some possible
"What if . . ." ideas, using any of the previous idea triggers
discussed. Let's say you pick: take an ordinary object in your
immediate vicinity. I'll pick what is in front of me now, a
small Swiss army knife. A word association with knife might
be *cut:* "What if I cut my living expenses in half?" or "What
if I cut down on the number of hours I work but increase the
amount I get for each hour?" (Other word associations might
be "sharpen," "slice," "stab," or "clip.")

Now pick your problem and the trigger you wish to work
with. While working on your questions, don't exclude any-

thing that comes to mind. Elimination comes later.

What new ideas did this method generate?

After you have enough "What ifs . . ." to suit you, ask yourself what your problem question and the "What ifs . . ." you generated suggest about your desires? (Birdseye's, "What ifs . . ." had to do with love of fish, risk-taking, and marketing foods for convenience. My "What ifs . . ." might mean I want a reduction of hours to have more time to compose.)

Finally, look at the "What ifs . . ." you generated. "What if . . ." you picked one of them to begin working on today?

HELP! I'VE GOT (TOO MANY) IDEAS!

Some people (usually Motivators) actually bubble over with ideas. Like a flood, those ideas spill over the river's banks without shape and direction, turning it into a delta.

GLEN THE GENERATOR

Glen, a creative free-lance photographer, had about as many ideas for missions as there are rides at Disneyland. Since he had received a healthy inheritance from a rich aunt, he felt for a long time that he didn't "need" to make a choice. Eventually, he sensed the lack of a mission in his life, grew restless and impatient, and flitted about from one idea to the other. But he realized that his mission, although as yet unknown to him, could not be ignored.

His task was to decide which choice was best for him in any given situation. I asked him to list those careers he was most attracted to emotionally. He produced a computer print-out of more than one hundred! Then he prioritized them on a scale of one to ten, coming up with twenty-five, reluctant to "reduce" his options for fear he would have to give up the others.

Glen's dilemma illustrates the fact that he didn't know precisely which of all his options he really preferred most. His inability to decide was like craving something to eat, but not knowing what. I helped him see that his craving would only be satiated when he identified precisely what he wanted.

When you identify your need, you can then do something about fulfilling that need, and the craving for it will stop. But during his entire life Glen had been told what to like or dislike. His own agenda had become clouded and buried. Glen also didn't believe he had the right to have specific, focused desires, and that's why he proliferated options. Giving himself permission to go for something he liked specifically seemed selfish, like going on an ego-trip.

Once he recognized the necessity (and advantage) of being specific, of precisely identifying his desires, he could now make some choices based on his true desires.

Glen admitted to himself that above all, he wanted to write screenplays. He had bought a computer and was passionate about it. Up to then, he had used it solely for correspondence! Part of him had already figured out that he loved writing. A growing mission emerged as Glen began to make scenes with words.

He took a week to clear out his apartment (Motivators like Glen tend to gather clutter). He gave away $1,500 in books, did some more clearing out of clothes and furniture, sat down and wrote out ideas for a screenplay, and then finished it in a week. He now has an agent and is busy looking for a producer for his movie script.

INCUBATION: PUTTING IDEAS ON HOLD

Part of any creative process is incubation. As any farmer knows, there is a period after planting seeds when you give them time to sprout and blossom according to a plan that has its own rules and timing. Mission ideas need to incubate, too. Witness the cicada, which takes 17 years to grow from a larval state into its adult form. Those people who have difficulty with incubation often find themselves leaping before they look, rushing from one solution to another without allowing anything to come to fruition. They deny the natural growth and development of their mission.

Incubation of ideas need not necessarily last months (as Analyzers think). Sometimes incubation can be a matter of seconds (Doers like that). It might involve doing some deep breathing before handling the crisis, or periodically getting up for brief stretches before returning to the word processor, or pacing around the room before making a decision.

Practice putting your ideas to rest for awhile! In *How To Get Control of Your Time and Your Life*, Alan Lakein tells of advising a disorganized client to take a weekend trip to think things over. The client gained immensely from his quietude. Jesus went out to the desert for 40 days. Many people I know change their routine by playing 18 holes of golf. Other methods include meditation, visualization, sleep, dreams, exercise, breathing, guided imagery, playing music, doing "right brain" (non-verbal) exercises, and removing yourself from the company of others.

Many people already know about "sleeping on things," yet during the hectic day they can't or won't take time for reflection and solitude. There is a temptation for immediate action, to pounce upon ideas and implement them without taking time to let them percolate. It's like cooking your grandma's favorite stew in ten minutes.

Moreover, this is an age of instant gratification, of having what you want when you want it. Instead of letting ideas ripen in the process, you've been conditioned to the end result. Ideas require patience—and germination time.

INCUBATION AND YOUR PM

If you are a Doer type, you especially need to sleep on your ideas. They may seem wonderful and ready for implementation, but a day or two later they will probably be better. (When you wait an extra day for the tomato to ripen, it tastes more delicious.) Motivators need time for focusing and clarification of choices. Stabilizers will be comfortable with incubation—perhaps too comfortable, since they can slowly arrive at the most logical conclusion. Analyzers will need to stop gathering information. They need to stop, incubate, and then make a decision without succumbing to the temptation to remain indecisive.

THE VALUE OF LOGIC IN IDEATION

Successful people are those who know how to balance creative ideas, risk-taking, spontaneity, and incubation with their logical, critical side. After incubation, you can use logic as a check and balance. You narrow down the ideas and select the best one for you, using logic. Think of logic as your safety net. It's there to check any slip or fall but does not interfere with the creative highwire act. Logic can also save you time. If you're busily cutting the lawn with a pair of scissors, it might be creative for whatever reason but not terribly logical. (Unless you are doing it at midnight, and there is a ban against mowing during the day.)

Analyzers are the most prone to be logical and follow rules.

IDEAS FOR YOUR LIFE MISSION:

Make a general statement about your Life Mission from where you are now. Let's say it's "My mission is to make people see the funny side of life," or "My mission is to make order out of chaos," or "My mission is to live closer to nature." Turn the statement into a question. For example: "What if I bought a house in the country?" Use any of the above seven methods that appeal to you. Open the dictionary and find a word that you can link to that mission.

Think of your Life Mission as clay to be shaped by you—a process. List any options, draw a line underneath the last one, and put the paper away. That's called incubation.

Craft a tentative, working Life Mission statement only when you have taken enough time for your creative and your logical side to mull your ideas over. It might be a matter of days, but it could be weeks or even longer. When the time is right, you will know which idea makes most sense to pursue.

If you are already bursting with ideas, and have chosen your best one, now what? An idea is useful only if you follow it through. Before it becomes a reality, you need to feel it in every fiber of your body and test it in the laboratory of your mind.

Before going from ideas/incubation to positive action, you need to use your inner eye. It's now time to journey within.

10

※

Visualize Solutions

I never saw a moor,
I never saw the sea;
Yet know I how the heather looks
And what a wave must be.

—EMILY DICKINSON

"See" comes from the Sanskrit word *veda,* which means knowledge, particularly sacred knowledge. Vision gives us the mental and spiritual blueprint to manifest desires. Visualization has little to do with the physical ability of sight. Instead, it's a process of seeing your needs on an interior level.

SEEING THE LIGHT

If the light in your tunnel has gone out and you are blocked from seeing your mission, this chapter will help you clear that vision and let the light radiate outward into your consciousness to help you see what you want.

We'll discuss a form of visualization called guided imagery and learn how to interpret the seemingly random information it supplies so that this information will guide you to your mission path.

Visualization might seem like some sort of hocus pocus or underhanded method like insider trading, because in using it you don't have to "do" anything. But it does require inner work: persistence, patience, faith, discipline, focus, and the willingness to give up control—qualities I have discussed many times in this book.

Neglecting your visual resource is like overlooking the parking spaces available at the far end of a shopping center lot. It seems to take longer to get where you want, but in the end, it's easier, and it's accomplished with far less hassle.

Internal work, of which visualization—manifesting your desire—is a part, always begins with the vision of what you want, and it comes from "tuning in" every bit as much as from actual action.

Everything comes in due season and proceeds according to plan. If you simply sit down and put a Mercedes, a mansion, or a yacht into your visual hopper of desire, then look at your watch and expect them to appear in five minutes, you're going to be disappointed. Leave the production and final say to your Source while going about your business.

Visualization is paradoxical: You visualize what you need by thinking of what you want and then wait for divine action to obtain the perfect solution at the perfect time. And, if you don't get what you hoped to, then affirm: "If not this, then something much better." That way, you'll always get what you need!

SEEING BY THE SEA

When I was going through a difficult time in my career, I made the decision to resign from a tenured university position in favor of an uncertain future. Nothing appeared to materialize. My vision for the future was blocked, a sure sign that I was not in the right place. I decided to move to Southern California.

I wanted to relocate to Santa Monica because it had the best air. I knew that apartments near the ocean were hard to get. People had told me horror stories of looking there for a year and giving up. But I had clear visions of the apartment and even the street where it was located. I made a "random" call to a local Women's Center and asked if the director knew of any apartments in Santa Monica. "No," she replied, "but I do have the name of a woman whom I had contacted three years ago. She manages of a lot of apartments; she might know of something."

A large apartment, exactly like I had envisioned, was available: with high cathedral ceilings, balconies, a loft, security parking, and situated in the precise location where I had visualized it. Too good not to be true! I told the manager it was a miracle such a beautiful apartment was available. She smiled and said: "Well, I guess this apartment was meant for you." But how to pay for the rent? I moved in anyway. A week later, my sister phoned to say she was moving to California and needed a place to stay. She shared the expenses for ten months, which was just what I needed to get on my feet financially, and the plan helped her too. This story of things appearing just when I needed them, has continued its pattern up to this day. The important thing was always to visualize what I wanted.

LEARNING HOW TO VISUALIZE

Senses help the brain connect to memory and emotion. You can encourage your ability to recall an entire past experience—and, for our purposes here, the visual aspects of that experience—by using as triggers the sensorial associations of sound, taste, smell, sight and touch.

WELL "BREAD" DESIRES

You have probably had the experience of seeing something and remembering the sound or smell attached to it. Maybe on a trip to your old hometown you visited your grade school and could actually recall your teacher's voice resounding through the halls. Perhaps the smell of clover reminds you of summer vacations. These sensory associations are also linked to *emotions*. That smell of clover can jog your memory of the happiness you felt in summertime at your aunt and uncle's farm.

Once I saw a highway billboard with the enticing ad: "See Palms Springs for Half the Bread." A half-loaf of bread, hot and steaming, was visible in the background. The ad was effective not only because it appealed to the viewer's creativity but also because it conjured up all the associations with the smell of fresh baked bread that make a vacation attractive: nurturing, food, and the comfort of home. The advertisers used sensory associations to capitalize our need for feeling at home during a vacation.

EYE OPENERS

We'll examine visualization from two perspectives: first, the ability to give yourself emotional permission to visualize just what you desire, and second, the technical ability of visualising your dream job or a delicious vacation spot in your mind. For example, David Karr, a classical doublebass player, was asked how he would describe the sound of the doublebass. Karr, a passionate lover of his instrument, replied without hesitation: "Like chocolate—sweet, smooth, creamy, and dark."

Desire is a word people use gingerly. It is often linked to sexual or primordial urges. But desire is actually a fundamental and intense longing that means "to regret the absence of something." You must be able to visualize what you truly desire.

By using and encouraging your senses, you strengthen your desires by giving them dimension and substance. Coaxing your desire through the senses is a primary aspect of visualization.

EXERCISE: COMING TO YOUR SENSES

The next exercise will take you through various sensory stages, supplying you with the emotional needs for your mission from a sensorial point of view. Do this with a friend, or record it and listen to it on a cassette tape so that you can go through it without interruption.

- Imagine the taste of your favorite childhood food. Describe the experience surrounding this food (peeling tangerines under the Christmas tree, for example), and then recall the taste of the food.
- Imagine the feel of a favorite childhood pet. Describe the animal, and then see yourself petting it.
- Imagine the smell of early morning after a rain.
- Imagine the sound of children playing on a distant playground.
- Recall your first childhood friend, then visualize her or him.
- Add a favorite sensory remembrance to this list.

Now continue with these active exercises

- Go for a walk in the morning, and concentrate on one sense each morning. Concentrate on taking your walk with only that sense in operation. What kinds of things did you notice that were different? How much more did you hear, see, smell, on the day you devoted to that particular sense? Which one did you respond to most vividly?
- Observe how you describe or remember things. Did you talk about a recent vacation in terms of what you saw, or the quiet you experienced, or how the food tasted?
- Review your material from these exercises. Which sense seems to be dominant?

- After these preparations, list on a sheet of paper the way you want your mission to feel, touch, taste, look, and smell. Be specific. If you want it to be sweet, that isn't enough. You have to link it to something focused, like lily-of-the-valley, or burning autumn leaves, or apple pies cooling on the windowsill. One person's sweet may be another's saccharine. Your specific associations give your Life Mission personal and specific information.

- Finally, take your dominant sense and work on your associations with that sense, linking them to your mission.

Let's look at how Paul did this.

THE SCENT OF A MISSION

Paul, a prep school art teacher, had always loved art, but he was frustrated at not making more personal use of it. And his concern about supporting a family was telling him to abandon art altogether for something more "practical," like administrative or corporate work. After working on his sensorial associations, he was able to generate some very specific information about his mission.

Paul identified his dominant sense as smell. He had been unaware of that preference, and during our work he discovered a poem he had written in high school which had almost entirely used olfactory descriptions.

Paul then related the smell of his mission to scented cathedrals. Growing up in France, he would wander as a boy through candle-lit cathedrals and remembered especially the smell of incense just after mass.

Scented cathedrals, Paul discovered, were associated with his love of art. I had Paul pick an additional association with smell. He came up with clean sheets!

Suddenly a personal childhood experience in a hospital gave him the clue: he now associated incense with medical care!

He knew now that the combination *medical care & art* had to do with his mission—but what? He went through several possibilities linking the two. After meditative thought, he felt his preferences had more to do with indirect care through art than teaching (which was what he had been doing previously). Paul came up with the following possibilities:

- Create toys for doctor's offices.

- Become an art therapist.

- Manage an art therapy program at a hospital.

- Organize art events for patients recovering from illness.

- Write about the use of art in recovery.

- Design art seminars for health care professionals.

Now Paul was focused and ready to attract an answer. Soon after, two opportunities arose: one, a position in a children's hospital and the other as a marketing director for a hospital. The children's hospital was a spanking clean new building, the other an older (somewhat scented) religious institution. Coincidence? Paul took the hospital marketing job in the "scented" building.

As Paul's example shows, associations with your senses can give you clues for a mission and a career that express your mission. These associations are personal design elements which set the stage for your own script. For example: the combination of children and art might result in one person's choice to become a lobbyist for art education in a state legislature; yet for someone else, it might translate into being a child therapist or a cartoonist. *Your mix based on your associa-*

tions gives you the palette you need to understand your passions and your career needs.

Even if you had the same sensorial associations as Paul's clean sheets, the connections you make are unique to you. Clean sheets might mean travel, family unity, crickets chirping at night, or a host of other clues.

Paul's new career required time for reflection. As I have emphasized again and again, your higher source will guide and help you if you have done the spade work—if you are specific as to your needs. You can't fulfill fuzzy goals. If you visualize your need as reaching the Mojave desert, you'll know you've achieved that goal when you are there. But if you visualize yourself "being happy" how will you know when you've gotten what you want?

The more specific you are, the easier it is to manifest your visions! What does being happy mean in concrete terms? Be specific enough, yet non-controlling of the outcome so your mission desire can appear on its own terms. Be sure to state clearly what you want! If you tell a caterer to "make any old thing" for a party you may end up with trayloads of turkey for the annual vegetarian Thanksgiving dinner.

To summarize:

1. Encourage your sensory faculties by practicing on your earlier memories.

2. Sharpen your senses with daily work focusing on one sense.

3. Pick your dominant sense.

4. Pick the top one or two associations and what they suggest to you. This is body work of the deepest (and most profound) order!

5. Connect the associations to something specific.

6. Relate this object to a desire.

7. Find possible expressions of missions suggested by this desire.

A final point. Most goal-setting exercises stop at identifying the goal. I think it helps to visualize the goal beyond the goal. If you want to win a prize, that's fine, but you must also see yourself doing something with the award money, and specify that, too. That's wanting the tree to bear fruit, seeing the fruit and eating it. You deserve to have your cake and eat it, too!

Clients often tell me they have trouble fantasizing because they fear it might mean they will have to follow through on their desires. They tell themselves that fantasies are unrealistic, a waste of time, something only kids would do (idea-killers in essence). They'll do anything to prevent accessing their mission! They are blocked and refuse to let their mission in.

Goethe said once that what you dream and imagine you can do, you can fulfill. Einstein was once quoted as saying that fantasy is our mind's preview of coming attractions. In other words, you must first be able to imagine something before you can manifest it.

Here are some techniques that will help stimulate your ability to visualize. In the following series of short scenes, spend as long as you need until you are satisfied you have gotten a specific image or are feeling connected with the suggestion. Avoid forcing anything. Instead, allow your inner eye to open up. Give this exercise time, and avoid judging yourself on how fast you see something.

Today: Recall what you had for breakfast. Be as specific as you can. What did the things you ate taste like? Include the color or feel of the plate, the shape of the cup, the table, chair, and so on. Add any smells or sounds, if that helps. (Did your cat *meow* during breakfast, did the phone ring or your child cry?)

Yesterday: Focus on an event from yesterday and see yourself recreating this event. If you were upset, bring that feeling up again. Or if you talked to someone, recollect the sound of the person's voice, any colors or temperature connected with it. Include anything that helps you make the situation vivid.

Recent Past: Go back to a recent incident—maybe it was an award you received, or a festive occasion you attended. Remember as many of the details as you can in your mind's eye.

Tomorrow: Now visualize a familiar place you're going to tomorrow and imagine how it looks, sounds, or smells. Be specific.

Future: Visualize a place you haven't yet seen but would like to visit—maybe someplace you would like to go on vacation. See yourself in the setting, what you are wearing, and what you will be doing. Take along some special objects from your immediate surroundings.

Fantasy: Create something that does not yet exist, perhaps a dream house, a baby not yet born, how you will look in ten years, or your first book. Draw a picture of it, or describe it in a journal in great detail. Include as much sensory items as possible.

EXERCISE: OPEN MY EYES AND I SHALL SEE . . .

Another way to get around any blocked visions is to use guided imagery. Have a friend read the following guided imagery exercise, or record it on tape for playback during the visualization. Use anything you hear as suggestions for what to see. Remember, nothing is at stake here: it is purely an exercise. This is a process, so for now think of it as NO BIG DEAL.

Prior to any guided imagery:

1. Sit comfortably on the floor with back erect and legs uncrossed.

2. Take deep breaths to center yourself and prepare for the quieting effects of the imagery. (Doers and Motivators need to spend longer getting centered.)

3. When your breathing has become calm, steady, and deep, begin your visualization.

4. When a suggestion comes to you, go with it, and do not analyze it. If you find yourself straying from the original direction, that's okay, because there is no right or wrong. (You Analyzers will struggle with this a bit more.) Go with the flow, and neither chase an image away nor block inviting it.

EXERCISE: GUIDED IMAGERY: "MY FANTASY WORK DAY"

(You may wish to tape record this for future use.)

Begin by closing your eyes and focusing on your breath until it becomes steady and even. Let your breath come in and leave your body easily and calmly. Feel your chest and diaphragm moving.

Now imagine that you are about five years in the future, on a day in which you are living your mission. It's morning, you've just awakened from a good night's sleep. Get up and walk slowly over to the window of your bedroom. Take a moment to look out the window and see what there is to see. Then walk over to the bedroom door and down the stairs. Before continuing downstairs, pause on the landing to look at the old grandfather clock and note the time.

Now head for the front door to fetch the newspaper, because today it contains an article about you. You get the paper, go to your breakfast area, and open the newspaper to the section in which your article appears. (Pause) Notice how you feel when you do this. Look at the article and make note of its title. (Pause) Then look at the photograph of you that accompanies the article. Make note of where you are, what you are wearing, and the expression on your face. Are you sitting or standing? Alone or with people? Take time now to scan the article, and observe your reactions to it. What is the tone of the article? What does it say about you? Note your feelings while reading the article.

When you have finished, take a pad of paper and a pencil and write down on the pad the first word that describes your emotional response to the article. Draw a line beneath that word and write down three things you are going to do today in connection with that article. When you have finished, return to your present space, bringing your note pad with you. Open your eyes when you're back.

Here are some guidelines to help you interpret what you saw. Remember, everything that occurred came from you, so everything is a valuable message. There is no right or wrong, only things you observed.

1. How did you feel upon getting up at the beginning of the visualization?

2. What did you see from the bedroom window?

3. What time was it when you passed the grandfather clock?

4. Did you feel relaxed, rushed, or stressed as you went down the stairs? How were you dressed?

5. How did you feel as you went to the door to get the newspaper?

6. In what section did your article appear in the newspaper?

7. What was the title and content of the article?

8. Describe the picture of you accompanying the article.

9. How did you respond to reading the article?

10. What do the words on your list suggest about your desires and mission?

11. What did you decide to do on that day after reading the article (refer to your three words)?

12. Make any additional observations of your own.

Armed with the raw data from your visualization, you can now analyze it for the clues it gives you about your mission.

1. What does the scenery outside the window tell me about the location I wish to live in?

2. What does the time on the grandfather clock tell me about how I want to structure my day?

3. What does my attire tell me about the kind of work I might prefer to be doing?

4. What clues does the newspaper section in which the article appears give me about my interests and desires? What do I want to be recognized for?

5. What does the content of the article tell me about my talents and skills?

6. How might these talents, skills, and desires relate to my mission?

7. What does my reaction to the article tell me about my needs at this moment?

8. What do the words on the pad of paper suggest about how I wish to live my entire work day?

9. What, if any, of the things I experienced in this visualization am I doing now?

10. What part of the visualization felt best to me? Why?

11. How would I feel if the visualization were true for my life now?

12. What can I begin to do to manifest any of the above parts of the visualization now?

13. What does all of this information tell me about my mission?

"My Fantasy Work Day" addresses such questions as: What setting would I like to be in? What do I want to be recognized for (newspaper article)? How would I like my day to be structured (what time was it on the clock)? Where do I want to live? How am I most comfortable? What does all this reveal about my mission?

Although you might know the gist of it, you may have had trouble seeing the article clearly. You may even resist being in the paper. No matter. You may believe that your visual response is either fantastic or irrelevant. But you can be sure that your Source is providing you a wealth of information. Don't discount it!

Some people are astonished to find that they are not rushing out in a business suit to hit the freeways, or that the newspaper article portrayed them as people very different from the ones they would otherwise have permitted themselves. One client of mine saw herself as having given a grand benefit for retarded children, raising more than $200,000. She was elegantly dressed and seemed perfectly at ease in that attire.

JOE GOES HOME

It was the first time Joe, an insurance agent, had ever worked on guided imagery. He was surprised that he saw himself staying home. Home? He had been working for ten years outside the home. He had always felt he really needed a place to escape to, an office, since he felt being at home all the time would drive him crazy. Joe realized that he wanted to be home for other reasons than self-employment. But what?

The fuzzy cloud slowly became clear. Part of his mission was to provide a more supportive environment for his kids, to participate in their growth and development, to be a caretaker—qualities that he had always used in his business. The combination of office and home began to make sense to him, and it had crystallized in the visualization.

VISUALIZATIONS: MAKING THINGS COMPUTE

A visualization stimulates apparently "irrelevant" information from within. Did you know that by age thirty you have inside of you the equivalent of over 20,000 volumes of information? Much of this knowledge is not available immediately because you have stashed it away. The things you need to forget are generally discarded. And that's just as well. If you remembered everything, you'd go crazy. (There is a man in the Soviet Union who literally cannot forget anything. He remembers, for instance, when and where—and even how old he was—when he first heard a word. This knowledge gives him no peace.)

So your interior mechanism stores material for selective retrieval. From time to time, when you need enlightenment, data is presented to you from you for interpretation. Your inner wise Source is saying "Here are some things for you to reflect upon."

Let's say you're taking a walk, thinking about a problem in your life, and seemingly random words pop into your head. You might, for instance, dismiss words such as "shrimp," "tables," and "bank accounts," as coincidental items, perhaps because you couldn't immediately find meaning in the combinations. Nothing is accidental, however. Whatever you conjure up is information you need to process. Try those three words right now as an exercise. What do they have in common?

The objective of visualizations is that you can call up specific information on a particular subject. At first, the information might seem disconnected. But everything your Source provides computes. Any manifestation has meaning; it's just up to you to find out what it is. Disconnected or "unrelated" images, words, feelings, associations, such as occur in visualizations, have been preselected from our vast interior store-house of knowledge to give insight on your mission. We'll call those "disconnected" items *approximately relevant.*

In the same way, you can link random things that appeared to you in the visualization. They all make sense, since you put them there. What relation do they have to each other? Do not pay attention to whether your conclusions seem right or wrong.

Trust that an offering from within is given to you as a clue. Receive it gratefully and analyze it. You know what it is only when you uncover it. Treat each visualization as an opportunity to access your internal resources. You have so much wisdom to draw upon! Intuition helps you process that wisdom quickly. And you'll learn to see that inner resource as a loving guide, confidante, lover, and sage.

In the next chapter, we'll visit this special friend.

Mission wanted: inquire within.

11

*Inquire Within: Your
Inner Quest*

Nach innen geht der Weg. (The way goes within.)
—*GERMAN ROMANTIC POET*

"So if you don't know it, know it!" I heard thundering from
the house next door to us at our vacation spot in Florida.
Those were true words of wisdom that accompanied hurled
plates smashing against the kitchen wall. As the angry
neighbor recognized, each person has a mandate to find the
truth. There is no excuse for ignorance, for not knowing.

Well, how do you learn to know what you know?
Inquire Within! You are the font of your knowledge. It's an
inside job. Inquire Within means you are taking a radical
turn from working on any other agendas to follow your
own desires. So if you don't know it, know it!

Inquire Within (IW) is the method, inner quest the means
to do so, and inner wisdom the desired treasure you seek.

INNER QUEST: DEFINING OUR TERMS

A quest, according to the dictionary, is a search, often for treasure. In this case, the search goes no further than within you. I have already discussed the interconnection between your inner wisdom and your soul. Inquire Within (IW) is done by means of an inner quest, which helps you access the wise information needed to do your soul's bidding.

YOUR INNER QUEST: YOUR REAL I.Q.

Your inner quest requires a kind of voluntary retreat, a willingness to exclude everything and deal just with you, honestly and fairly. It's a journey made just by you alone, in order to consult with your internal guides. This inner quest is the real I.Q. worth having.

You Doers and Motivators must remember that your inner quest requires patience. It's not like instant coffee. A client called me several days ago and told me she had finally figured out an exercise that I had given her more than two years earlier! Stabilizers will need the courage to trust their own voice, and Analyzers will need to shut off their rational, critical voice.

TURNING ON YOUR INNER LIGHT: YOUR INNER WISDOM

Much as a mustard seed contains the blueprint of an entire plant, your inner wisdom contains the seed to fruition within you. When you nurture your own seeds of wisdom, they will seek the light above, just as a planted seed grows towards sunlight. Your soul's path needs enlightenment, and inner wisdom provides the illumination.

The goal of this chapter is to demonstrate that:

1. IW is vital to your mission—your soul's assign ment for this life.

2. The answers to your search are within.

3. IW requires a shift in focus from outward to inward.

4. You must consult with yourself to the absolute exclusion of external influences.

5. Your inner quest requires total self-honesty.

Finally, we'll discuss ways to tap your inner wisdom to realize your quest.

Your interior self is filled with marvelous information. Once you begin accessing that source, your fantasy and imagination will blossom and clues to your mission will rise to the surface. Look at the example of Geri.

BEING WARY OF GERI

Geri had great difficulty knowing exactly what her mission was. I asked her to tell me when she felt most alive and excited. Her face suddenly brightened as she told me of a vacation she had taken to Ireland and the thrill she had experienced "seeing all those old build-ings and the lovely green of the countryside." A bit o' the wisdom had emerged! Would she like to spend two to three months combing through Ireland? "No way," she said. "I can't leave my husband alone."

Geri had always been wary of listening to herself, but she agreed to try. After several weeks of an intense inner quest, it became clear that she was really seeking preservation and greenery, luxurious surroundings and peace. She discovered that she felt most at home on campuses and botanical gardens because of the feeling of contentment they evoked in her body.

Suddenly, her inner wisdom began to supply her

with information. She sensed her love of plants reawakening. She had always tended to them with great love and affection, and friends often asked her to care for their plants while they were on vacation. Her Life Mission began to emerge: to create beautiful and uplifting environments for people's homes. She happened to live in a lush part of town. Geri had tapped a love and a location right around her where she could explore and start to live her mission.

At first Geri resisted her mission since she thought her husband would be adversely affected. She had neatly boxed herself in, telling herself that her desire would dramatically affect other aspects of her life. But she also realized that she would be unhappy forever if she refused to change herself. She began to understand that her commitment was a response to an inner urge.

Even if your treasured answer lies buried deep within, you get constant clues to unearth it. IW leads to the truth about yourself—and compels positive action on behalf of your soul. Your inner quest unlocks the desire within you that is always there, which is to express the very mission you are equipped to carry out—everyday!

IW REQUIRES A SHIFT IN FOCUS FROM OUTWARD TO INWARD

IW demands surrender to your mind, body, and spirit. To make this shift within, you must tune out the voices of authority, friends, loved ones, or family. Remember, people are always willing to share a piece of their mind. And it's easy for people to make suggestions, especially when they don't have to act on what they suggest. A verse from the J. B. Phillips translation of the Bible says: "Do not let the world squeeze you into its own mold." You are the potter, creator and shaper of yourself. Your inner wisdom is the repository of your knowledge. And, as a jazz lyric reminds us: "Only you can tell how deep the well. The well is your soul."

DUTIFUL DALE

A gentle, caring individual, Dale had lived his life for others. His family had grown accustomed to an affluent lifestyle, but he felt helpless because he couldn't meet his own needs. A right-brained visionary, he had worked for more than ten years in a structured left-brain environment. He had imprisoned himself in a corporate legal department that demanded long hours of tedious fact-finding and research. On the weekends, Dale would literally head for the hills to spend all his available time outdoors, only to return to his dungeon during the week. You could say he was paid dearly—or rather he *paid* dearly—for his trouble.

Dale used his family's demands for an affluent lifestyle as an excuse to avoid dealing with his own issues. I encouraged him to go within and look at his problems independently of anyone else. After visiting a monastery retreat, where he spent three days consulting with himself, Dale came to an important insight. He realized he had been in denial for many years by telling himself he had to maintain his family's expectations while ignoring his own need for creativity and freedom.

He decided to keep his city job for another year or so while exploring a law practice in a rural community near the mountains, where he could enjoy a practice as a small-town lawyer/environmental advocate and operate on a more personal basis with his clients. Now meditation and inner dialogue are a regular part of his life. His family resisted at first, but when they saw the change in Dale's behavior, they gradually accepted his needs. (And they got more in touch with their own, since Dale wasn't holding up the sky for them anymore.)

THE MACH ONE EXPERIENCE

If you knock on the door of your inner wisdom, open it a crack, get scared and slam it shut at first, it's all right! But do it! It will strengthen your resolve to open up more the next time. You validate yourself every time you decide to look inward for answers.

The going gets rough as you approach the threshold of truth. You might be willing to trust yourself on low risk questions, but for the biggies, such as "What is my soul's path?" "How can I accept the artist, negotiator, business executive, neighborhood activist, or beekeeper in me?" or even "How can I juggle all this with the mortgage payments?" it will be more difficult. If you need to resort to logic and reason, you'll find that these two "friends" usually put the kibosh on any internal desires.

In the movie *The Right Stuff,* there was a scene about breaking the sound barrier. Just before the pilot, Chuck Yaeger, went through Mach One (the speed of sound), the plane shuddered, shook, and resisted. We didn't know if it would make it. Suddenly, the plane soared into serene, glorious, thrilling silence. No more resistance or difficulty, just a smooth, peaceful ride.

I call that the Mach One Experience. The willingness to go through the disturbance of Mach One made the rest easy. If you go up to a certain point and then say, "This is too painful; I don't want to deal with it," you keep that barrier before you. There is no better way to break through the resistance to your Life Mission than go through it! Allow yourself to be "shaken up" so you'll get to experience the smooth ride of a focused calling.

Here's another way to look at it. Larry Dossey, in his book *Space, Time and Medicine,* discusses a shaking-up process in nature first identified by Ilya Priogogine in his Theory of Dissipative Structures. (It won Priogogine a Nobel prize.)

Priogogine's ideas have to do with molecular structures in nature. Those structures that evolve into greater complexity— that is, escape to a higher order—acquire the quality of fragility, the capacity for being shaken up, that is paradoxically also the key to growth. "Structures that are insulated from disturbance are protected from change. They are stagnant and never evolve toward a more complex form," Dossey notes.

DO DISTURB

Applying Priogogine's theory to the human condition: if you want to grow, change, and evolve toward living your Life Mission, you must be vulnerable to disturbance, especially if you are a complex being (which you are). Of course, if you opt for the mundane and the safe, this process isn't for you. Without the willingness to be "disturbed," there is no complexity and no chance for growth. Avoiding the Mach One Experience protects you from experiencing disturbance but blocks movement towards change. Absence of movement means stagnation and death. Evolving demands that you let yourself be shaken up. Avoiding your inner wisdom is dangerous because it keeps you static, as Priogogine's theory shows. The going can get rough as you approach the threshold of truth, but the reward is smooth sailing.

Dossey quotes from F. Barron's studies of creative individuals in which he found that they are comfortable with complexity and disorder, the irrational, the magical, the primitive, the nonsensical. "The truly creative individual stands ready to abandon old classifications and to acknowledge that life, particularly [her or] his own unique life, is rich with new possibilities."

The payoff for trusting your inner wisdom is enormous because you are investing in yourself! Trust the melody within you, and dare to be "irrational."

A PERSONAL MACH ONE EXPERIENCE:
PAM FACES THE MUSIC WITHIN

Pam, a V. P. of a large institution, was clearly no longer able to function in the well-paying job she "enjoyed." Her lower back was giving her enormous pain (she was putting too much stress on it by denying her true feelings). Her creativity was at an ebb. Yet she wanted to hang in there until she could retire and sail around the world with her husband. I said if she continued in this manner, there might not be any retirement benefits or world cruise. But Pam clung to this destructive job for two more months, as I worked with her to break through her resistance.

Pam finally agreed to the thing she had dreaded most: leaving a position she knew well and in which she had "made it." Her fears about quitting were enormous. She had to face herself. Who was she without that title? Where would she go now, and who would pay the bills? Still, she decided to cut the ties.

As she allowed herself to be shaken up by leaving, her creativity slowly reemerged, and her health improved. She rediscovered latent capacities in herself, one of which was singing! Whereas she had thought it would be the end of her identity, Pam experienced renewed health, vitality, and energy (akin to the "soaring" of the airplane after Mach One). Pam returned to work for a smaller, more low-key neighborhood financial institution, without the stress of her old job, and nearer home. This lower stress work and reduced commute gave Pam time to devote her energies to her reawakened hobbies. She put the music back in her life, improved her health, and got more in touch with her desire to combine her leadership and artistic talents.

CONSULTING WITH SELF:
I'M ALL FOR YOU BODY AND SOUL

Remember the safety instructions on your last airplane flight? "Put the oxygen mask on yourself first before assisting those traveling with you." Why? You're useful to others only after first taking care of yourself. IW means you are willing to surrender to yourself and say: "Okay, I won't interfere. This time I'll listen to YOU."

Where is the wisdom of knowledge located within? Well—actually, everywhere. You think with your whole being, not just with a specific organ. We'll begin with the brain.

The neo-cortex, that "new bark" (as the term means in Latin) on the outer rim of the brain contains the area most commonly associated with cognition, higher levels of functioning, fantasy, spirituality, higher consciousness, reason, and intuition. The neo-cortex has two primary ways of processing things. The left generally draws conclusions based on reason and observation, which are largely conveyed verbally. The right side processes holistically—almost mystically—and likes to go beyond the five senses to create new contexts of reality.

The neo-cortex, together with the "older" evolutionary parts, the "mammalian" and the "reptilian," form the triune brain. Like the neo-cortex, each of the older parts of the brain is responsible for a specific kind of function. The mammalian brain (present, for example, in horses, dogs, and cats), governs the knowing we get through our emotions. Our triune brain, then, actually processes through action, emotions and reasoning. Information is not confined just to our head, but is an affair of the entire body.

One role of the neo-cortex, as the "newest" brain, is to

help us moderate and process any information from the two older parts, provided we are open to this exchange of information. That is why we must pay attention especially to the feelings (and body reactions) from the older brain parts as conduits of knowledge for our mission. Although we may not always be able to immediately explain the reason for our feelings, they do reveal powerful urges and desires which we cannot afford to ignore.

IGNORING THE WISDOM OF YOUR FEELINGS: A HEART BY-PASS

At times, you've undoubtedly left home sensing full well that you've forgotten something, but couldn't "think" what it was. Your feelings gave you information that you acted upon. Information was also triggered through your senses. Perhaps a sensory experience made you remember (think of it: re-member, that's a body term!) a favorite Aunt when you smelled red cabbage just like she prepared it. Or your muscles tightened when you had to return to work on Monday morning. The point is that feelings from emotions, the senses, and even muscles provide us with powerful mission information. Mission is expressed in every fiber of our being.

The problem is that frequently, we humans have learned to bypass our heartfelt feelings. When we tune out the body and its feeling messages, or block emotions through fear-based survival mechanisms, we diminish the ability of our neo-cortex to help process that information. Thus, we close off an important avenue to discovery of our soul's purpose.

According to Paul McLean, "The human brain suffers from a quasi-schizophrenic split between reason, emotion and survival drives, all based on inadequate integration between the neo-cortex and the older (reptilian and mammalian) brains."

Ingrid illustrates the consequences of disconnecting from her body's clear messages about her mission.

INGRID IGNORES BODY LANGUAGE

A rugged and independent Swede, Ingrid had come to the United States from Scandinavia in the sixties with a degree in chemistry. After enjoying several good jobs with pharmaceutical companies, she landed a position with a leading aerospace corporation. Six years later, her career crashed in front of her eyes when she was laid off. In the meantime she had become a citizen and wanted to remain in the United States. But after sending out 150 resumes and exhausting her 26 weeks of unemployment compensation, Ingrid despaired of ever getting off first base. Nothing seemed to work for her. (Life Mission was also not a working concept for her.)

I noticed that although she claimed to be depressed about her lack of work? ("I need a job" she would say every time I saw her), she seemed to be having a great time. She got involved in politics, did volunteer work for a couple of service organizations, read books and saw movies she'd never had time for. She had time to reflect on her life. She was in the best of moods when working on environmental projects and humanitarian issues to "while" away the time.

But Ingrid rigidly refused to admit she wanted to do anything new. "Besides," she said, "I can get a good salary doing work on missiles." (Logic!)

One day, Ingrid watched a movie on Mother Teresa in which Mother Teresa exhorted people to "follow their heart." She felt an instant dizziness and pain. Without warning, she was sick all the next day. Usually a picture of health, she now couldn't get out of bed. "Was there a connection between her illness and Mother Teresa's message?" I asked. "Just coincidence," Ingrid insisted.

Her body had spoken, even if she didn't listen to it. Ingrid finally got a job doing the same old thing. When she announced it, I thought she was describing a disaster that had befallen her. If her spirits were uplifted with her new position, I missed it (and she did, too).

EXERCISE: "ULTIMATE BEING"

This exercise helps you tap into your body. Stand erect and still for a few minutes. During this time, say everything you notice or experience in your body. If you wiggle a finger, twitch, hear something, make a gesture, sigh, or whatever, take it into your immediate awareness. As much as possible, keep in the present. You will begin to see how much your feelings and thoughts are expressed through your body in subtle ways. An excerpt might sound something like this:

"I'm blinking my eyes. I feel uncomfortable doing this. I put my hand to my ear. I hear a car go by. I am swallowing. I lower my head. I shift back and forth from my left foot to my right foot. I am thinking about what I am going to say. I feel my heart beat. I am aware of tension in my lower back. I just folded my hands. I looked down to get an idea. I curled my little finger. I hear a car roar by and children laughing and shouting. I am thinking about this evening. I notice my thoughts are wandering. I'm feeling energized after having read a chapter of Naomi's book."

Do this exercise each day for several weeks. You'll develop an awareness of the way your body reflects what you feel and think, and you'll start listening for its wisdom.

DEB'S HAIRDO

Body gestures, for example, provide information about a person's thinking. Debbie, a young post-graduate student of philosophy, avoided her feelings on just about any subject. She had thought out her life "to the max" and was able to theorize on her condition from every angle. When I attempted to get Debbie to discuss her feelings about her mission, she invariably ran a hand through her hair. When I asked about her habit, she was totally unaware of it. Debbie needed to get out of a mental straitjacket and connect to her feelings. Her body knew she was overloaded.

TONY'S TWIST

For thirty years, Tony was an accountant in a manufacturing firm. At one of our sessions, he slumped down on the couch and, while turning and twisting his wedding ring, immediately sighed about having no time for himself He had accepted the burden of going to work every day but was growing tired of this responsibility.

Did he resent his wife staying home and not having a career? "No" (twist). Did he wish he could have some time to himself like his wife? "Yes." (twist) Could he give up his need to be the sole provider? "No." (twist) Would he consider doing something his wife would not approve of? "No." (twist) I asked Tony about his feelings of being the breadwinner. Only after I made him aware of the ring twisting did he admit that he was angry and resentful at his wife for her "easy life." How he wished he could have the luxury of six months "off." The twist became very obvious in meaning.

Had he ever wanted his wife to work before this?

"No," Tony said proudly. "I felt it was my role to earn the money." Some time later, Tony admitted that the anger was really self-directed, because with his "sole provider status" he had not only boxed himself in, he had also kept his wife from developing her mission as well.

I credit Frau Dr. Margarethe Mitscherlich of Düsseldorf, Germany for explaining to me how she used this technique of the "significant gesture" in her therapy. With every client she discovered a revealing, habitual body movement that shed light on a problem she or he was working through. We'll pursue this body language a bit further.

THE PAINFUL TRUTH

Body pain is an indicator of blocked energy. Like those unconscious gestures, body pain, if you pay attention to it, can supply you with a lot of feedback. Language reflects "body wisdom," someone is a "pain in the neck," you "feel it in your gut," you don't "have the heart to do it," and so on. Rather than looking at pain as a nuisance, get in touch with that discomfort and find out what it's trying to tell you. Try the following exercise:

EXERCISE: PROBING YOUR PAIN

Sit comfortably or lie on the floor and relax your entire body. Now scan it for any pain, discomfort or stress. As soon as you find the greatest ache, intensify it, exaggerate it, make it as sharp as you can. While in this state, ask this part of your body for help. Become that place in your body and tell yourself what's the matter. What is the source of the pain? What does the location have to do with your life? Here are some body insights clients have come up with:

Hearing or ear aches	— Need to trust self and shut out outside influences
Seeing problems or blurred vision	— Need to see things clearly or be willing to focus on objectives
Throat conditions	— Communication problems (need to express feelings and love)
Chest pains	— Need to unblock emotions (try softer approaches)
Breast pain	— Need nourishment
Back pain	— Burden of having to support world; harboring unexpressed sadness
Colon problems	— Holding suppressed anger

Pains make you think. What are your aches and pains telling you?

CARLA: FLYING "BUT"RESS

Carla's PM was Analyzer, with some secondary Motivator traits. She had main interests: dancing, creative writing, and biology. Approaching 30, she was terrified of not being able to make that triple combination (or any parts thereof) work. She continued her job of managing a family-owned furniture store, allotting little time to inner work. As a result, she was experiencing enormous headaches and eye trouble.

Carla felt that to follow her path would be self-indulgent (that is, giving in to her body), although each time she wrote, danced, or took a science course she felt fine for that period of time. Besides, her family wanted her to do something "real," like go into business. Carla's devotion to "reality" was doing her in, and her body knew it.

Carla's eye trouble was the clue for her. For a long time she had been focusing her sights on the present, seeing only what her family wanted her to see. She began to direct her thoughts inward (whereupon the headaches diminished, too) and discovered she needed to attend graduate school to integrate her desires of science and writing. She began to feel a surge of energy and took up ballet once again!

RIGOROUS SELF-HONESTY PRECEDES AN INNER QUEST

Your inner quest demands rigorous standards of honesty and ethics. That's not so easy in a society that promotes and encourages duplicity and self-deceit. How many times have you heard "she's away from her desk" and you knew it wasn't true? A favorite rejection slip from editors is: "It doesn't fit into our plans," when you know it really means "We didn't like your stuff." Disinformation, euphemisms, fibs—call it what you will—are, well, lies (and I don't mean white). In fact, lying is so pervasive in our society that *Time Magazine* featured this subject on its front cover!

A client recalled the story of his aunt and nephew sitting together in the living room watching TV.

Aunt: "Is the light from the lamp bothering you?"

Nephew: "No."

The aunt asked the question three times but stopped when her nephew's voice quivered with irritation. She then got up, went into her bedroom, and reemerged wearing a hat with an oversized brim. The aunt was in denial. It was she, not the boy, who was irritated by the lamp.

Family communication is often the setting for misleading and evasive communication. You learn early on how to decode your parent's messages and translate them into what was actually meant. You were actually dealing with dishonesty (no matter if it was unconscious or conscious) whenever you unveiled the message. Parents may have admonished you with the question, "Who do you think you are?" But they really meant, "I don't like the way you are, and I want you to stop being that way." If you had answered "I think I am being myself," you might have come away with a knuckle sandwich.

How many of you have experienced honest communication with siblings and friends, either? If you have experienced much miscommunication, it will affect the way you talk with yourself. You may fool some of the people some of the time, and they may fool you, but fooling yourself even some of the time will result in depression, distrust, lack of self-esteem and a derailed mission track.

HONESTY AND LIFE MISSION

Give yourself direct, honest and unmixed messages about what you want. Any con job you do on yourself will result in a delayed or missed mission. When I asked Rae, a successful manager of a merchandising firm, to describe how she was conning herself, she fell silent; then her face contorted, as if a spirit guide were entering her body for a channeling. Actually, Rae was making a first attempt at an inner quest (the art of self-channeling). Staring dejectedly at the floor, she admitted that she really didn't want to be Number One. "I'd rather be a good follower. I want my mission to play out behind the scenes."

It was a breakthrough for Rae. Her endless striving for the elusive laurel wreath never matched her true desires. It was her father who wanted Rae to be Ms. Prima. She freed herself from the imprisonment of the lie of competition, perfection, and being Number One.

WAYS TO TAP YOUR INNER WISDOM

Your inner wisdom communicates to you in uncustomary ways. How can you know how to recognize that inner wisdom at work?

Look for the following clues:

- rewards for your inner quest
- less resistance
- feelings of timelessness
- feelings of passion

Make note of the moments when these things occur. Keep a notebook and record the contexts. Invariably, they will happen after you have consulted with yourself. They will empower you to spend energy in the service of your mission.

Rewards.   You are always rewarded for going with your inner wisdom. Be on the lookout for immediate payoffs for following your inner quest. It might be getting fired from a job you hate (hardly ever seen as a bonus!), it might be a phone call or it might be an unexpected check in the mail.

Identify, for example, a particular gift you use infrequently, or one you feel is not "practical." When your intention shifts to actually use it for its own sake, amazing things can happen. One client who was in his fifties had not played the viola since high school; it had sat in his closet for thirty years. I recommended he play it fifteen minutes a day without concern for "producing " anything. A week later he had the complete outline in his head for a screenplay that "popped up out of nowhere."

Less Resistance. When you follow your inner wisdom, things flow easier, and you don't have to strain as much. When you are on your path, you will experience a smoothness you hadn't imagined possible—the Mach One experience.

If you are experiencing obstacles, examine what's causing them. Is it the activity itself or another factor? For instance: I resisted this book at first, struggling and straining to get fifteen pages written. Although I knew from my inner work that I must write this book, I was resisting the shaking-up process. I'd find excuses to do anything else but write. Everything came slowly, painfully, and reluctantly. I also learned that I needed to get a computer. But I was afraid of using a computer. A speech by Dr. Richard Byrne on computer-phobia convinced me I could do it. I acted on that advice, although I had to borrow money for the computer. When I began using it, however, things literally flowed out of my hands and onto the screen. I was using a gift I had been neglecting. My inner wisdom knew I could do it.

Feelings of Timelessness. Acute awareness of time, when it either drags or races, is a sign that something is wrong. When you say "time flies," for example, you are having fun. The irony is that when you are having fun you seem to have less time, because it flies!

On the other hand, when time feels like the interval between paychecks, it can weight you down. You look at your watch constantly and think about when you can be free. When you are bored or unhappy, time seems to drag. What a mess! Unbearable times never seem to end, but when you're having fun, time flies. (The only way to have time slow down, then, is to be bored!) That's the tyranny of thinking about time. If you find yourself saying, "Time dragged on that picnic," "I wasted my time on that novel," or "I frittered away my time at the office this weekend," examine the reasons you engaged in these activities and try to avoid engaging in them.

Living according to your inner wisdom releases you from the tyranny of time. When you go onto an inner quest and contact your inner wisdom, then follow its advice with action, you can lose a sense of time during that activity. An artist friend described it this way: "When I paint, I almost step outside of time. If anything, time appears to be suspended." Only when you are acting out of desire do you have the luxury of standing outside of the tyranny of time.

Dossey cites the example of the Zen meditator who experiences five minutes of deep meditation as though it were an hour. (Maybe that's why I won't meditate in the dentist's chair.) In five minutes of time, the meditator has processed a lot of information—an hour's worth. Time seems to stretch to accommodate that information, but without being a drag.

Feelings of Passion. Your mission search must give you a rush, a thrill—perhaps even an erotic feeling. Doing your soul's bidding must provide your libido with lots of stimulation and sizzle. One way to tell if you're even in the sizzle arena is to examine your job. When I ask clients what is sexy about their jobs, they usually laugh or look dumbfounded. "That's something I never really connected with work!" Why not? Who ever said jobs had to be dull, drab, tedious, and uninteresting?

Of course, there will be times when things are routine—vexing valleys among the passionate peaks. A steady diet of climaxes would be too much even for the most rabid pursuer of a Life Mission. But if the sizzle factor has left your career, then it means, as in a relationship, that something is missing.

FOLLOW THE CLUES ON WHERE TO SPEND YOUR ENERGY

Be aware of where you put your energy. Energy itself is neutral, but it can be wasted or put to good use. I found that I tended to work harder on things that were not part of my mission. If something challenged me, I piled on the effort. (Doers and Analyzers are prone to this type of behavior.) I poured time and toil into my teaching at college. I prepared endless lecture notes and read books copiously in order to be informed. The more I hated it, the harder I struggled.

Make your efforts count. If you have committed to something you do not want to do, then stop doing it! It could be anything from quitting a compulsive, addictive habit, resisting the temptation to do low-priority things or terminating your job. Listen to yourself carefully.

If you like something, and devote time to your path, your attitude toward the process will change. You'll say: this is fun, thrilling—I love doing this! And the idea of spending time (an interesting concept in itself) on it simply doesn't enter your mind. Even the less glamorous parts will be okay if the overall process is exciting. After all, renovating a house includes less enjoyable acttivities like cleaning up, getting rid of the trash, or ordering materials. But if it contributes to something you love, you'll not find it a drag.

EXERCISE: CREATING YOUR PERSONAL MYTH

Myth is "a story or belief that attempts to express or explain a basic truth." Each of us has a private image of ourselves aching to be revealed. It is the truth about us as we feel it. A final stage of inner work is to redesign the person—YOU—from the inside out according to what you want to be. *Create the you of your mythology.*

What is this image of your myth based upon? You can supply themes for private myths from a variety of sources. Find a character from history, lore, or literature whom you admire and who characterizes what you feel. You can also draw a picture, write a song, poem, or description, or create an abstract collage to describe your myth.

Write down everything you can think of pertaining to the person of your mythology. Supply all the details about that person. What time does she/he live in? What place, situation or environment does this person live in? What does this person do and with whom does she or he associate? Do not show your description to anyone. Once you get in touch within, your inner wisdom will flood you with suggestions and encouragement.

Next write a statement of purpose for this mythological figure, preferably one that is worded in a fantastic or unusual way.

Let's say your myth is that of Snow White. Your statement of purpose is: to find a kingdom in which you can provide foster care for orphaned children.

Next, visualize yourself as this person in a present setting: talking with your friends, working, interacting with others. Imagine how you feel when you are this person and what you can accomplish as a result. You can incorporate your work experience into the visualization. (Be careful not to include anything you don't want to do.)

Act out this myth in ceremonial fashion. Get dressed up as this character, make cards with the character's name on it, act the role of the person in front of a mirror, be the person every day for an allotted period of time, call yourself by the person's name! Get into the part that you desire! With this personal image, you could then set out to revolutionize the care of orphans. Then everyone in this world of yours would truly whistle while they work!

The more you live your myth, the easier it will be for you to become the person you want to be. This is not a con job. Your myth is the person you have been hiding from yourself! She or he is there in vibrant, pulsating color, full of energy and passion. Take off the veil of deceit and live your myth! In turn, you will become a model to yourself and to the world.

Jacques Cousteau responded to his personal myth, which said to pursue three things: medicine, diving and film-making. Instead of denying the message he devoted his life to all three: studies on the psychology and physiology of diving (medicine), exploring the ocean from the ship *Calypso* (diving), and documentaries (film-making), and he thereby created the Cousteau myth we all know so well. Cousteau demonstrated what can happen when you respond to internal signals and leave the integration of desires to your wisdom. Your life can be apples and orange—and a bowl of cherries!

When you look for guidance, be the kind of thoughtful person who never forgets to include yourself. What better source for all you need could you possibly imagine than your own self? Inquiring within is evidence of your self-love, self-trust, and self-reliance.

Poke around in the coals of a fire, stir them up, give them a puff of breath, and they will rekindle. And so it is with the flame of your Life Mission. It often lies smoldering in the embers and needs reviving. IW sparks the passionate fire of deepest wishes, desires, and passions. Answering the call means responding to your inner voice, the voice of your soul.

We'll turn now to the gentle, soft path to assist in helping you find your Life Mission.

12

Try Softer

Less is more.
MIES VAN DER ROHE

The previous three chapters discussed the vital work of going within. This chapter emphasizes the *soft* quality of that work. *Try Softer* challenges you to use the gentle way to get results. *Try Softer* is more lasting because it operates in tune with internal wisdom, and it is healthier because it permits the wise use of your energy. You'll realize your mission more smoothly when you are efficient with your resources.

If you have to be in control, if you define outcomes, if you are into workaholism, or programming results or anything else that seeks to make things happen by sheer force of muscle or will, then this chapter is especially for you.

THE SOFT TRUTH

Much of the Western world is terminally addicted to the value of hard work. "If at first you don't succeed, try, try again" (harder, of course).   Or how about Churchill's famous "Blood, sweat, tears, and toil." Or, "Work hard and you'll amount to something." "You don't get something for nothing" was the phrase I remember from home.

But just look at the enormous toll the hard approach takes on people's physical, spiritual and emotional health. It's often referred to as Type A behavior: people chomping at the bit at traffic lights, fighting for the last car space in a parking lot or working 60 hours a week (usually at jobs that themselves require a *Try Harder* attitude). People who cannot take breaks often break down in other ways.

The trouble is, Type A behavior usually benefits physicians, therapists, funeral directors, cocaine dealers and anyone else trying to patch up, pacify, or put away people. One word used for drug dealers is "pusher," while booze with high alcohol content is called "hard liquor." And that's not accidental. *Try Harder* imposes on you and your body; *Try Softer* disposes of pain and obstacles.

The word *radical* means "coming from the root, to derive from the soil, to grow out of, or from something." *Try Softer* is a radical concept because following this approach gets at a major clue to your Life Mission. If it's easy, then start doing it.

TRY SOFTER: OR STRONG IS WRONG

There are three major factors combatting the *Try Softer* approach: cause and effect thinking; hard is better (is stronger); and instant mania.

Remember the county fair? There were always guys hitting a gong with a hammer. You could see the cause/effect relationship between the force of their blows and the height of the ball—the harder they swung, the higher the ball would rise. When it came to this game, muscle seemed to work. Of course, sheer strength is useful for some things like lifting heavy packages. The problem occurs when the superiority of muscle power is generalized to all endeavors.

The myth that "hard" is better for everything stubbornly persists. "Hard" means tough, beefy, macho or durable. "Soft," on the other hand, connotes such things as wimpy, a pushover, feminine, and weak. Students would hardly admit they "studied easily" for a test in school. Anyway, it would be almost anti-American! Rarely are people rewarded for doing something with grace and ease. It's as if they were going against the rules. (They are!)

The age of instant gratification and "masculine" values favors the hard way because it seems to show immediate results. In living a Life Mission, the centuries-old dependence on trying harder no longer applies. Your soul is not impressed by the muscle, big-boss approach.

SOFT IS HARD (AT FIRST)

Try Softer is a principle by which you allow things to happen, events to take place, and processes to unfold on their own terms. *Try Softer* relies on the intention and direction of energy to achieve effective goals rather than fast results. Inner energy replaces cause-and-effect thinking and sheer force of will.

Try Softer uses the law of attraction. Things come to you because you have created the environment, set the stage, provided the culture so that what you need will gravitate to you.

Caution! *Try Softer* is NOT a brand of California-style Tofu, or meditation pillows accompanied by soft New Age music and mantras, with the expectation that everything is going to fall from the sky. It's a challenging business, requiring trust, surrender, and faith that the fulfillment of your desires and mission happens via the path of least resistance. With *Try Softer* things appear to "just happen."

TRY SOFTER: "JUST" DESSERTS

Ever since my early teens I dreamt of going to Europe. I listened to music from foreign countries, saved my money and began to learn German. One day Ursula, a German exchange student attending my high school, just happened to ask me to spend the following year in her home. I said yes immediately and was off to Germany that fall.

However, the stay with her family didn't work out, and I decided instead to go to Nuremburg to visit a friend of my family who had just returned to Germany from studying in the States. She had no idea I was coming to visit. Upon arrival, I discovered that she had just broken her foot and needed someone to do things around the house. Staying at her house forced me to practice German. Since she just happened to be a language teacher, she was able to help me in ways most untrained people could not. And since she just happened to be laid up at home, I received 24 -hour language instruction and became fluent in a short time. Make up your own "just" desserts list. What can you identify that "just" happened, especially when you let go of making it happen?

WHAT YOU KNOW WON'T HURT YOU: BE A(WARE)!

You must be fully conscious that you are *Trying Softer*. During my European adventure, I didn't know I was using *Try Softer*. Every time something went my way, I found a perfectly reasonable explanation for the reason I got what I wanted: good old cause-and-effect stuff.

I told myself I had worked hard to save money and earn my way to Europe. Having done all the work myself, I was convinced that I deserved full credit for it. That was the Puritan ethic: you got it when you earned it. No one else contributed to my success.

So far so good. But here's the rub. Nothing ever felt easy during that time! And whenever something went wrong, I found myself obsessing over every little mistake. It felt like going upstream. Each time things worked out I breathed a huge sigh of relief. Anxiety came from a feeling that I had to control everything.

In retrospect I know I experienced *Try Softer*, even though at the time things seemed hard. It was as if I had done my laundry in a washing machine but felt as if I had washed all my clothes by hand.

Practice *Try Softer* consciously. Learn from it, give it credit, nurture and appreciate it. Be aware that it is in operation!

TO DO AND NOT TO DO: THAT'S THE ANSWER

The *Try Softer* process is a paradoxical combination of preparation and not doing anything. A colleague of my father used to say: "God looks good when you're prepared." Well, your Source looks great if you let it operate on your behalf.

Notice that I didn't sit around waiting for things to happen to get me to Europe. In fact, there was a lot to prepare for: learning a foreign language, visualizing desires, getting a part-time job, saving money, looking into inexpensive travel, and thinking about a place to stay. But all of this action really wasn't hard because it was happening in the service of my mission.

Stop pushing; abandon trying to make things happen, and relinquish being in control—all action verbs! "Let It Be" as the Beatles' song says. With *Try Softer* you are in effect saying that less achieves more. Look at the things you do well—I'll bet they are much easier to do than anything else! It's like hitting a golf ball in a relaxed and easy manner. It seems illogical, but that's precisely the way to do it for maximum effectiveness. Nice and easy does it every time. And the same method is true for your life.

WAYS TO SOFTEN UP

Here are some softener tips you can use to undo any hardness in preparation for the *Try Softer* program I'll introduce later.

Examine your life. The most successful experiences of life flow easily. Individual parts may be "illogical," and setbacks can occur, but they don't matter, because the outcome will give you what you envisioned, and that's what counts. Identify one successful experience of your life, take it apart (as I did for Europe) and look at the process.

1. Trace the sequence of events. Did things "add up"? (Did you, for example, program events to happen in just the way they did?)

2. Did you have to work "hard" to make the events happen? When? How did you feel during those times? What did *"Try Harder"* net you?

3. Was your entire experience without any setbacks? If not, what were they?

4. When did you surrender to the process—that is, pull instead of push?

5. During that time were you focused on the experience and the outcome you wanted from it? Was it easier than when you pushed?

Look for *Try Softer* Examples in Others. Ask people to tell you about their successful experiences. It makes for wonderful conversation, since people love to talk about their successes. Ask why they thought things happened in the way they did. Look for the "illogical," "fantastic," or "nonsensical" aspects to their stories. Were they focused on what they wanted? Did the script go as they had expected?

A songwriter I know got his big break while selling shoes on Venice Beach in California. A producer chanced by, and in the course of the conversation, the struggling artist mentioned that he wrote songs. "Send me a tape," said the producer. Later that week, the producer called in the middle of the night and said, "I like your songs." A record contract followed. Logical? No. If I told you the way to song writing was to sell shoes at the beach, you'd say I was crazy. Precisely. Following your passion knows no logic.

The fulfillment of my vision came five years after it had entered my mind, five years of apparently "aimless" dreaming and wishing. Change your direction of thinking. Where you end up is where you need to be, so why aim first? You are the arrow, not the archer. Let your mission go where it needs to go.

As the poet Theodore Roethke said in his poem, *The Waking:*

> I learn by going where
> I have to go.

Accept your Life Mission as a gift. It's easy to get presents. But do you accept the one important gift that has been given to you? You must be able to do that before you can give it to others. Only when you recognize your gift can you pass it on in the form of a career, vocation, or pastime.

In a television interview, the opera singer Renata Scotto, was asked how she would like to be remembered, and she replied:

> "I would like to be remembered that on stage I always loved my audience so much and that the most important thing is the voice was a gift that I received that is not mine. It's something I have to share with my audience. I would like to be remembered as someone who shared her career with her audience." [Italics mine.]

A gift is something that comes to a person. It is one that is then to be shared and given to others. *Try Softer* is receiving and accepting the gift that is yours.

Apply the five-step program below to finding your mission.

Your Five-Step Try Softer Program:

1. Connect to Your Desire
2. Focus
3. Trust Your Source
4. Use *Less is More*
5. Look for Results

CONNECT TO YOUR DESIRE

Try Softer depends first and foremost on letting your desire rather than muscle power carry you. You'll push less whenever you wish more. Nothing ought to be easier than saying "I want this." Closing yourself off from desires will block you from ever having them. Look at cats: they don't seem to mind asking for what they want. Learn from your furry friends and make your mission purr with your fulfilled desire.

Desire and Your PM. Each profile has differing approaches and difficulties with the desire part of the *Try Softer* process. Doers work with results, not feelings, making wishing tedious because it takes too long or seems too soft. Meditation is especially helpful for you Doers. You Motivators, on the other hand, tend to shower the world with desires and have trouble focusing on one. You think in all-or-nothing terms.

Stabilizers want to know where they are each step of the way, whereas desires thrive on the spontaneous and unbridled approach. Stabilizers need to be more flexible. A straight line is not always the most logical way to get to desires. Analyzers want to be right, but desires cannot guarantee logic because they operate on laws different from cause-and-effect. Analyzers need to develop greater trust in the "irrational."

Identify anything that you desire strongly. Keep it simple and measurable. "Happiness" is too vague to quantify. "One half day a week to read in the library," on the other hand, is much clearer. Other examples:

1. Three hours a week for hiking

2. A new summer business suit

3. Saturday mornings with my child

Now see yourself in the situation you desire. Example: "I'd like to visit archaeological sites in Greece." How would you feel if you followed through on that wish? "Elated and invigorated!" Then write a sentence saying the reward you'll get from your desire. "I'll be able to plan my trip wisely and know just which archaeological sites to see on my next trip to Europe. And I'll appreciate these sites much more with my knowledge."

Seizing the Moment. Operating out of your desires creates a magnet that attracts what it is you need in order to achieve specific goals. Don't work at cross purposes with your desires (that's trying harder). "Oh, I'll just do this job that I hate for a little while longer so I can earn the money to pay the bills," or "As soon as I rack up ten years in the company, I can take early retirement and then . . ." Then what? The "what" will never get addressed during the limbo period of waiting. If you don't care about your desires, then any reason is good enough to postpone them. When will the moment be right? The only moment you have is the present. Seize it!

SEEING STARS

Juanita sat impatiently on the edge of her chair when she came to see me. A dynamic and intense Latina in her mid-thirties, she dominated the session, explaining her dissatisfaction with the progress she was making in the film industry. Although she had impressive credentials, she feared she wasn't ready for the big time. Being a woman still isn't exactly a plus in the entertainment industry. But Juanita also wasn't sure what her exact desires were: she felt she could go in a number of different directions.

A Doer, Juanita didn't like to sit still very long. But excessive "doing" wasn't helping her. Since nothing else had worked, what could she lose? She spent the next month concentrating on clarifying her desires.

They included a higher-level management position and work on a foreign film project in India. Soon she got an interview for a high-level job in a well-known entertainment firm. Her interviewers only had to see her for the rest to be history. Juanita later called me to say she got the job. "It's everything we talked about," she told me on the phone. "I'm really excited. As you said, 'Seeds I plant sprout daily.' "

Desires manifest when you stick with them. When clients finally connect to what they want, they say: "You'll never guess what happened to me!" "Just by chance I was doing such and such," "A funny thing happened to me," or "Out of nowhere this person called (or popped up)." I listen with an inner smile, because it's evidence that their desires have brought results.

FOCUS

Focusing requires the commitment and concentration of all your energy on what you desire. It also helps translate your vision into something vividly recognizable, passionately dear, and intensely close. I remember going to a friend's house to see her slides of Europe. Most of them were blurred. Was that a cathedral or a chateau? The few pictures in focus were a relief because we could recognize what we were seeing! Then we could devote attention to the slide.

EXERCISE: THE EYES HAVE IT

1. Take a common object and spend two minutes inspecting every detail; look at the way the light strikes it, how it feels, smells, tastes, and sounds. Look at the shape, size, texture, color, and volume of the object. Then put your choice away and recreate it in your mind with as much detail as possible. At first, you may overlook obvious details. In time you'll discover you are more attentive to seemingly unimportant features of an object.

2. Practice the exercise twice a day at least three times a week.

3. Focusing attention on something will increase your interest in it. After practicing a week, pick one of your objects and write a page expressing the feelings you have for this object. One client went on and on about paper for three pages! She knew more about types, uses, origins, manufacture, and selection than anyone else would even care to know. As it turned out, paper was an emotional issue for her, and she had never suspected it until she focused. "Who would have thought," she said, "that I was harboring such passions!" And she had resisted the exercise up to one hour before we met. Don't thumb your nose at a common object. There is a woman who is so passionate about rubber bands that she now commands a six-figure income by importing them to the U.S..

The application of these exercises to your Life Mission process fine-tunes your focus and increases the desire for your mission. When you are looking at a diamond you'd like to purchase, you focus your attention on each facet. Treat your Life Mission the same way. It's precious, just like the diamond. Focus your attention and love on it!

It would be frustrating to hear someone tell you, "I love you but I don't know exactly why." *Be clear about what you desire and focus on it. Then and only then can you realize what you want.*

Focus and Your PM. Focusing for Motivators is particularly difficult. They have so many projects and dreams to fulfill. To give up any one of them is like losing an arm. Doers are often impatient with concentrating on goals (or objects). Analyzers can focus much easier (almost to a fault), and Stabilizers must assert their need for concentrating on their desires.

"YES, BUT . . ."

Cindy, a free-lance cartoonist, looked at me uncomfortably through her horn-rimmed glasses when I asked her to focus on what she wanted. A serious, articulate, and precise woman in her mid-thirties, she seemed to be the kind of woman who had the skill to achieve whatever she wanted. But every time I asked her to describe a desire, she began, only to stop in midstream with negative rebuttals, such as "But I know I won't get that" or "But I'll have to settle for a small beach shack instead of a house overlooking the ocean." We went through about 20 minutes interrupted by "buts."

Cindy's parents had contributed to the pattern by saying she could do anything she wanted in life—that meant that they were giving unfocused advice. All her life Cindy had looked for things to do which were difficult so she could prove she could "do anything." In the meantime, her desire had been kept at bay. Then she would skip to something else, only to repeat the process.

I suggested that during the week Cindy review how often she blurred her desires. She was first to focus on the one thing she most wanted. Then she was to complete that wish before going on to another one. First wish: enrolling in a design course at a local college. Cindy had never allowed herself to focus on that. She called up the next day for registration information.

TRUST YOUR SOURCE FOR HELP

A key figure in the *Try Softer* method is your Source. Think of your Source as the CEO of the firm, supporting you and providing you with support for the job you are to do. Think of your mission as a loving attendant or clerk, in the business of helping you express your soul's intention. If you ordered from a catalog and said to a clerk, "I'd like something, but I don't know what," you'd get a puzzled look. The clerk needs specific information as to item, page, size, color, price, style, and whatever else is relevant.

Your mission needs conscious visions, not vagueness or pot-shot wishes. It is not in the position to be the decision maker without your consent.

To tell people what they need before they are ready is to ensure either confusion, resistance, or a disruption of the process. Would you like a clerk to tell you what you want before you even know what it is? You must give the green light before that clerk can proceed. The same is true of your mission, which, paradoxically, operates in your best interest only if given specific desires and permission to carry them out. That's where trust comes in.

It's not easy to turn over management to someone else (especially for Doers). But the *Try Softer* method involves surrendering your questions and concerns to your mission. It is there at your beck and call, ready when you are. Ask for guidance and encouragement—that's doing it the easy way. When you give up the need to control the outcome or to dominate the process, then your mission has room to figure out the best plan.

USE *LESS IS MORE*

Pick an appropriately safe area to practice this step. *Less is more* in paying bills might not endear you to your creditors. Try something in an aspect of life where you may have been successful but pushed a lot. Make sure you like whatever the activity is, but choose one for which you haven't gotten the results you want. You may feel as if you're in neutral when you'd like to go into fourth gear. But remember: idling, not driving hard, is what we're talking about here.

REMAINING SPEECHLESS

Brad decided to apply less is more to speechmaking. An amiable, ambitious, worried looking man in his mid-fifties, he described his shift from university teaching to public speaking. But, he complained anxiously, no matter how often he gave speeches, their quality hadn't improved much. He enjoyed talking and was good at it but got bogged down in preparation. He remembered that at the university he had also spent a great deal of time on his lectures. A pattern!

I asked Brad to review his most successful presentations. His worried face began to lighten as he reflected that most of them had been spontaneous, with very little practice. To his surprise, the feedback he got was always quite good. "I substituted for some instructors from time to time and did quite well, considering the fact that I had no advance notice," he grinned. "And then there were the times," he continued, "that I 'winged it' for my own classes. Instead of being a dreadful flop, the session actually went over better than usual!" I asked Brad to apply the same process to giving speeches.

Brad waited until his next speaking engagement to experiment with some less is more methods of speech-making. Every time he wanted to jot down some notes or say something into the tape recorder, he reminded himself to refrain from fully preparing the speech. He simplified his outline, identifying three main points to get across and visualized the speech and a (thunderous) audience reaction. He avoided all further preparation.

The next time I saw him, Brad was beaming. The anxious, withdrawn expression on his face had disappeared. "The reception to my last speech bowled me over," he announced proudly. Brad now worked on presenting his speeches spontaneously.

The interaction between Brad and the audience was alive, direct, and electric. No one knew of his experiment, of course. Brad figured it out. "People saw my willingness to risk and go with the moment. It was a relief not to have that obsessing beforehand."

Brad's *less is more* method was a new way of *being* rather than *doing.* His success impressed upon him the need to include spontaneous motivation in his life. As a result of making this one speech, he received three further speaking engagements alone.

Practice *less is more* now! Maybe it's time, for instance, to put this book down and take a break. Go out and smell the fresh air, or listen to the birds sing. Treat yourself to an ice cream cone or non-fat yogurt. Lubricate your soul by loosening the brittle, exhausting way you have been approaching things. Then you will see desires flow, the struggle release its grip on you, and, like the clay on the potter's wheel, your mission taking new shape.

LOOK FOR (BUT DON'T PUSH FOR) RESULTS

If you have been specific in your desire, have been focused, and have let go of the process, you will find the yield much more than you could ever imagine. Like Brad, you will see an increase in the success of your project and a decrease in the effort you put into it, and it's more fun in the process!

It all comes out in the wash: when you begin to use softeners, things get smoother. Keep a record of the things that begin to happen when you surrender to the results rather than push for them. Check it out for yourself. When did you push, and when did you allow things to work for you? Which was more successful? What was the difference in results?

Give yourself enough of *Try Softer*, and you'll wonder why you ever tried any other way. The most difficult lesson is to go soft on yourself!

Stop the macho-muscle-manic approach. Instead of wasting your precious energy on agendas not meant for you, honor the softness of your path now!

To return to the poem by Theodore Roethke:

Of those so close beside me, which are you?
God bless the Ground! I shall walk softly there.
And learn by going where I have to go.

That's *Try Softer* in action.

13

Yield to Your Intuition

*"Intuit? I'm not into it," said the
left brain to the right.*

Compare the items in column A with those in column B.
Check the one you prefer for each number:

A		B
____1. What I see		____What I feel
____2. The present		____The future
____3. Solving problems by experience		____By ingenuity
____4. Using things		____Designing things
____5. What I know		____What I find
____6. Working with facts		____With hunches
____7. Controlling the situation		____Going with the flow
____8. The steps of a process		____The purpose of it
____9. Things as they are		____As they could be
____10. Right and wrong situations		____Ambiguous situations
____total		**____total**

If you chose more answers on the left, you're probably
someone who thinks your neighbors must be at home if
their radio is on. If most of your check marks were on the

right, you're the person who figured out that they left the radio on to ward off burglars.

Preferring the intuitive approach (items in the right column) doesn't make you superior over the person who prefers the logical way. There is, however, an advantage for the intuitive person: free access to additional and often important information unavailable from any other source. What could be more exciting than to access the incredible wisdom stored within you? And like a radio program, this intuition is available the moment you turn it on and tune it in.

This chapter shows how to train and access your marvelous resource of intuition and put it in the service of your mission. It also identifies the barriers to intuition and shows how to overcome them. Finally, it examines the relationships between intuition, Life Mission, self-acceptance, trust, and surrender.

INTUITION DEFINED

Intuition, according to *Webster's Dictionary*, is a "direct perception of truth, fact, etc., independent of any reasoning process, a keen and quick insight." It is a quality that goes beyond the five senses and immediate perceptions, a conduit from your interior that conveys a direct, singular, intense, and unmistakable message when it connects to your consciousness. It has been variously described as a "hunch," a "gut feeling," a "funny sensation deep inside," a "knowledge that goes beyond all understanding," or "illumination." No matter what you call it, intuition is an invaluable consultant to you in your Life Mission process.

Many people think that intuition is only for women, creative types, artists or gypsies. Everybody is intuitive, yet many fail to take full advantage of it. To access your own font of knowledge, you don't need special faculties, just the tools to learn how to do so.

INTUITION AND MISSION: INSIDER TRADING

Too much "outsight" detracts from your mission search. Intuition keeps you internally grounded and in tune with your subconscious self. Insight, as the word connotes, is internal vision. A mission can be apprehended only from within you. It is axiomatic that intuition—since it also comes from an inner source—serves as a kind of side-kick for your quest. It goes something like this: intuition is advice from spirit and provides you with just the appropriate information needed for your mission search. It is a private exchange of communication between you and yourself. This is insider trading that's good!

With your intuition, you will access your precise internal areas of interest, desire, and expertise. You will discover that intuition likes nothing better than to give inside guidance, advice, secrets, information, and help on matters of importance to you, such as your mission. Listening to your intuition will automatically connect you closer to that calling. In fact, the aspects of life in which you get greatest intuitive insights will always pertain to your mission.

INTUITION: BODY LANGUAGE

Common to all these descriptions is the fact that intuition operates through feelings and desires on a psycho-physical level. The knowledge it imparts occurs through sensations, desires, emotions, and feelings.

As discussed in the previous chapter, in order to yield to intuition you must trust your body as the place containing this special kind of inner wisdom. Mission and intuition will seem like ships passing each other in the night if their inner connectedness fails to reach your conscious self. It is imperative, then, to risk yielding to the one resource that can enlighten and reveal your desires on a conscious level.

Using intuition is like going "in" on a limb. But that's where the fruit is! The real risk is ignoring intuition. Use it, and you'll find the right limb—and exactly the piece of fruit you want.

INTUITION: WHO IS INTO IT

Intuition is a lot like sex: it's a major factor in life, yet people are reluctant to talk about it. Why keep it hush-hush? Intuition has been verified by people in all walks of life from every century. It is a quality unique to humankind and one of our most important endowments.

Laurence Loewy, the daughter of designer Raymond Loewy, related to an interviewer that after her father had finished his conceptualization of the Studebaker automobile, he turned off the lights, put some jazz on the phonograph, and ran his hands along the clay model. He wanted feel and intuition to have the final word in the car's design. Einstein regularly used his intuition before cross-checking results with his logical side. General Patton, too, patently consulted his intuition before making critical campaign decisions in World War II. And a CEO of a Midwest corporation started a day-care center at his company because he "figured" it would help increase worker productivity. (Self-evident, you say? How many companies in the 1990s have yet to initiate day care?)

But we don't need famous people to validate intuition. In every workshop I did on creativity, participants told fascinating stories of ways they have used their intuition in business, at home, on trips, in relationships, and in virtually every situation of human life. Intuition is your guardian angel.

THE DUAL ROLE OF INTUITION

Intuition is powerful because it serves a dual function. It contributes to inner wisdom, *and* it provides a pipeline to universal knowledge. Who doesn't like a bargain? In accessing intuition you receive a double return on your investment: *collective knowledge made particular* to your situation. The following anecdote will show how remarkably this two-for-one deal works:

"UNSER STEINWALD"

I went on a trip to Europe with my friend Sue and her mother Eunice. Eunice's desire was to locate the place where her brother Dane had been killed in World War II. Although he was buried in Epinal, which is west of Alsace, Eunice thought Dane had died somewhere to the east, near Colmar. She had only the name of the forest, Steinwald, where the battle that took his life occurred. (The Alsace is an area in France where until 1918 German had been the dominant language.)

When we visited Dane's grave at the United States cemetery, I checked the battle records, but I was able to come up only with some names of Alsatian towns through which Dane might have passed during the campaign. Eunice talked about an area around Colmar, but that didn't feel right to me. Somehow, I felt it had to be further north, around Strasbourg, close to the Rhine. We had just driven through that section on the way south, and I remember feeling a prickly sensation in my stomach when I saw a sign for the Alsatian town of Gambsheim. I gave it no further heed. We couldn't find the Steinwald Forest around Colmar, and all inquiries were to no avail.

We headed back north in the direction of Strasbourg, comforted by the fact that Eunice had at least seen Dane's military grave. I still felt that Steinwald forest was located in an area north of Strasbourg, but since time was running out before

we had to return to the airport in Frankfurt, the
chances of verifying this hunch seemed bleak. But
my sensation that we were near Steinwald persisted
even though there was no evidence of such a forest
even on detailed maps of the Strasbourg area. I was
going on pure intuition.

There was time to visit only one of the three
Alsatian villages. I had no proof that my choice
would be correct, but I was guided to pick the one
that felt right to me: Gambsheim. Then I gave Eunice
the names, and asked her to choose. "Gambsheim,"
she said without hesitation. I knew that funny-sound-
ing town was it. At that moment I recalled the sensation I felt when I saw the sign a few days earlier.

As we neared Gambsheim, I glanced over my
shoulder at a small patch of trees and felt goose
bumps on my arms. We passed into the village,
only to discover it was lunchtime and the streets
were deserted. (In France the midday lunch period
lasts until three.) I was not about to go up to a house
and disturb anyone. Perhaps somebody would be
on the street—an old person who had survived the
war and was a native speaker of German.
Suddenly, we rounded a corner and saw a prim-
looking old man dressed in black, resting on his
cane. "Stop the car!" I shouted. Had the old gen-
tleman heard of a forest called Steinwald? "Unser
Steinwald!", he exclaimed in German ("our
Steinwald Forest"). I was overjoyed, and Eunice
gasped from the back seat as she heard the long-
awaited word.

After getting directions, we drove straight over to
the forest, pulled off the road, and looked in silence
at the kaleidoscope of trees, now so quiet and
resplendent with fall colors. For the next half hour

Eunice walked through the forest, taking in the place where her brother had spent his last few hours. It was a moment of sadness and yet extreme satisfaction. Her search had been successful. Later, I checked the local Michelin map for the area and located a tiny green patch, not more than an eighth of an inch, just outside of Gambsheim. Too tiny for a name. But it was *"unser Steinwald."*

Gambsheim would be etched in my memory forever as the validation of intuition. Eunice and I had listened to it, and what a yield it had given! Where did our shared knowledge come from? From universal wisdom, the same collective repository where all available information is registered.

BLOCKS TO YOUR INTUITION

The pressure in our society to conform to logic and facts is enormous. For that reason intuition often stays under cover. No wonder, then, that you might be reluctant to use it.

I have identified some common blocks that contribute to an underuse of intuition:

- Distrust
- Difficulty with self-acceptance
- Fear of intuition
- Need for control
- Giving in to the pressure of others

DISTRUST

There is a certain uneasiness about intuition, even for those using it. Imagine a coach saying, "Smith, you go in for Jones. I intuit that you can win the game for us." But in their books and private memories, almost all sports figures admit to relying heavily on intuition. The word itself is problematic. "Hunch" or "gut feeling" are more macho and acceptable words for the same thing. Imagine General Patton, who studied Napoleon and the Greeks extensively, using the word *intuition* when urging his men on to battle (although, as I mentioned, that is exactly how he made many of his major decisions).

Many people distrust their intuitive wisdom, too, because it seems too easy or elusive. Anything that comes effortlessly is greeted with suspicion. I remember my old Latin teacher's phrase on the board: *Ad astra per aspera!* (To the stars through difficulty.) It was like a warning to the class: Beware, nothing comes easily! Not so. Intuition comes easily if we are open to its gifts.

Clients have dismissed their intuitive insights because they came without struggle! They were uncomfortable with short-cuts that came to them like manna from heaven (except if they happened to be Moses in Egypt). Moreover, they argued, if they did trust intuition, would it provide tangible results? Too many people opt for the "sure thing" of logic rather than the greater yield from intuition. A bird in the hand is worth two in the bush.

DIFFICULTY WITH SELF-ACCEPTANCE

How can intuition go wrong? Only when you lack trust in its message. Intuition is a part of you. All those beliefs about inadequacy reinforce a distrust of any internal messages. The results are predictable: "Why would I want to consult with myself? I'm not worth the trouble. I don't have the knowledge, I can't possibly know the facts, better stick with the safe stuff, like 2+2= 4."

When you take the two parts: distrust of self and the distrust of the intuitive process, and put them together, you've cooked up a marvelous piece de resistance.

FEAR OF INTUITION

You may tend to use your intuition to a certain point, but when you begin to see things in powerful ways, you stop. I am reminded of a Schiller poem about the veil of Isis, behind which truth lies hidden. A servant rushes in, lifts the veil, sees truth, and dies. (A similar theme in romantic poetry involves death for the person who sees pure beauty.)

The same sort of fear exists with intuition. I've observed that clients become uneasy when they they begin to consult their intuition intimately. When they listen to their intuitive voice on Life Mission matters, they get information that they have often denied or ignored.

By not listening to intuition you can fool yourself into thinking you lack information. That kind of thinking becomes a vicious circle, because the fear of hearing the truth mounts with avoidance.

Many, too, are paralyzed by the thought of acting on their internal powers. When you know you are empowered, then you have to act on it.

You can't lose by following your intuition! Because it is an integral part of you, it cannot be used against you. Only your interpretation of intuition can be misleading. Intuition is not the culprit, it's fear of facing the truth about yourself that is the problem. Why?

Well, you will learn about the good and the bad (intuition doesn't make judgments): You'll see your self-deceptions, compromises of relationships, jobs, and mates, and of course you'll get to know your talents in a more honest way. Any contradictions, discrepancies and dishonesty present in you will now become glaringly apparent when intuition lights the way.

The resulting illumination (literally, making light what was dark for you) will demand a response, and that's the scary part.

NEED FOR CONTROL

Sticking to one way of doing things or one-answer solutions can be a difficult habit to break. The need to be in control is one of the most powerful addictions in society. If you are a person who sees things in terms of right and wrong, one way and one way only (Analyzers often do), you will be wary of your intuition and tend to shy away from its seemingly ambiguous nature. When you use logic, you avoid choice, for logic must perform in a single-minded way. But logic doesn't give information about what you want or what you desire, because it doesn't deal with feelings. If you have spent $40,000 getting a degree in accounting, and you really never liked the subject, what's logical about continuing to pursue it?

As my father used to say, "I may not always be right, but I'm never wrong." When you yield to your intuition, you in effect relinquish control (and dependence on logic) by surrendering to forces *inside* yourself. You dance on the crest of your own power to achieve your desires.

LAURA'S HOT FLASH

A young, bright, and energetic woman with piercing blue eyes, Laura had finally landed a job in a professional firm. Although she had a degree with honors in journalism, she could not get the newspaper job she desired and had settled for a position as an administrative assistant in an unrelated field. She felt defeated almost from the start, and had abandoned her journalism dreams.

At first, Laura didn't believe my contention that intuition can be a valuable tool for discovering what a person loved—and for learning how to go about manifesting it in life.

At my request, she compared two projects she had recently completed—one that went well and the other that didn't. (I didn't mention my hidden agenda of the differing role intuition played in these projects.) She picked "writing a magazine article" and "landing a job." I asked her to explain her process for each project.

To get her administrative assistant job, Laura related in a disgusted tone, she went from agency to agency, newspaper ad to newspaper ad, exhaustively looking for anything that would pay her enough. She eventually got the job after three months. To get a job, she reasoned, demanded a rigid sequence. If she called x number of agencies in x amount of time, she would find a job eventually. Laura took strict control, since she "knew" that was the only way you got a job in a tough market.

For her article, on the other hand, she was unable to identify any strict guidelines she had used. In fact, while relating her process to me (in an excited tone), she described how in a meditation, she had "flashed on" the magazine where she would submit her article, and she even got information on the format and slant it was to have. She called the editor of that magazine and was hired on the spot to write the article. She did not have to call dozens of magazines.

The difference between the success of the two processes lay in her method. Getting the article published was much easier because her intuition had offered advice—and Laura was open to it. She finished the article with ease. No muss, no fuss, no bother. She hadn't pushed. Instead, she had given intuition control, space, and opportunity to provide the way and the tools. With the job search, Laura had determined every step of the way and steered a rigid course. And she had got it by gosh and by golly. The irony was, she used "the logical way" for something she didn't want!

An added bonus: we know intuition helps us even more when we are dealing with our heart's desire! It's no accident that Laura *much preferred* writing the article to searching for a low-paying, dissatisfying job. Laura's success with her magazine article made her rethink her discouragement with journalism and gave her courage to determine exactly what direction she wanted to take in that field. She busily began working on a second article, and of course, allowed her intuition to take charge in the future.

GIVING IN TO GROUP PRESSURE

Friendly intuition can falter under the test of group pressure. In an experiment, five people were seated in a darkened room and shown slides of four colored columns of various lengths. Their objective was to determine which column was longest. At first the four columns were obviously very different in length, and all subjects agreed as to the correct answer. But as the experiment progressed, they became increasingly similar in length.

Four of the five participants had been told what answers to give. When the four stooges gave the first obviously wrong answer, the unsuspecting participant hesitated but stuck to his own answer. Thereafter, the stooges always agreed unanimously about the "correct" answer. Soon the unsuspecting person changed his mind to agree with the others' answers. He didn't trust his own judgment! How much opportunity would your intuition have in situations when it is pitted against reason? Intuition is a solitary endeavor; you need to ignore the cries of the crowd and listen only to your voice within.

FIVE WAYS TO TAP YOUR INTUITION

Use these five ways for tapping into your intuition:

1. Practice daily.
2. Observe a lot.
3. Trust your intuition.
4. Make connections.
5. Listen to your intuition.

Practice daily. To fine-tune your intuition, you need to exercise it. You can do mini-practice sessions as well as structured, longer ones. The next time the phone rings, try to guess who it might be, or anticipate what the nature of that phone call will be. Hocus-pocus? No, that's what intuition is: simply knowing a little more fully about things beyond the facts. Keep notes on what interests you. Let's say it's buying a car. Then when you get around to your purchase, your intuition will be better informed to help you make a decision because you have done your preparation. Your intuition always looks better if you have done your homework.

Guess what people are going to say before they begin speaking. Sometimes you'll even be able to predict individual words. Have someone open a magazine to a picture and, without looking, you try to describe what is on the picture. Keep a log of your answers. Think of someone you'd like to hear from, and wait to see if the person contacts you. Ask that person how she or he happened to think of you.

You can also identify an object hidden in a box. Use as clues any feelings, words, or associations which come up for you. "Chubby toes," blurted out Edith, a workshop participant, while gazing at the box. She felt the object must be something owned by a person with chubby toes. A small piece of jewelry came to mind. She knew only one person with chubby toes. And that person wore a very distinctive ring. Edith guessed "ring." The object in the box was indeed a ring.

Follow up on your hunches, particularly when they are "illogical" yet persistent.

Observe a lot. Intuition comes through an ability to interpret information inside and outside you. Indeed, the only way to intuit is to tune in. You'll need to devote keen attention to what you are feeling and desiring. Ask other people how they use their intuition and when it has worked for them. Imagine using this as a party opener: "Hi! How's your intuition been doing?"

Watch how you come to know about things, and keep a journal about it. Give yourself credit when you observe correctly. When things don't turn out the way you thought you intuited them, identify the source of the confusion. Did any ego demands or force of mind get in the way? Read about how people have used their intuition and the results they have achieved.

Trust your intuition to come from your inner wisdom. Your own day-to-day information comes from individual perceptions, awareness, and visual and aural fields; in short, from whatever you give your immediate attention. Two people can have differing views of an event because each is coming from her or his own limited perspective. Intuition transcends personal limitations and perceptions to access a universal source of truth.

We all know people who took a job even if they felt in their gut that it was wrong. Did that job ever turn out right? Doubtful. But what made you pick up this book? You had a feeling it would do you some good. (My intuition tells me you're right.)

If there is a discrepancy between what your intuition tells you and what you think is logical, practice going with your feelings even if the facts to back them up are not evident. Work with low-risk items at first. Don't start by using your intuition to put all your fortune in a certain stock or quit your job.

SANDY'S SIXTH SENSE

Sandy, a single mother with two kids, woke one morning with an inexplicable urge to go halfway across town on a weekday to have a cappuccino before work. "But you usually jog in the morning," she protested to herself. Yet the urge wouldn't leave her. She knew there was a reason, even if she couldn't figure it out at the moment. So she scrapped the jogging and drove her vintage Mazda to a little coffee house she loved near the ocean. While sitting over the cappuccino and writing a letter to her mother, she tried to figure out why she had come. She knew it wasn't really to have coffee or communicate with her mom. But why *was* she there?

Just then a Dodge van pulled into the parking lot. "Gee, just like the one I'd thought about getting for me and the kids," she sighed. As the driver turned the van into a parking space, Sandy could make out the "For Sale" sign pasted on the window. She dashed out and looked it over. It was outfitted for camping, complete with toilet, sink, fridge, TV and three beds, just what she had always wanted. She asked the owner what his asking price was. "Actually," the man shrugged, "I hadn't thought of a sale. I'm really looking for a small car in trade. A Mazda or something—maybe around ten years old."

"It's a deal—I've got the Mazda you're looking for!" Sandy exclaimed. Within an hour they had made the trade. "So it wasn't really the cappuccino!" she said to me. "It was my intuition that told me to go there. I know now that when it speaks, I don't ask why. I just follow it!"

Make connections. Observe the times when you link two things together accidentally or coincidentally. For example: how often do you think of someone only to have that person turn up in your life? A friend recorded at least ten "accidental" occurrences in three days, including a phone call from someone he was just thinking about, but whom he hadn't talked to in over two years. How about that new word you just learned which crops up again later in the day?

Intuition connects you to knowledge that is pure, unhampered by restrictions, and often shared by more than one person at any given time. That is why Eunice and I could both come up with Gambsheim! We were connecting to our mutual source.

Listen to your intuition. Go deep inside to a place where only you can talk with you. When you lend an ear, you will find intuition to be your soul-mate, your guide and your counselor. What do you really need to be in your life? How do you make use of your gift? Intuition will gently guide you. If you drop the "shoulds" and "ought-tos," intuition may even be able to help you forget the "reasonable" way to be. I must emphasize again that most people are overwhelmed not by what their intuition says, but by the prospect of following through on it!

Listen to yourself as you would listen to a loved one. Let that voice implore, beseech, motivate, cajole, and otherwise cause you to rise up, throw off any burden of guilt and fear, and follow your own voice. Be your own Pied Piper and dance to your own intuitive melody! Intuition is that vital, generous, and necessary partner to which we all have the luxury of access. Pursue your necessary luxury.

Remember Laura and her use of intuition to get the magazine article accepted? Because Laura still lacked the funds to quit her job, I suggested she use her intuition for the next step. Shortly thereafter, she began an in-house newsletter for her company. It didn't take long for her talent to be recognized, and she eventually took over as full-time editor of the company newsletter.

Bloom Where You Are Planted. One recent Christmas holiday, I paid a visit to a friend recovering from a serious operation. We went to a mall one afternoon to shop, and as we descended the concrete steps leading from an older parking structure, I noticed a plant bursting through a crack in the pavement. There was no vegetation within sight, yet somehow this fragile plant had found a place to bloom where it had been planted.

No matter where you are, there is no place too inhospitable, no place without some possibility of growth and flowering. Would the plant flourish better in a field amidst its own kind, in a place it was "supposed" to be? The question for the plant is really irrelevant. It simply did what came naturally: grow! There was no other choice. Learn from nature's example.

"Bloom where you are planted" means you must make a go of it even if your ultimate objective would be to flourish in another setting. It means accepting where you are at any given moment, even if your plans envision something else in the future.

To make the most of any circumstance, situation, or place you are in, your task, like the plant's, is to take root and blossom. As the poet Goethe said, "Manifest according to the law unto which you were born." And that law is your soul's design for you, your mission.

Bloom where you are planted. Making peace with the situation in which you currently find yourself results not from some sort of complacency or fatalistic "Oh, well" attitude—"now that I'm stuck here I might as well like it." No, it comes from a genuine desire to follow your soul's intent wherever you are, using whatever it takes. Manifesting a mission requires you to enter into a very special relationship, just as in a marriage, wherein you vow to hold fast to your beloved in sickness and in health, for better or worse, till death do you part. We are all responsible for our actions; we must take full credit for the good we manifest and the mistakes we make. Things happen for a reason, from which we are to learn and understand. Circumstances are not out of our control; we still have the choice of acceptance or not of anything that crosses our path. Unlike the plant, you have the option of moving to a different location. But, like the plant, you must at the same time make the most of where you are now. And that is the dilemma that besets many people: how to get on with an identified mission in the here and now.

Not everyone will experience blockage to moving forward with their mission. But for many, the discovery of a mission can and often does initiate a challenging phase in which people learn to respond to what they have just uncovered. It's like unwrapping an exciting gift, or embracing a new person, baby, or relationship in your life. You have something that hadn't been there before. It makes demands on you. You now have to give it time, attention, and room for nurturing and growth.

Many people are affected by tough economic conditions: a client who can't move because health care benefits would be cut for a spouse with breast cancer, or a family stuck with a house that won't sell. Other people are in a location they want to be, yet they experience difficulty in getting on with their mission because of real considerations, such as grandchildren who have moved in just when the grandparents were about to relocate to a smaller apartment.

Whatever the cause, the result is that some people must stay put longer, or they must take more time between moves. Others are beset with delusional thinking, fear-based emotions, or scattered energy. The mission, so clearly in mind, gets blocked.

Maintaining the expression of a mission during an apparent "slowdown" of a timetable is best done with the help of your intuition. Use the five ways you can tap your intuition to help you unblock your progress toward your mission.

As with the "yield" sign, intuition tells you when it's right to go ahead or when to wait a few moments. But forward you will go at just the right time. Yield to your trusted friend, your intuition.

PART

Three

14

Mission Accomplished

'Tis the gift to be simple
'Tis the gift to be free
'Tis the gift to come down where we ought to be.
And when we find ourselves in the place just right
'Twill be in the valley of love and delight.
—*SHAKER HYMN*

This book begins and ends with gifts. They're really quite
simple. You don't need to write a doctoral thesis or paint
the Sistine Chapel to prove you have them. Take Martha,
who wanted to beautify the environment, Gene, who wanted to farm, and Dan, who discovered his love for nurturing
young people. Ordinary stuff, so much so that you almost
wonder what all the fuss is about. The extraordinary thing
about them is that they followed through on their calling.
They "came down where they ought to be."

You'll reach that "valley of love and delight" the
Shakers sang about if you keep these simple ideas in mind:

Everyone has a gift.
You, too, have a gift, and it is special.
Your gift is within.
You are responsible for finding out what it is.
Accept your gift fully.
Give your particular gift back to the world.
Use your gift and you'll "come down where
   you ought to be."
Keep on keeping on with the process.
Accept where you are at any given time.

The core of your mission is that simple gift you receive and pass on. It is your beacon, anchor, and path. It's what you are here for.

If you haven't yet "found the place just right," take heart. If you go on the quest of discovery you'll reach your mission as surely as the people in this book did. You'll learn, then, that your calling is an ongoing process. How you express it may differ from stage to stage in your life. There will always be new dimensions, and fresh insights. But the theme of your life will be your constant companion and support through any and all change.

Being willing to do what it takes is the first step. No one can meet and fulfill your Life Mission challenge except you. Friends may offer advice and mates encouragement, but the final decision will be yours. If you make that decision for reasons other than your own you are saying that others' agendas are more important than yours. There is a difference between taking something into account and doing something on account of someone else. You must know and understand that difference.

If you think you have neglected your Life Mission up to now, take heart. When you picked up this book, you might have been experiencing a time of contraction, a sense of being "off track." The paradox is that you are never off track! When your lungs are contracted it takes time before you can expand them. That's a simple law of nature. So contraction always precedes expansion. Your mission gives you the power to inspire yourself and others. It allows you to breathe in (in fact *inspire* means *to breathe in*) and experience expansion.

Let's look at one example, that of Elizabeth. She is a woman who met the challenge and is living her mission. Observe how she managed her exercises and tasks, how she dealt with fears and discomfort, how she kept on going in spite of resistance from others and how she overcame negative thoughts. Notice her PM and the way she approached her goals as a result.

ELIZABETH: FROM RESISTER TO SISTER

A wiry 54 year-old woman with graying hair, Elizabeth was a Division Head of a computer research firm. She characterized her dilemma this way: "I was having lunch with one of the CEOs in the executive dining room overlooking the entire city. I had everything I wanted, but I felt an emptiness inside."

Elizabeth had taken at least a half-dozen career tests (she was a Stabilizer, with some secondary Analyzer traits) but felt none the wiser from the results. Burned out and unhappy in the city where she was living, she was despondent because she feared, and thus resisted, change. She thought a new job would never bring her the salary she was presently commanding. If she relocated, she thought it would disrupt her partner's work.

Elizabeth explored her interests, her past, and her needs, and worked intensely on her desires. She kept a copious journal, wrote about her past and taped her thoughts. She realized that her mission

had always dealt with doing quiet things that bring
people closer together. Words and phrases like "big
band playing on the lake," "summers on the farm,"
and "family photos" came up in her journals. She
still felt the attraction to technology, but now it
appeared more in the service of communications.

Her fondest hope was to move closer to her sister
in Illinois. Elizabeth's need for a haven, for close-
ness to the community where she had grown up and
for a closer bond with her sister was almost stronger
than her career. (And characteristic of her PM!)
Once she accepted those needs as "okay," she could
affirm them and make them come true.

For a Stabilizer, any change creates anxiety, and
has to be prepared for carefully. Self-employment
for Elizabeth turned out to be an unlikely option
because she needed security. If that wasn't enough,
she and her partner were unable to sell their house
because of the slow real estate market.

Then Elizabeth made some further attitudinal
changes. She decided first to give up the attachment
to the house that was chaining her to her present city
of employment and job. Then she identified the
changes she wanted to make. She wanted to work for
a firm that manufactured products to foster communication in an atmosphere less demanding and stress-
ful than her present position.

Elizabeth was able to feel, taste, experience, and
smell the location she wanted. All of a sudden, a
number of astonishing things happened: (1) She
received a job offer from an optics firm in a town
near her mother; (2) Although housing was tight,
the house right next to her sister was put on the
market to lease! (3) It became possible for her to
take the job offer without undue financial strain;

(4) Suddenly Elizabeth's house sold; and (5) Her partner was able to continue a career in the new location.

All of the above happened *within a month!* The optics firm rekindled Elizabeth's love of photography. Soon she began a small portrait business, and in just three years she expanded it to a full-time business with her partner.

Within three months Elizabeth went from despair of ever getting what she wanted to having a splendid outcome to her wishes. She never stopped pursuing her dreams in spite of recurring doubts and fears. She trusted her inner wisdom and the guidance of her inner wisdom. It was a joy to see Elizabeth's face as she got the news of her transfer. Although I was sorry to bid her farewell, I knew that leaving was right for her.

SORRY, WRONG NUMBER . . .

Wherever you turn, there are examples of missions never undertaken, never fulfilled, never realized, or gone haywire. Hitler's attempts to gain (self-)acceptance as an artist is an infamous example that comes to mind.

But you don't need to find examples of well-known people. Those with missed callings languish all around: the neighbor who never got beyond all those years of childbearing: your brother who could have reached for the stars but stayed on safe ground to carry on the family tradition; that brilliant, eccentric aunt who stayed in a menial job and provided gossip at family reunions; or a high school friend whose talents were obvious to everybody but him.

Contrast these sad examples with those people who have been shining lights. Perhaps there was a teacher who inspired you to bring out a special talent, a person in your community who never seemed to stop making waves, or a relative who quietly followed his dreams and became an example for you.

A LOOK INTO THE FUTURE

What would the world be like if right from the start people were totally involved with pursuing a dream uniquely theirs? How would the world look if everyone were living a mission with determined passion and unencumbered joy? What would be the emotional, economic, and societal effect on all of us if people were not running away from something but heading toward the realization of their desires?

More to the point, how would that world look if it were *harvesting the fruits of your calling?* Try for a moment to imagine your gift spreading out into the world, seeing your gift working for global good. Here's my vision of the way the planet will look when your gift (indeed everyone's gift) becomes global.

The planet will hum. You'll devote time, money, energy, and resources to the things you need to fulfill your dreams. You'll know your priorities because you've identified your own needs.

You'll trust your decisions and take greater risks to meet them as you begin to use your soul for guidance and your source for nurturing and comfort. You'll no longer be going through the motions of driving listlessly to work in the service of earning money. Instead, you'll "come down where you want to be" to complete a specific assignment in the service of your mission.

When you are living your own mission, there will be no need to aggress against others out of feelings of deprivation, no need to see the world in terms of "you have what I want." *Lebensraum*—new frontiers, expansion, exploration, and discovery of new worlds—will refer not to a conquest of property, people or land but to *conquest of space within yourself*. You'll feel the need to give of the overflowing gift that you have rather than envy what someone else has.

You will learn how to attract the good to yourself rather than push to make it come to you. When you begin to actively and consciously live your mission, your life will be more harmonious and congruent, with less conflict. Values such as pursuing the latest fad, keeping up with the Yuppies, wearing a certain style because that's what one does, will no longer matter.

Since you are responsible for your space and are working on your own agenda, you'll not be concerned with what others are doing. Any need to do things on the behalf of others will come not at the beginning of the decision-making process but as a result of making decisions. In meeting your own needs, you'll be the ultimate beneficiary of your choice.

When you feel the effects of responding to your inner calling, you'll want to pass the torch and encourage others to find their own missions.

When you live your mission, you'll have options and choices rather than restrictions and closed doors. You will make clear and positive decisions based on your desires. Your creativity and fantasy will thrive as you find more time to explore and invent things. You'll spend more time on developing your intuition because you'll see it as a necessary partner in the mission process.

You'll eagerly spend time with yourself, and you'll love yourself for that care and attention. You will accept your need to pursue your own interests even if it means spending less time with others. Doing something for yourself—say, on a weekend—will be seen as natural, congruent and sensible as opposed to sitting around drinking endless cups of coffee when you would really rather be doing something else. The bumper stickers you see everywhere: "I'D RATHER BE _____ " will change to "I'M DOING WHAT I WANT TO RIGHT NOW!"

You'll spend less time frittering away the day on excuses,

sidetracks, diversions, and procrastinations. You'll go directly to what you want. You will start to live through yourself rather than through others. You'll take healthy risks and break out of old patterns and ruts, because you are no longer dependent on people, substances, or distractions for fulfillment.

You'll be much happier at home because you will know how to negotiate a relationship according to the mission you are here to fulfill. Instead of choosing someone on whom you are dependent, you'll make choices based on how your dreams will be realized. If a relationship is not conducive to your growth, you will have the courage and wisdom to sever it lovingly and promptly.

You will recognize that long relationships must produce a fulfilling and growth-producing environment and nothing else. People will negotiate with each other out of true desire rather than based on what they are supposed to want.

Paradoxically, you'll now be able to respond to the needs of loved ones more compassionately because you can detach yourself from feelings of competition and envy. And you will model the thrill of living your soul's purpose and seeing the benefit to others.

They, in turn, will feel no need to protest that you are being selfish and ignoring them, because they now have a model to meet their own needs. These people will recognize that they need to be going in a different direction. People will listen to their own dreams and support their mates' passions, and offspring or siblings will stop living through others and become themselves.

Can you add to this list?

YOU ARE NOT ALONE

Let's review the relationship of mission to Source and spirit. No matter what your situation, whether you are in a relationship, a single parent, living alone, divorced, or widowed, all your work is in partnership, collaboration and cooperation with your mission. It's a duo. Your mission stays with you even when the going gets rough. In fact, for all the roughing up you do of your mission, it is amazing to think of its resilience, loyalty, and perseverance. You must think of it as the channel for your well-being, the wise silent observer, the nurturer of your good, the expression of your talents.

Remember also, that you have a Source, a complete and perfect support for your striving toward wholeness. Each mission lived brings you into further alignment and atunement with that Source. You need only to listen to a Bach chorale, see a Gothic cathedral, work on a computer, or admire a poem by Emily Dickinson to realize that a Source is operative in their creation—indeed in all creations. It is also in you.

Much in the twentieth century has enticed us away from a feeling of spiritual support. Be assured there is something beyond you, as well as in you, that supports and protects your being. You are actually a part of this creative nurturing, not separated from it in a sort of I-Thou dichotomy.

Your energy is evidence of your spirit in action. When you are creative, you give this energy back to the universe in an ever-flowing cycle. What is divine in you is both an expression of your own spirit and a reflection of the spiritual energy radiating out from your source. It is both in you and reflective of you. That's the paradox. The Life Mission process provides a creative interchange among soul, spirit, inner wisdom, intuition and mission in a spiral of energy to your Source.

TRUST YOUR PATH

The paradox continues. You have only one task to perform in this life: being yourself. It's momentous yet simple. You are charged with fulfilling the unique role you have been called to perform.

No, this is not selfishness! It's the most responsible

thing you can do for yourself. Much of the unhappiness in the world is caused by placing demands on others instead of fulfilling one's own needs. You will find that when you commit to your role, you will contribute more to others, to society, and to the world at large.

KEEP ON KEEPING ON

"Nothing succeeds like success" is a well-known adage. But success is often a string of failures dared to be experienced. Success actually comes from perseverance: not the bang-your-head-against-the-wall type of keeping on, but the type in which you try again another way, a creative way.

As the clients presented to you in this book have illustrated, you must affirm your path and say yes to what you need as well as no to those who would keep you from it.

EXERCISE RIGOROUS SELF-HONESTY

Never lie to yourself about who you are or how you want to express yourself. A con job on yourself sentences you to imprisonment within a stranger. Don't spend your life with someone you are not! Be honest, faithful, and devoted to expressing who you are designed to be. Be devoted to yourself, to your calling, and to your mission.

NO BIG DEAL: DO IT YOURSELF

This book has given you exercises, signs, appeals, admonitions, encouragement, examples, and steps to make you trust the process that you alone must carry out. But, take it easy. Stamp the process with a great big NBD: NO BIG DEAL. Each step is only a mosaic tile in the bigger picture. "Life is just a bowl of cherries," as the lyric says.

EMBRACE YOUR DESIRES

Part of finding your Life Mission is to acknowledge the desires that you feel and affirm them daily. Somehow people have gotten the message that being desirous of something is suspect. Schiller, the great 18th century German poet, once said that true freedom resulted from fusing what one wants to do with what one must do. Imagine living each day knowing you want to do what you must!

SPREAD THE GOOD NEWS

Motivate others to follow their path. Encourage them toward their goals by making positive and supportive comments. I remember one client who clearly identified what she wanted to do, only to have her partner bristle and throw barbs the minute she even talked about it. The partner had a path in mind—hers! The client never regained her courage to complete the process.

Form support groups to offer mutual inspiration, exchange of information, and role modeling. The more you begin to spread the good news of self-actualization and self-fulfillment to others, the more you exemplify these values in your life, the more you will further your own—and everyone else's journey.

LOVE YOURSELF

Finally, the simplest way to answer your call is to love yourself. This is what you are all about, what you have been created to express, and what you are here to do. The greatest love for yourself is to fulfill your dream, accept your path, carry out your vision, and love the gift you have been endowed with. Remember, you are called to do something that is entirely within your capability, interest and talent to do!

Love the mission that you have set for yourself, for in the final analysis it is your gift, your challenge to you, your commitment to you. Your mission is love. Embrace it as you would a loved one, and it will return that love with abundance and joy.

Your Life Mission is the talent and sending, the light that shines within you that must be revealed. Enlightenment will be the inevitable result. Illuminate your path, accept and follow it, and your life will be congruent, focused, successful and authentic. Trust that you are guided and protected during this journey.

You'll discover when you answer the call of your soul that it will permeate everything you do. As a stonemason expressed it in Studs Terkel's book *Working,* "Stone's my life. I daydream all the time most time it's on stone. Oh, I'm gonna build me a stone cabin down on Green River. I'm gonna build stone cabinets in the kitchen . . . . All my dreams, it seems like its got to have a piece of rock mixed in it." Another mason named Michelangelo picked out a block of marble in the quarries near Florence. When he found the block he wanted, he immediately began chipping away at it. What are you doing?" cried one of the quarry workers nearby. "I'm looking for the angel within," Michelangelo replied.

Find your angel within.

15

―――――――― ❧ ――――――――

Living Your Mission: Soul Nourishment

CONNECT TO YOUR SOUL

Over the years, I've learned that finding our Life Mission is even more basically important that I originally thought, for it opens the way to link up with our soul.

If we listen to the intentions of our souls, we will learn why we are here, what we are here to create, and the steps needed to get where we need to be. Surrendering to the guidance of the soul and to the way to live your mission is to establish and maintain a deep connection between you and your soul. Surrender to this process is key.

Some of you may have trouble with the concept of soul. I know I did. I came from a traditional religious background, in which the word *soul* was used but not really defined adequately. I guess I always thought there was a soul, but I never knew what it was supposed to be or do. Now I believe the soul is that indestructible part of me that goes on into other dimensions after I have departed. It is that part of me that cannot be removed. My spirit can be challenged, weakened, my life force can grow dim, but the soul remains intact.

What is, then, the role of the soul in this Life Mission process? The soul is the author of your script, whereas you are the player in that drama, the actor of your mission. Finding your mission is the main focus of this book. After that is accomplished your next objective is to carry out your mission, your soul's intention for this life.

Each of you, after realizing your mission, must communicate with your soul for your continued instruction. The soul, in turn, needs attention, your willingness to follow its guidance in order to manifest your mission. Above all, it needs your constant contact and support, which I call soul nourishment.

Soul nourishment refers to that deeper level of mission work required to manifest the mission. I'll liken it to the process of making champagne. In France, you have to go down very deep into the earth to reach the champagne cellars. There you can observe the 63 steps that Vintners go through to produce the bubbly brew.

Making champagne involves a more intricate process than making wine (or grape juice). Think of the wine process as analogous to the mission—as foundation, as groundwork. The champagne process is analogous to the domain of the soul in that it takes place on a deeper level under the earth. Whereas the mission is what you are here to be on the earth plane—how you are to be, your role, melody, unique path, destiny—the soul is your inner deep guide from the cellars below, advising you on how to proceed on your path. Soul and mission must work in partnership, just as the grapes for champagne originate from the earth above. Tune into that soul and it will help you carry out your mission.

But for many the soul can seem awfully far away, very distant.

Because the soul operates at such a deep level, you may not always hear its message. These are times of assaults on our souls. Your soul can thus combat a lot of interference when it tries to communicate with you. Greed, fear, feelings of lack, violence, international strife, and a host of other non-heavenly hosts vie for our souls. If you feel that your mission is not moving forward, how do you learn from—and conquer—the blockages, resistance, abandonment, or neglect of your soul to open a positive open channel of communication?

How do you strengthen the connection to that indestructible part of you when it is under assault, or when you are not listening to it? These assaults bring about a conditioned response from your soul. When the self slips off track, the soul becomes very quiet, receding into a corner to get in a position of safety. It's almost like a small animal when it is in danger of being attacked. It withdraws or takes cover.

What is to be done in this moment of soul recession? How do you nourish the soul so it doesn't have to retreat, withdraw, or remove itself from your "stuff"? How do you encourage yourself to hear the soul, to listen to what it needs to tell you? In short, how do you keep it nourished, supported, loved? That's what this chapter is all about.

STEPS TO NOURISHING THE SOUL IN THE HERE AND NOW WHETHER YOU ARE MOVING OR STAYING PUT

Express Your Talents. The soul is a rich entity within you that provides the repository for all your talents. It carries your DNA, your own individual stamp. You are the sole determiner of whether or not you use these talents. First, your soul really gets fed from any direct expression of your gifts. When you do anything you truly love, then you act out your soul's script, and that's when the soul feels nourished.

In spite of how much else seems to be on your agenda, set up a schedule or a regular time to do mission/soul work. Do it especially when it seems you have absolutely no time for it.

Imagine you wanted to start a relationship with someone, but you stated to that person that you had very little time to spend on the relationship. What would that person think? What would you think if she or he said that to you? You'd undoubtedly feel hurt, angry, or deflated. All right, then, how could your Number One relationship—your mission—survive under such conditions and stipulations?

Give us this day our daily bread. Your daily bread is your mission. The more you spend on anything connected to it, the more you will experience the thrilling feeling it brings you, and the more you will want to taste of it.

Do not question the process, and stay away from demanding a product, a poem, composition, or something tangible for now. Your task at this stage is to give time and attention to your mission without questioning the outcome.

Recognize The Magic Connection. Magic always involves a soul connection. For me, it is a transcendent, mystical feeling, when there is no difference between me and the surrounding world. Learn to recognize the internal signs that show, that you and your soul are in nourishing contact. Rather than listening to your head, monitor you feelings. It is a connection that cannot be put into words. "Who can explain it, who can tell you why? Fools give you reasons," but, as the song continues "wise men never try." Give your fullest attention to the way your body responds to events. Have you ever said yes to something, but find that afterwards your heart is heavy, or you can't sleep because of anxiety? What do you do when your mission says "yes" but your head says "no?"

Synchronicity. Watch for events that transpire magically, yet have no logical causation. In particular, watch for a form of magic called synchronicity—that is, two significant events that occur simultaneously, yet have no apparent causal relationship.

Here's an example. I received a phone call letting me know that a recording of one of my compositions was to be played at a national choral convention not twenty minutes from my house. When I went to the convention, whom should I meet but a college friend I had not seen for twenty-five years. When I met her I was in the midst of a conversation about organizing a women composer's symposium. My friend showed me a brochure about precisely that sort of symposium, which she had already organized. After hearing my piece later in the day, she asked me to write a composition for that symposium. The first convention thus led to a further convention and further important contacts for my musical compositions.

And on it goes. I could not have programmed this sequence of events as wonderfully as they programmed themselves.

Synchronicity occurred, I believe, because I had set the stage for it to occur. Devotion to music—choral music specifically—was uppermost in my mind. The events simply unfolded in a magical way on my behalf.

Be on the alert, therefore, when you encounter serendipity and surprise. I know they're on to something when clients come to me and say, "You'll never guess what happened!" Beware, however, of delusion, and always give your plans a reality check after you have cleared them with your body.

Truth or Consequences. Develop total honesty with yourself. Are you connecting to something within you that is your divine destiny? Is it within your purview to do, your calling, your path? Or are you doing a huge con job on yourself?

You can delude yourself into thinking you are communicating with the true needs of your soul. Often the distinction between delusional effort and nourishing your soul can be quite subtle. How do you recognize the difference between the genuine article and delusion? What are some symptoms of delusional effort?

Let's first define what delusion is. Delusion derives from the word ludicrous and denotes a "false mental conception resistant to reason." You've probably had the experience, for example, of eating a meal and not feeling nourished at all. Yes, you have eaten, that's the truth. But it does not mean that you were nourished, that the food was good for you. It might have been something too rich, or maybe it was sprayed with chemicals, or it was just plain junk food. You've filled your stomach, yet you have no feeling of health. But you deny that you are malnourished, and so you continue your eating habit day after day.

Look what is generated by delusional effort. We humans practice delusion on a mass scale, so we are well tuned to this type of acting and thinking. Hitler, for example, masterfully capitalized on mass delusional thinking by promising a *Reich* of a thousand years, a car affordable to everyone, and a country free of any "undesirables" (homosexuals, Jews, misfits, and the mentally retarded).

Environmental pollution is another form of delusion. That for years we could spew carbon monoxide, chemicals, and garbage into the atmosphere or onto the earth without questioning what the effects on our biosphere and food chain might be is a notorious example.

Examine any of your limiting equations. "Since I am so good at teaching, and I'm getting good results, I must be doing the right thing, I must be connecting with my soul." But check it out with your body. If you drag home at the end of the day, your reasoning is delusional (that is, ludicrous)!

Monitor Your Energy Connection. The soul connection is also an energy connection. You'll find that an indescribable energy and clarity will come over you when your mission is being expressed.

Conversely, a depletion of energy is a clue you're going in the opposite direction your soul intends you to take. You know the signs: When your energy is down, depressed, when you say, "Do I have to do this?" or when you are feeling resistive (not the same as being blocked), when you are in agony over what you are doing, when you're experiencing headaches, backaches, neck pains, foot pains, ear aches. You *feel* it when you are not connecting.

Here's how to go for the positive energy connection to the soul. For the next thirty days, do as much as possible that energizes you. Your energy level is like a line on a seismograph. A rumble means there is a change in activity—a rise in energy—and that is a clue. It may happen for a couple of seconds, a couple of minutes, several hours—there's no telling how long it might last. But when you've noticed it, you are now in dialogue with your soul. Your high energy level reflects that connection. You'll say, "Aha! I feel it now." And your creativity and sense of well-being will flow as a result. You are looking to feel that way as much as possible.

Eliminate the energy drains. Let's be realistic. Most of us are living in constant battle with noise, pollution, and crime. Furthermore, we now face the damaging effects of electromagnetic radiation (EMR) created by television, radio waves, electronic equipment, car phones, utility poles, nuclear submarines and nuclear plants. All of these attack our bodies, and thus deplete and fragment our life force.

To counteract the massive dosages of urban life, technology, and EMR, you must take very good care of yourself by eating right, living right, thinking right. If you live in an urban environment, you may have take refuge in the mountains or smaller towns, where these forces fields are less complicated and chaotic. (That's why I have moved from an urban area to a smaller town.)

You have to stop struggling to maintain an energy level just to have the wherewithal to get to work next day, just to be able to complete the nine-to-five stuff. That's not the ideal. The goal of soul nourishment is to empower you to be of service on the planet. Of service with your unique talents. That can happen only when you keep your energy level high.

Get Off of the Surface and Take the Plunge. Superficial means staying on the surface. You'll achieve little by staying in a comfort zone on the surface of things. Soul work is intense, deep, committed. Dare to plunge beneath the surface to reach the depths of your soul. Learn to intensify your relationship with the core of your mission and do what it takes to have it fully.

Your mission involves one central love, around which many attendant loves revolve. It's like a family—each member is equal, but in the clan is one central figure who commands greatest respect. That's exactly the way your soul operates. It is in direct communication with all your loves, and keeps you connected to them, particularly to the main member of the clan. It's so easy to get caught up in all the satellite loves and forget the main one (as I did for so long with my music). The main love has to be in your consciousness AT ALL TIMES. Your soul will see to it that you keep on track, if you will but ask it for assistance.

Your main love lives at the center of your soul—in other words, at the greatest depth. To access it requires effort and commitment. If you want to dive for pearls, you have to be willing to make the climb—the climb to a height needed to reach the depths where the pearls are. If you are not willing to go high enough and dive deep enough, then you won't get the pearls.

You have to climb past people's nay-saying, past your own fears, beyond the expectations that people have of you, surpassing your own limitations. You have to keep on going up that mountain to reach the point where you are willing to make that dive.

Love for the soul and its guidance will take you to dizzying heights, out on a limb. It can be terrifying. That's where you feel most vulnerable. The air is pretty thin up there. When the bough breaks, the baby will fall. That creates a fear of falling (failing?). Maybe you'll fall flat on your face. It sometimes feels so much safer staying superficial—on the surface.

Do Daily Devotion. Develop an attitude of devotion. Devote as much time as possible to your soul work—5 minutes, 15 minutes, 5 hours. Just start doing it. You haven't got time to put it off. People say "you don't understand, I have to earn a living!" But when you realize it, the only living is living your mission. The first duty is to feed the soul. Without food, the soul languishes, and the body goes limp. Without a healthy soul, that mortgage, important meeting, or new car won't seem so important. Indeed, not even your mission functions without a healthy soul.

Avoid Fragmentation by Keeping Focused. Clients often labor under a proliferation of options. They like so many things about their mission. Which step do they undertake first? A lot of people are good at a lot of things. Some people go from love to love, a sort of serial love affair. Doing many things well in constant alternation does not necessarily mean you are carrying out your mission. The time spent on any aspect of your mission has to have an organic, integral connection to the core of that mission. Then there is a soul connection. The trick with so many loves is first to establish expertise at the very core love you are meant to express—that is, your mission.

Listen to the soul guidance within you for help to tune in to your *sine qua non*—the thing without which nothing else in your clan of loves matters. When you have spent sufficient fundamental time with that core love, you can then express other facets of it without feeling fragmented or guilty. (As I am doing right now, with my writing. My compositions wait for my attention, but at this moment it is important for me to finish the chapter.) Your soul will tell you what comes first, what second—and more important—what IS first, and second. At any given time, you'll know when and how to take any plunge.

Fear of Failure of Mission. Some of you may fear embarking on a mission, because that might mean you'll have to deal with failure along the way. Of course, real failure is to leave your mission in the lurch.

Rework Your Beliefs. What would happen if you rephrase—at least, in your mind—some of your old statements or your old equations. Most people need to clear the decks for their souls with such statements as: "I won't find time to be with _____," "I refuse to go to that awful job one more day," or "I cannot tolerate another evening with those relatives." If you can't be honest with yourself and the way you spend time, then you are in effect saying: "I'm not prepared to spend time with my soul!" You've got to start being honest with yourself and scrutinize everything you do: does it relate to what nourishes you?

I know there are times of anxiety, fear, dilemma or even paralysis. But those times are often useful and productive. They offer us lessons. How many of us can create something that moves us unless we've been through sadness or depression? Mind you, no pain, no gain is not my game. But if you feel pain, then what is the lesson? Keep on keeping on, because if you don't, you'll not get to the pearls.

Keep Up the Clue Work. Clue work, so important to the Life Mission process, doesn't end when you find your mission. I have almost daily insights into my mission through new clues. This doesn't change my mission; it only brings a deeper understanding of it, further insights or greater clarity.

Practice looking at clues. Each day we get scores of clues: tips, messages, sensations of the ingredients of our mission.

The soul is like a well-tuned engine. It hums when you work on your mission. Lubricate that soul with mission work.

Exercise With Your Soul. Allow positive statements to nourish you, and your soul will be strengthened. Everyone needs a healthy, vibrant soul. Compare such statements as, "Why bother about composing choral music? Who would want to hear it anyway?" versus: "I'm going to spend an hour with my music and enjoy myself!" Which of the two statements nourishes the soul? Try testing your muscle strength when you make a positive statement as opposed to a negative one. Your energy will sag with the negative ones, and increase with the positive ones. Avoid excuses to run from your soul. The ironic fact is that the soul is with you, in you, a part of you. It's waiting for you to connect. Someone once said that, what matters is what happens *in* us, not *to* us.

A vibrant soul, you see, enables you to release all your other talents to express your mission. One talent begets another as it were. People have discovered, after they begin to activate their soul, that they possess all sorts of talents they were unaware of. I gave energy to composing, and poetry followed (not a bad combo). The soul will always provide us more of what we need. There is no loss! Think of gain, not loss. A vegetarian client lamented the loss of his former cooking style—but I suggested he look at having gained a new—and more healthful diet.

Let in the only thing that matters: your soul's desire, the desire that you carry out the mission for which you came into the world.

Start on your soul's path. Do it now, do it lovingly, do it with gusto.

BIBLIOGRAPHY

In addition to the works cited in the text, I recommend, for further reading, the following list of books dealing with related topics.

Bingen, Hildegard von. *Illuminations. With Commentary by Matthew, Fox.* Santa Fe, N.M.: Bear & Co., 1985.

Caple, John. *Finding the Hat that Fits.* New York: Dutton, 1993.

Chopra, Deepak. *Quantum Healing: Exploring the Frontiers of Mind/Body Medicine.* New York: Bantam: 1989.

Csikszentmihalyi, Mihaly. *Flow: The Psychology of Optimal Experience.* New York: Harper Perennial, 1991.

De Bono, E. *Serious Creativity: Using the Power of Lateral Thining to Create New Ides.* New York: HarperBusiness, 1993.

Diamond, John. *Life Energy: Using the Meridians to Unlock the Hidden Power of Your Emotions.* New York: Paragon House, 1990.

Dominguez, Joe, and Robin, Vicki. *Your Money or Your Life: Transforming Your Relationship with Money and Achieving Financial Independence.* New York: Viking, 1992

Edwards, Betty. *Drawing on the Right Side of the Brain.* Rev. ed., Los Angeles: J.P. Tarcher, Inc.,1989.

Fox, Matthew, *The Reinvention of Work; A New Vision of Livelihood for Our Time.* San Francisco: Harper, 1994

Frager, Robert. *Who Am I? Personality Types for Self-Discovery.* Los Angeles: J.P. Tarcher, Inc., 1994.

Fritz, Robert. *Creating*. New York: Fawcett Columbine, 1991.

Garfield, Charles. *Peak Performers: The New Heroes of American Business*. New York: Avon Books, 1987.

Hawley, Jack. *Reawakening the Spirit in Work*. San Francisco: Berret-Koehler, 1993.

Lakein, Alan, *How To Get Control of Your Time and Your Life*. New York: New American Library, 1989.

McMakin, Jacqueline, and Dyer, Sonya. *Working from the Heart: A Guide to Cultivating the Soul at Work*. San Francisco: Harper, 1993.

Markham, Ursula. *Living with Courage*. Rockport, Maryland: Element Books, Unlimited, 1993.

Masters, Robert, and Houston, Jean. *Listening to the Body*. New York: Delacorte, 1979.

Moore, Thomas. *Care of the Soul: A Guide for Cultivating Depth and Sacredness in Everyday Life*. New York: Harper Collins, 1992.

Moore, Sue, and Stephan, Naomi. *The Finding Your Life Mission™ Workbook: A Guide to Self-Study*. Life Mission Press, 1991. (800) 957-8888

Myers, Isabel Briggs, and Briggs, Peter. *Gifts Differing*. Palo Alto: Consulting Psychologists Press, 1993.

Dick Leider, Ed., *On Purpose: A Journal about Taking Charge of Your Life/Work*. The Inventure Group, Minneapolis, MN.

Ponder, Catherine. *The Dynamic Laws of Prosperity*. Cutchoque, N.Y.; Lightyear Press, 1993.

Raudsepp, Eugene. *Creative Growth Games*. New York: Putnam Publishing Group, 1980.

Saltzman, Amy. *Downshifting: Reinventing Success on a Slower Track*. New York: Harper & Row, 1991

Sher, Barbara, and Smith, Barbara. *I Could Do Anything If I Only Knew What It Was: How to Discover What Your Really Want and How To Get It*. New York: Delacorte, 1994.

Steinem, Gloria. *Outrageous Acts and Everyday Rebellions*. New York: New American Library, 1986.

Tieger, Paul D., and Barron-Tieger, Barbara. *Do What You Are: Discover the Perfect Career For You Through the Secrets of Personality Type.* New York: Little, Brown & Co., 1992.

Thurston, Mark. *Soul-Purpose: Discovering and Fulfilling Your Destiny.* San Francisco: Harper & Row, 1989.

Yogananda, Paramahansa, *The Autobiography of a Yogi.* Los Angeles: Self-Realization Fellowship, 1981.

ABOUT THE AUTHOR

Naomi Irene Stephan, Ph.D., lives her mission to create a sound world through music and word as a composer, writer, motivational speaker, and educator. Her choral works have been performed throughout the United States and she has published her own workbook companion to this book.

Since 1982 she has headed her own Life Mission coaching practice offering consultations by telephone, individual Life Mission coaching intensives, as well as books and tapes.

Those interested in her services or her music may contact her at 1-800-957-8888.